The International Labour Organization
and the quest for social justice, 1919–2009

# The International Labour Organization and the quest for social justice, 1919–2009

Gerry Rodgers, Eddy Lee, Lee Swepston,
and Jasmien Van Daele

ILR Press
an imprint of
CORNELL UNIVERSITY PRESS · ITHACA
and
INTERNATIONAL LABOUR OFFICE · GENEVA

Cloth edition first published in 2009 by Cornell University Press (available for sale in North America only)

Paperback edition first published in 2009 by the International Labour Office, CH-1211, Geneva 22, Switzerland

Librarians: A CIP catalog record for this book is available from the Library of Congress.

ISBN: 978-0-8014-4849-2

Printed in the United States of America

Cloth printing    10  9  8  7  6  5  4  3  2  1

# Contents

## Figures

## Boxes

# Foreword

On the wall of the temple of Apollo at Delphi in ancient Greece were written the words, "Know thyself". That 2,500-year-old lemma can be a guide for us all in our personal and professional lives. But it is equally important for institutions. And those of us who have the privilege to work with and for the International Labour Organization have a rich heritage that informs our work and guides our actions, often without our knowing it. To know this heritage can help us understand both the responsibilities of today and the mission that our founders and successive generations have placed in our tripartite hands.

When Dharam Ghai came to me with the proposal that we document better the ILO's history and its achievements in time for its 90th anniversary in 2009, the idea was instantly appealing. Dharam, with whom I have worked in different contexts and who headed my transition team after my election as Director-General, has been a source of inspiration and support to many of us who have been working to strengthen international social policy, and his understanding of our possibilities and our goals is second to none.

He was sowing on fertile ground. Some years before, I had mentioned in my annual address to the ILO Conference the fact that we won the Nobel Peace Prize in 1969. Throughout that meeting, I was struck by the number of delegates who were unaware of a key facet of our history. Clearly, we needed to do something about it.

And so this book was conceived, and the idea of the "Century Project" to celebrate our 100th anniversary in 2019 was born.

The ILO is a large community, more broadly based than the other United Nations organizations because we include not only governments, but also workers' and employers' representatives, each with their own global networks. Thousands of national and local organizations belong to the ILO through their representatives at our Conference. Then there are those who work in the ILO's secretariat, and our loyal corps of former ILO officials and delegates around the world, as well as the many more who belong to a wider community concerned with work, with workers, with enterprises, with social justice, with decent work, with gender equality and non-discrimination, within each country and in the international system.

This book is for that wider community and beyond. It explores some of the main ideas which the ILO has seized, developed and applied, examines their history and tells how they were pursued in different geographical and historical settings. And, since the ILO revolves around ideas, that helps us understand why the ILO has sometimes thrived, sometimes suffered, but always survived and persisted to pursue its goals through the political and economic upheavals of the last 90 years.

What lessons can we draw?

First, the institutions on which the ILO is founded have proved their worth. That includes labour laws which frame national action; social dialogue which builds understanding and expands the common interest; and tripartism, the bedrock of the ILO, which provides for the democratic participation in decisions of the key social and economic actors.

Second, the effectiveness of the ILO – the role it can play and its ability to respond to the demands that are put upon it – depends on major world events: economic crises, social conflicts, war, and in recent years globalization policies which are inimical to ILO values. But, in all of these extreme situations, in the end the ILO is an indispensable partner because of the balance it brings between state and market, between society and individual and, today, between economic, social and environmental policies for sustainable development.

Third, the ILO has often been swimming against the tide. Its mandate for social justice can be thwarted by economic and political forces, and pursuing its goals is often a long struggle, as is today the struggle for decent work.

The book has four authors, three of them long-serving former ILO officials, with a total of over 100 years of experience working in the ILO, the fourth an academic who has looked at the ILO from the outside; two economists, a lawyer and a historian. This book is their view.

Gerry Rodgers, who led this project, was a member of the team that worked with me to construct the Decent Work strategy after my election as Director-General, and subsequently helped put it into effect. He has a long experience of, and personal commitment to, research and policy on employment, labour markets and poverty in different parts of the world.

Eddy Lee has been the ILO's leading economist for many years and has published widely on topics such as employment policies, development strategies, the social impact of globalization, and international economic and social policies.

Lee Swepston brings to the book 35 years of experience in promoting human rights as an ILO official, with major contributions and writing on discrimination, the rights of indigenous and tribal peoples, and child labour, among others. He is now teaching international human rights and international labour law to the next generation.

Jasmien Van Daele is a young historian who joined us from the University of Ghent (Belgium) after completing a PhD on the origins and the early history of the ILO. She has brought to the team an understanding of public history, its methods and how it can be applied to the ILO, a wide knowledge of the literature and a network of external expertise which has contributed many useful ideas.

This book is the creation of its authors. It was never intended to be the definitive history, but rather to start to tell a story. It is a story with which you may agree or disagree, and there are opinions here as well as facts – but in my view it captures much of the essence of this organization, its spirit, its commitment and its work.

This is just a starting point. The key anniversary will be not the 90th, but the Centenary in 2019. I believe that the ILO must reach its Centenary knowing itself better. Confucius said it long ago as well: "Study the past if you would define the future". There are many ways in which a better understanding of our past can help us. And so this book is just the first outcome of what I have called the Century Project. The aim is to build a more systematic understanding of what the ILO has done and how – its successes; its failures; its contributions to both thinking and action; its work to embed rights in the global economy and to ensure that the goals of employment and socio-economic security are addressed at all levels; its principles of justice, representation and democracy; its method of reaching consensus through informed dialogue among representative social actors; and its key objective, which we now sum up in the concept of decent work. The ILO has played a role at key historical junctures – the Great Depression, decolonization, the creation of Solidarność, the victory over apartheid – and today in the building of an ethical and productive framework for a fair globalization. We should know more about the many inspiring figures in the ILO's history. That requires a mix of history, biography and autobiography.

All of this material must be the subject of informed social dialogue, if the ILO's tripartite community is to build the agenda for its second century. For if one thing is clear, it is that a century of effort has brought progress to some, indeed to many, but certainly not to all. The need remains for an international organization devoted to social justice and a fair globalization, as an essential foundation for the world's future peace and stability. An international organization in which the actors of the production system work together towards just and inclusive societies, built on decent, productive work, which respect rights, reflect needs and provide avenues for fulfilment and achievement.

The story of the ILO has not always been smooth, but we, and our predecessors, have always been looking towards that goal and facing up to new challenges. And, in order to strengthen our ability to do so, future generations need to know where we come from, and the story of our struggle.

I am writing this foreword when the global financial crisis of 2008 and its impact on the real economy have moved us from an era of change to a change of era. The 2008 ILO Declaration on Social Justice for a Fair Globalization gives the Organization the vision and the contemporary tools to continue with its historical mission.

JUAN SOMAVIA
*Geneva, October 2008*

# Authors' preface

There have been many excellent publications on the ILO's past and present, and we list a selection in an appendix to this book. They tell us a great deal about the institution and how it has evolved.

Our aim has been not to repeat this existing work, but to complement it. Drawing on our own experience and our own disciplines, we tell a story of the ILO's goals and ideas, and how the institution has pursued them at different times, under different circumstances and in different fields.

We look into what has been done, by whom, and how, and consider the influence of the Organization in a world in which the ILO is one actor among many. In so doing, we have highlighted some periods and parts of the world and neglected others, discussed some topics and passed others by. This is a personal selection, rather than a comprehensive account, and there are many other important topics in the work of the Organization which we have not attempted to cover.

It is also only one output of a wider project, the ILO Century Project, which aims to strengthen the ILO's knowledge base in a variety of ways in the period running up to its Centenary in 2019. Information about the Century Project can be found on its website, http://www.ilocentury.org.

We start in Chapter 1 with an overview of the ILO as whole – what it stands for, how it was created, how it works. The last section of this chapter looks at some of the essential political, social and economic developments of the last century, and discusses how they have impinged on the ILO's action and its priorities.

Chapters 2 to 5 then deal with some of the central themes of the ILO's work in the last 90 years: human rights, the quality of work, income protection and employment and poverty reduction. Each chapter tells its own story, in its own way, reviewing the development over time of the ILO's ideas and its work, the strategies adopted by both the Office and the employer, worker and government constituents of the Organization and the influence on national and international policy. The pattern is different for each of the themes, with both progress and difficulties to report. There are many successes, but also powerful countervailing forces.

Finally, Chapter 6 paints a broader picture of the development of the international social policy agenda, how it has conditioned the ILO's work and the way the Organization has responded, most recently with the Decent Work Agenda. It ends with some pointers to the future.

Many people have contributed to this book, and without their help it could not have been completed. First, there are those who have participated in the work of the Century Project, many of them preparing papers which have been used as source material for different parts of this book. That includes Claude Akpokavie, Roger Böhning, Thomas Cayet, Ben Chigara, Marianne Dahlén, Nigel Haworth, Stephen Hughes, George Kanawaty, Sandrine Kott, Frédéric Lapeyre, Kristoffel Lieten, Andres Marinakis, Daniel Maul, Deirdre McCann, Jill Murray, Jean-Jacques Oechslin, Catarina Pimenta, Paul-André Rosental, Neville Rubin, Jeremy Seekings, Marie Thébaud-Sorger, Lisa Tortell, Anne Trebilcock and Oksana Wolfson. Marcel van der Linden, Research Director at the International Institute of Social History in Amsterdam, has helped the project as a whole in important ways.

Second, we would also like to acknowledge the help of a number of readers of earlier versions of the text: Dharam Ghai, P. Gopinath, Richard Jolly, Sandrine Kott, Virginia Leary, Manuel Montt, José Antonio Ocampo, Kari Tapiola and Victor Tokman. A number of other ILO colleagues have read drafts of some chapters, or provided information and inputs, including Sam Afridi, Lin Lim, Francis Maupain, Stephen Pursey, Emmanuel Reynaud and Manuela Tomei. Sandrine Kott and Richard Jolly provided much additional source material, in addition to their comments. Dharam Ghai played a particular role because not only was he a reader of the manuscript but also the originator of the idea of the book. He, Richard Jolly and other participants in the UN Intellectual History Project have provided examples and points of reference for our work. None of the readers is responsible for the final outcome, but their views and comments have been invaluable.

Juan Somavia, whose foreword precedes this preface, gave a great deal of support to the project, contributed ideas and information, and read and commented on parts of the text.

Special thanks are due to the ILO Archives (Remo Becci, Renée Berthon) and the Library (Lauren Dryden, Ariel Golan) for their assistance in the project. Research assistance was provided by Jaci Eisenberg and Véronique Plata. The project was hosted by the International Institute for Labour Studies (IILS), which arranged administrative, organizational and computing support, provided by A.V. Jose, Cyrena Beranek, Vanna Rougier and Françoise Weeks. One of us (Gerry Rodgers) was Director of the IILS at the time the project was launched; we are grateful to Raymond Torres, who took over as Director in September 2007, for his continued support.

The manuscript was edited and revised by Frances Papazafiropoulos, who also participated in the overall planning and design of the volume, and made many helpful suggestions. We are also indebted to Charlotte Beauchamp for her capable management of the publication process and the finalization of the text.

While gratefully acknowledging the assistance that all these have provided, we take final responsibility for this text, which necessarily reflects our views and opinions, and so does not in any way constitute an official ILO position.

GERRY RODGERS, EDDY LEE, LEE SWEPSTON and
JASMIEN VAN DAELE
*October 2008*

# An international organization for social justice

**1**

## A "wild dream"

In 1941, 22 years after it was founded, the International Labour Organization (ILO) held an extraordinary Conference in New York. The goal was survival. Exiled in Montreal, its work was severely hampered by the war. The League of Nations, with which the ILO was associated, was defunct. If the ILO were not to suffer the fate of the League, it was important to establish that the Organization, and all that it stood for, should play an important role in the reconstruction of the world order after the war. Its fate hung in the balance.

The position of the United States, which had joined the ILO in 1934, was key. And on 6 November 1941, President Franklin Roosevelt came down strongly on the side of the ILO. Inviting the delegates to the White House on the last day of the Conference, he told them that he had helped organize the ILO's first Conference, in 1919.

> I well remember that in those days the ILO was still a dream. To many it was a wild dream. Who had ever heard of Governments getting together to raise the standards of labor on an international plane? Wilder still was the idea that the people themselves who were directly affected – the workers and the employers of the various countries – should have a hand with Government in determining these labor standards. Now 22 years have passed. The ILO has been tried and tested ...

He underlined some of the Organization's achievements since its foundation and, pointing to the challenges ahead after the war, concluded that the ILO

... will be an invaluable instrument for peace. Your organization will have an essential part to play in building up a stable international system of social justice for all peoples everywhere.[1]

Twenty-eight years after Roosevelt's decisive intervention, the ILO's contribution was recognized again in a different setting. In awarding its 1969 Peace Prize to the ILO, the Nobel Prize Committee reiterated the connection between peace and social justice. "There are few organizations," said Mrs Aase Lionaes, Chair of the Nobel Committee, "that have succeeded to the extent that the ILO has, in translating into action the fundamental moral idea on which it is based ... Working earnestly and untiringly, the ILO has succeeded in introducing reforms that have removed the most flagrant injustices in a great many countries ...."[2]

The ILO was created in 1919 as a means to promote social progress and overcome social and economic conflicts of interest through dialogue and cooperation. In contrast to the revolutionary movements of the time, it brought together workers, employers and governments at the international level – not in confrontation, but in a search for common rules, policies and behaviours from which all could benefit. It included a number of unique features. Above all, it gave these economic actors equal power of decision with states, and it introduced new forms of international treaty concerned with social aims, along with new ways to apply them. Politically it drew on the main European democratic political currents of the time, in particular social democracy, Christian democracy and social liberalism, and actors from each of these perspectives participated in its work and contributed to its development.

The two triggers for the creation of the ILO were war and revolution. The twentieth century, even more so than in earlier times, was a century in which human activity seemed to be largely structured around war and work. And this was partly because both war and work had become global. The scope and brutality of twentieth-century war far exceeded anything which had occurred before, for the first time killing many millions of civilians – and not only in the two world wars, but in the immense number of large- and small-scale conflicts around the world throughout the century, from Manchuria to the Congo. In the wake of the First World War, with its savagery, mass mobilization and widespread social repercussions, political leaders were open to fundamental change in politics, economy and society, and to the building of international institutions which could engage

---

[1] Franklin D. Roosevelt, Address to the International Labor Organization, 6 Nov. 1941. Available at J. Woolley and G. Peters: *The American Presidency Project* (Santa Barbara, CA, University of California) available at: http://www.presidency.ucsb.edu/ws/index.php?pid=16037

[2] http://nobelprize.org/nobel_prizes/peace/laureates/1969/press.html

all countries in a common effort. The same openness to change emerged again after the Second World War, and led to the creation of the United Nations and the construction of a new agenda of social progress and human rights. This pattern has been repeated many times at the local and regional levels because successful emergence from conflict has to be built on a framework of rights and social justice, as the world's peacemakers know, or should know.

But the twentieth-century world was also structured around work. Work was at the centre of most people's lives, as it always has been, but it increasingly became a concern beyond the sphere of the family or the firm. The character of work itself changed, as the flow of people from agriculture to industry accelerated. Workers organized and demanded dialogue, opportunity, decent incomes and dignity. Waves of economic crisis and mass unemployment destroyed individuals, firms and societies. There was growing awareness that labour markets were interconnected across borders, that public action was needed to achieve common standards. Above all, work dominated the political agenda. The growing contradictions of capitalism contributed not only to the Bolshevik Revolution, but also to the many later revolutionary movements and the subsequent fault lines of the world political system. They also conditioned the development of a variety of streams of socialist and liberal thinking in all countries. The ownership and organization of the means of production, the role of the state and the interests which it served, the pattern of organization of social forces, equality and equity, were all closely connected with the fundamental role played by work in society.

In the creation of the ILO, these two streams came together. "Whereas universal and lasting peace can be established only if it is based upon social justice," declares its Constitution, "and whereas conditions of labour exist involving such injustice, hardship and privation to large numbers of people as to produce unrest so great that the peace and harmony of the world are imperilled; and an improvement of those conditions is urgently required". Born in the aftermath of the First World War, the ILO was built on the belief that peace and justice go hand in hand. Not in the sense that war is always the result of injustice, but rather that social justice is an essential foundation of peace. This fundamental idea would later have applications that the drafters of the Constitution might not have imagined – for instance when the Solidarność trade union in Poland demanded application of the ILO's Convention on freedom of association as one pillar of a new political order in the 1980s; or when an ILO Convention on the rights of indigenous peoples contributed to the peace agreement in Guatemala in 1996. And there have been other examples on all continents.

The origins of the ILO lie further back, in the nineteenth century. As industrialization began to transform economies and societies, a central political issue was the so-called "social question" – how to deal with the social consequences of industrialization, and to redress the deep inequities and injustices of the Industrial Revolution.

Workers had been organizing throughout the latter part of the nineteenth century, as social conflicts increasingly shifted to the workplace. This movement began to internationalize early on. The International Working Men's Association was formed in 1864 with the goal of protection, advancement and emancipation of the working classes. This brought together trade unionists, a diverse group of political activists and other forces in what became known as the First International. Its work was continued after 1889 by the Second International, whose demand for an eight-hour working day would ultimately be taken up in the first Convention adopted by the ILO. The first International Trade Secretariat was established in 1889 with the creation of international federations of typographers and printers, hatters, cigar makers, and tobacco workers, and boot and shoe operatives.[3] The International Secretariat of Trade Union Centres, created in 1901, was the first international trade union confederation composed of national trade union centres – renamed in 1913 as the International Federation of Trade Unions (IFTU).

In parallel with these developments, moves were afoot to establish interstate agreements on conditions of work, through the creation of the International Association for Labour Legislation (IALL) in 1900. The IALL brought together a group of private individuals from academia, politics, administration, labour and industry. In 1905, it successfully convened an international meeting of experts, which laid down the basis of two international Conventions, adopted at a conference in Berne in 1906. One of these prohibited night work for women in industry, and the second prohibited the use of white phosphorus in the manufacture of matches. As many as 41 states or colonies adhered to the international Convention prohibiting the use of white phosphorous, and 25 to that prohibiting night work for women. Although its activities were interrupted by the war, the Association provided an important laboratory for the subsequent work of the ILO. But, as its legitimacy and influence were limited to a few European states, there was no effective mechanism for the implementation of its conventions, and many governments preferred to develop bilateral treaties.[4]

---

[3] A. Carew et al. (eds): *The International Confederation of Free Trade Unions* (Berne, Peter Lang, 2000).

[4] See J.W. Follows: *Antecedents of the International Labour Organisation* (London, Oxford University Press, 1951); and R. Gregarek: "Une législation protectrice: Les Congrès des assurances sociales, l'Association pour la protection légale des travailleurs, l'Association pour la lutte contre le chômage, 1889–1914", in C. Topalov (ed.): *Laboratoires du nouveaux siècle: La nébuleuse réformatrice et ses réseaux en France, 1880–1914* (Paris, éditions de l'EHESS, 1999), pp. 317–333.

The impetus for the development of common standards was the growing integration of the world economy, under way throughout the "long 19th Century"[5]. Both workers and business had supported the efforts of the IALL for different reasons – not the last time that their interests would coincide based on different imperatives. The workers saw these efforts as coordinated international attempts to achieve better conditions of work and to control the adverse effects on labour of market forces, while employers favoured equalizing conditions of work in order to facilitate the expansion of trade and remove unequal conditions of international commercial competition.

War temporarily halted the growth of trade, but generated many other reasons to be concerned about labour matters. Labour unrest was widespread in the latter stages of the conflict and immediately afterwards, and this had a notable influence on the Peace Conference in 1919. As Edward Phelan, Director of the ILO from 1941 to 1948, and one of the drafters of its Constitution in 1919, recalled in a 1949 article entitled "The Contribution of the ILO to Peace":

> The three Great Powers, the United States of America, Great Britain and France were ... preoccupied [in 1919] with a critical post-war situation, more immediately dangerous than that which followed the Second World War. A revolutionary temper was widespread: the Bolshevik Revolution in Russia had been followed by the régime of Bela Kun in Hungary; the shop steward movement in Great Britain had honeycombed many of the larger trade unions and undermined the authority of their constitutional executives; the trade union movements in France and Italy showed signs of becoming more and more extremist; millions of men, trained in the use of arms, to whom extravagant promises had been freely made were about to be demobilised; the wave of unrest had spread even to such stable and peaceful democracies as the Netherlands and Switzerland. How gravely the situation was viewed may be indicated by the fact that during the Peace Conference itself, Clemenceau moved many thousands of troops into Paris as a precaution against rioting in the streets. The decision to give labour matters a prominent place in the Peace Treaty was essentially a reflection of this preoccupation. The Peace Conference accepted the proposals of its Labour Commission without much concern either for the generalisations of the Preamble or for the details of the proposed organisation. In other circumstances, it is indeed highly probable that some of the more daring innovations in the latter, such as the provision that non-Government delegates should enjoy equal voting power and equal status with

---

[5]  Eric Hobsbawm's expression for the period 1789 to 1914.

Government delegates in the International Labour Conference, would have been considered unacceptable.[6]

The Peace Conference was intended to build a new international framework – political, of course, but also economic. The point of departure was President Woodrow Wilson's "Fourteen Points", of which the third called for "the removal, so far as possible, of all economic barriers and the establishment of an equality of trade conditions among all the nations consenting to the peace".[7] The creation of the ILO was to provide a considerably more powerful instrument than had hitherto existed to expand and enforce a range of international labour standards. And, by establishing a social framework for economic exchange, it set out to provide the foundation of an equitable world trading system.

## The central ideas

The ILO's first Constitution was prepared by the Commission on International Labour Legislation[8] of the Peace Conference in 1919 and formed part of the Treaty of Versailles. This was the first attempt to construct universal organizations to address the social and economic problems facing the world of the early twentieth century. There were no models on which the ILO, and the League of Nations, created at the same time, could be built. Original solutions could thus be tried which might no longer be conceivable if the same kinds of institutions were to be created today. The ILO's Constitution laid out the rationale for the Organization, spelled out its aims and purposes as well as its detailed design and also identified certain "methods and principles for regulating labour conditions which all industrial communities should endeavour to apply, so far as their special circumstances will permit" which are of "special and urgent importance".

The vision of the original Constitution was taken a step further towards the end of the Second World War in a powerful declaration, which was adopted by the Organization at the Conference it held in Philadelphia 1944, and subsequently incorporated into its Constitution. The Declaration of Philadelphia

---

[6] E. Phelan: "The contribution of the ILO to peace", in *International Labour Review* (Geneva, ILO, 1949), Vol. LIX, No. 6.

[7] Discussed more fully in M. MacMillan: *Paris 1919: Six months that changed the world* (New York, Random House, 2003).

[8] Hereafter referred to as the "Labour Commission".

reasserted the principles and goals of the Organization, and in important respects reinforced and expanded them. It is a strong statement of the need for international and national action for universal social progress.[9]

Key passages from these documents are reproduced in Appendix II. Together, they identify the principles, issues and means of governance that lie at the heart of the ILO's work.

Five basic principles can be distinguished in these texts.

- Lasting peace cannot be achieved unless it is based on social justice, grounded in freedom, dignity, economic security and equal opportunity.

- Labour should not be regarded merely as a commodity or an article of commerce.

- There should be freedom of association, for both workers and employers, along with freedom of expression, and the right to collective bargaining.

- These principles are fully applicable to all human beings, irrespective of race, creed or sex.

- Poverty anywhere constitutes a danger to prosperity everywhere, and must be addressed through both national and international action.

These moral and political principles guide the action of the ILO, and provide the cognitive framework for its work – the spectacles through which the ILO sees the world. The first of these, that peace must be based on social justice, has been considered above. It lays out the overriding reason for the existence of the Organization. The second provides the fundamental principle guiding its action. It expresses the dignity of labour and the recognition of its value, in contrast to the Marxian notion that, under capitalism, labour becomes a commodity. In the ILO's vision, all forms of work can, if they are adequately regulated and organized, be a source of personal well-being and social integration. Of course, labour is bought and sold, but market mechanisms are subordinate to higher goals. The original 1919 Constitution states that "labour should not be regarded merely as a commodity". By the time of the Declaration of Philadelphia, the same idea is expressed more strongly: "Labour is not a commodity."

The remaining principles express commitments – to democracy, equality and the reduction of poverty. Freedom of association and expression is the foundation of a model of participatory democracy, based on free debate among independent actors. The goal of equality is reflected in the universal principles of

---

[9] See E. Lee: "The Declaration of Philadelphia: Retrospect and prospect", in *International Labour Review* (Geneva, ILO, 1994), Vol. 133, No. 4, pp. 467–485.

the Declaration of Philadelphia, which are "fully applicable to all peoples everywhere" – even if pro-colonial governments prevented the adoption of any such commitment by the ILO or the League of Nations until the Second World War was drawing to a close (see Chapter 2). This basic tenet has underpinned the Organization's action on decolonization as well as its contribution to the struggle for gender equality. Finally, the imperative of action against poverty at international as well as national levels is expressed in terms of the interests and moral obligations of all.

All of these five principles are, of course, regularly flouted. Labour is widely treated as a commodity, poverty persists alongside prosperity, equality and freedom of association are widely honoured in the breach, and peace and social justice still remain distant goals in many parts of the world. Realizing these principles therefore continues to frame the action of the ILO.

Progress towards the goals implicit in these principles requires action in many specific fields. Seven central policy concerns are stressed in the Constitution:

- The promotion of full employment and rising standards of living, in occupations in which workers can apply their capabilities and contribute to the common well-being – along with equal opportunity for men and women in achieving this end, and facilities for training and for migration.

- The provision of an adequate living wage for all those employed, calculated to ensure a just share of the fruits of progress to all.

- The regulation of hours of work, including the establishment of a maximum working day and week, and of weekly rest.

- The protection of children, young persons and women, including the abolition of child labour, limitations on the labour of young persons and the provision for child welfare and maternity protection.

- Protection of the economic and social interests of those workers who are employed in countries other than their own.

- The adequate protection of all workers against sickness, death and injury arising out of employment.

- The extension of social security measures to provide for old age and ill-health, a basic income to all those in need of protection, and comprehensive medical care.

Obviously this list does not exhaust the areas where action is needed, but it does identify priorities. The first two elements express the concern with work as a source of livelihood and fulfilment – hence the goal of full and satisfying employment, at adequate wages and incomes; the third, fourth and fifth aim to prevent exploitation – notably by limiting hours of work, and taking measures to protect those who might be particularly vulnerable; and the last two are concerned with the protection of workers, both against a dangerous or otherwise inadequate working environment, and in terms of income security in the face of life's contingencies.

The Constitution also identifies four means of governance:

- Tripartism: the representatives of workers and employers, enjoying equal status with that of governments, join with them in free discussion and democratic decision on social and economic measures, and collaborate in increasing productive efficiency.

- The adoption of international Conventions and Recommendations to be submitted to national authorities for ratification or other action.

- A system of inspection to ensure enforcement of the laws and regulations concerned.

- Collaboration among international bodies in order to ensure that all economic and financial policies contribute to social progress and well-being.

We discuss the first two of these means of governance in more detail in separate sections below. The third is straightforward, at least in principle. The last, however, is an important and complex assertion. It expresses the belief that economic and social goals are interdependent, and that an international organization concerned with social goals should therefore be able to influence the design of international economic policy. It has been hard for the ILO to realize this demand, notably since the creation of the Bretton Woods institutions after the Second World War, but the issue regularly returns to the table, as we shall see in Chapters 5 and 6.

These then are the building blocks for the ILO's work, which constitute the subject matter of this book. Most of these ideas did not originate in the ILO, but were built on foundations which were established elsewhere. Yet they are "ILO ideas" in the sense that the ILO seized them, developed them and gave them practical expression. Although they date from the period 1919 to 1944, they remain largely valid today. Of course, priorities have evolved, and there have been some major discontinuities. The promotion of human rights came to the fore after the Second World War. Decolonization called for new forms of action.

Over time, a variety of actions and programmes have developed, which have expanded the ideas further. The work of the World Employment Programme in the 1970s put employment creation and basic needs at the heart of development strategy. Work on social security has embraced additional contingencies. Sources of discrimination other than race, creed and gender are now acknowledged. The 1998 Declaration on Fundamental Principles and Rights at Work has led to new forms of action.

With such a diverse agenda, building a coherent and integrated approach has always been a challenge. Today the overall goal is formulated as "decent work", a concept which synthesizes rights at work, employment and social protection into an overall vision, pursued through social dialogue, and which pays particular attention to the mutual reinforcement of action in different fields. The decent work goal is embedded in the most recent ILO Declaration, on Social Justice for a Fair Globalization. We shall return to this issue in Chapter 6.

Some of the ideas pursued by the ILO have been developed and driven by the Director-General of the time, or by leading figures among the staff. Others have been constructed within the political constituency, by groups among governments, workers or employers. Many result from an interaction between the Secretariat and the membership. Some have clearly been consensual ideas with widespread support. Others have been conflictual and contested – the management of international labour migration is a case in point.[10] In many cases, the Organization has been only one participant in a broader debate. Often its position has been weakened by divergent views within the Organization, especially between workers and employers – on labour market flexibility, for instance, or the role of reduced working time in employment creation.

There is an important premise underlying all this work – that international action is required to pursue these issues. The raison d'être of an international organization lies in its ability to achieve goals that cannot be achieved by nation states acting independently. The need for action beyond the national level is questioned at intervals. Examples include the retreat from the international economy during the Great Depression in the 1930s, or when the end of the Cold War led to talk of "the end of history". But the need for international action in favour of social justice has always been reasserted.

---

[10] Discussed in W.R. Böhning: *A brief account of the ILO and policies on international migration*, paper prepared for the ILO Century Project, 2008, available at: http://www.ilocentury.org, and below in Chapter 2.

## Box 1 The International Labour Organization today – A brief description

The ILO is a Specialized Agency of the United Nations system, and the principal centre of authority in the international system on labour and social policy.

The Organization as a whole, in its intention and in its essence, is a global assembly of the representatives of the world of work. It is tripartite, in that representatives of workers' and employers' organizations decide its programme and adopt its instruments alongside representatives of governments. Its membership is virtually universal.

Three organs oversee and carry out its work: the annual International Labour Conference of the entire membership; the Governing Body, elected by the Conference, which meets three times per year; and the Office, managed by the Director-General, who is elected by the Governing Body.

The International Labour Office, the secretariat of the Organization, today has a regular staff of some 1,700 people, and manages an annual core budget of around 320 million US dollars, a budget which has fluctuated around a broadly constant real level over the last 25 years. It is composed of both the "technical" departments of the Organization, which undertake research and provide expertise on the main issues with which the Organization is concerned; and the services which support the work of the Organization as a whole, including the administration and management of its work, its relationships with the membership and outside partners, and the supervision of its standards. Some specialized institutions are linked to the Office, including a training centre and an institute for labour studies, and some regional institutions. Just over half of the regular staff are posted in Geneva, and the remainder in some 50 country and regional offices around the world, engaged to a large extent in responding to demands from the membership in the regions concerned.

The results of the work of the ILO appear in the formal instruments that the Organization adopts – Conventions, Recommendations, resolutions, declarations and codes of practice; in publications, both official and authored, which range from training manuals and brochures to in-depth empirical research; and in policy-related activities at both global and national levels. The latter include advocacy, technical support and policy advice in member States, and technical cooperation projects and programmes in over 140 countries financed by outside donors on subjects which range from eliminating child labour to enterprise development, from microfinance to policies against social exclusion. Technical cooperation currently adds some 50 per cent to the regular budget and staffing levels.

The work of the Office is today organized around the goal of decent work for all women and men, discussed in Chapter 6, and structured into four sectors which deal with rights at work, employment, social protection and social dialogue.

Some key dates (for a full timeline see Appendix I):

**1919** Creation of the ILO by the Paris Peace Conference;

**1944** Declaration of Philadelphia;

**1946** The ILO becomes a Specialized Agency of the United Nations;

**1969** The ILO receives the Nobel Peace Prize;

**1998** Declaration on Fundamental Principles and Rights at Work.

## Tripartism

The ILO differs from other intergovernmental organizations in two basic respects, which derive from two of the means of governance identified above. The first of these is *tripartism* – the participation of the representatives of workers' and employers' organizations in its work and governance. The second, less well known even to many international lawyers, lies in the particular ways in which *international labour standards* are adopted, ratified and supervised. We discuss the first here,[11] and the second in the next section.

The ILO is the only international intergovernmental institution in which governments do not have the exclusive voting power in setting standards and policies. Employers and workers have an equal voice with governments in its decision-making processes. This concept, known as "tripartism", is based on article 3 of the ILO Constitution, which with great simplicity states that: "The ... General Conference ... shall be composed of four representatives of each of the Members, of whom two shall be Government delegates and the two others shall be delegates representing respectively the employers and the workpeople of each of the Members." The General Conference, which meets once a year, is a meeting of the entire membership that adopts the ILO's instruments and approves its programme. Day-to-day governance is the responsibility of a Governing Body with more limited membership, which is also tripartite (currently with 14 Worker members, 14 Employer members, and 28 Government members), and the tripartite structure is reproduced in almost every formal meeting convened by the ILO.[12] The Employers' and Workers' groups even have units of the Office (the secretariat of the Organization) dedicated to their interests and staffed from their representatives.

This form of governance attaches limits to the concept of the exclusive right of states as decision-makers in intergovernmental organizations, and acknowledges that workers and employers share interests on a global basis, transcending national boundaries. The adoption of a tripartite approach in 1919 also implied that conditions of labour and of social policy were recognized from the beginning of the new era of international organizations as appropriate subjects for interstate

---

[11] This section relies heavily on the papers written by Claude Akpokavie and Jean-Jacques Oechslin as contributions to the ILO Century Project. See J.-J. Oechslin: *Tripartisme, dialogue social et democratie: Perspectives du monde des employeurs*; and C. Akpokavie: *Tripartism, social dialogue and democracy* (2008), available at: http://www.ilocentury.org

[12] The only two recurring parts of the ILO structure that are not tripartite are the Finance Committee of the International Labour Conference, composed exclusively of governments; and the Committee of Experts on the Application of Conventions and Recommendations, composed of independent experts.

action; and that those directly concerned should bear joint responsibility for the decisions taken and their implementation. Even more important, it translated to the international sphere a means of resolving conflict through negotiation rather than confrontation.

Some countries had begun to create tripartite structures to deal with social issues at the national level at the end of the nineteenth century, but the First World War made this type of approach far more urgent. In this new kind of conflict, military success was tightly bound up with the ability of nations to support increasing demands on their economies and to build ever more sophisticated weapons, which demanded concerted industrial efforts. Business and labour had to become involved in policy and cooperate to support the national effort. In France, Albert Thomas, a socialist who was shortly to become the first Director of the ILO, was Minister of Armaments in 1916, and thus in a position to help forge an alliance of trade unions and employers for national defence that resulted in building mutual respect between them. In Germany, meetings between trade unions and employers resulted in an agreement in November 1918, putting an end to revolutionary strikes that had broken out in sympathy with the Bolshevik Revolution in Russia. The agreement provided for generalizing the eight-hour day, systems for conflict resolution, joint placement agencies and other advances. These wartime alliances – which would be reproduced in the Second World War – risked disappearing with the coming of peace, however, leading among other things to their being taken into account in the peace negotiations.

We have already noted Phelan's comment that the decision to give "non-Government" representatives a right to participate in international conferences was an entirely radical suggestion. In the build-up to war, promises had been made to organized labour in Allied countries to ensure their contribution to the war effort. Trade unions and employers were invited to sit on governmental bodies in Great Britain, the United States and elsewhere. Moreover, unions were asked to forego acquired trade union rights for the sake of the war effort with promises that these rights would be restored after the conflict. For instance, in order to secure the needed output of ammunition, trade union safeguards such as opposition to the substitution of women for male skilled workers had to be abandoned or diluted in Great Britain.[13] Neither trade unions nor employers' organizations were involved directly in the negotiations in Paris, but the international trade union movement was greatly concerned with the Peace Conference. Indeed, it had made a number of proposals during the war as to its outcome, and some recognition of this fact

---

[13] E. Phelan: "British preparations", in J.T. Shotwell (ed.): *The origins of the International Labor Organisation* (New York, Columbia University Press, 1934), Vol. I, p. 106.

influenced the composition of two of the delegations. The United States Government appointed to its delegation Samuel Gompers, President of the American Federation of Labor, whom the United States successfully imposed as President of the Labour Commission of the Peace Conference. A second representative on the United States delegation was an employer, Mr A.N. Hurley, President of the American Shipping Board.[14] The French substitute delegate was Léon Jouhaux, General Secretary of the General Confederation of Labour (CGT), who was to play a significant role in the events leading up to the creation of the ILO and in the early decades of the Organization (and who later received the Nobel Peace Prize for his work).

The first draft of the labour proposals for the Peace Conference had been prepared by the British Government and became the basis for the discussions in the Labour Commission, and these proposals included the establishment of an international organization for labour legislation that would give a voting role to representatives of workers and employers. A similar proposal had been made by the Allied Trade Union Conference in Leeds in June 1916. The true originality of the design of the ILO was to transpose existing tripartite structures at the national level to the new international organization.[15] The principle of tripartite representation was not seriously contested, but there was a bitter fight over how the representation and votes were to be allocated, with workers demanding an equal voice with governments. In the end, as noted above, a 2:1:1 formula was adopted, with each country represented by two Government delegates, and one delegate representing employers and one workers. However, a 1:1:1 formula survived in the committees of the General Conference, giving non-governmental representatives a decisive role at the crucial negotiating stage for new standards and other important decisions.

In synthesis, as the fifth Director-General, David Morse, said in his lecture accepting the Nobel Peace Prize for the ILO in 1969:

> [The First World War] resulted in trade unions and organizations of employers acquiring a position at home which they would not otherwise have had, and encouraged the growth of independent interest groups where they might otherwise never have developed. It also gave the world a new approach to the resolution of social conflict, an approach based on dialogue between the two sides of industry, and between them and the state. The ILO in short offered the world an alternative to social strife; it provided it with the procedures and techniques of bargaining and

---

[14] However, Hurley only participated in the first session of the Labour Commission.

[15] Akpokavie, op. cit., p. 14.

negotiation to replace violent conflict as a means of securing more human and dignified conditions of work.[16]

While there have been problems along the way, tripartism has generally survived without successful challenge to the principle, despite attempts by the Soviet Union, in particular, to weaken it. As the Second World War wound to a close, the value of tripartism was reaffirmed in the Declaration of Philadelphia:

> The war against want requires to be carried on with unrelenting vigour within each nation, and by continuous and concerted international effort in which the representatives of workers and employers, enjoying equal status with those of governments, join with them in free discussion and democratic decision with a view to the promotion of the common welfare.[17]

## Tripartism in practice

Tripartism is based on a notion of society built around collaboration among structured interests rather than individual actors. Nevertheless, it is also constructed on a fundamental principle of freedom of choice and freedom of association, which has frequently put the ILO in conflict with its Members. Many countries have attempted to institutionalize the organization of workers and employers at the national level in ways that restrict their freedom to choose the organizations to which they belong, and the political orientation of those organizations. The ILO's understanding of tripartism presupposes real independence of its worker and employer constituents vis-à-vis other groups and their governments. For this reason, the ILO struggled with the implications of communism and fascism, and the centralized control both systems exercised over the workers' and employers' movements in their countries, throughout the first 75 years of its history – and it continues to do so in a number of states that are unready to allow freedom of association in the ILO sense.

The implications of tripartism in the ILO are manifold. To put it simply, the participation in ILO deliberations of delegates directly representing the interests of workers and employers adds a connection with economic reality that cannot be reproduced in an organization where governments are the only spokespersons.

---

[16] D.A. Morse: *ILO and the social infrastructure of peace*, Nobel speech, on the occasion of the ILO being awarded the Nobel Peace Prize, Oslo, 11 December 1969.

[17] The Declaration is given in full in Appendix II.

The "social partners" are willing to challenge political convenience and the views of Ministries, and to add the perspectives of enterprises and workers' rights to governments' priorities. Since the Employers' and Workers' groups together have the same voting strength as the Governments, but are much more internally united than the latter, if they agree with each other, they can often set the agenda for discussion, on the content of international labour standards, for instance. And they have an international view that goes beyond the interests of individual nations in a way that Government representatives cannot often achieve. Indeed, because they are chosen by their groups, Workers' and Employers' delegates in the ILO tend to remain far longer than individual Government delegates, and thus accumulate knowledge and power bases that can give them great advantages over government delegations with their shifting composition, although this longevity can also reflect a restricted selection process.

The roles played by representatives of workers and employers differ markedly. For workers, the ILO is a major instrument to pursue their goals, and they have a much more active agenda than employers. On the other hand, employers frequently play the role of the "brake" on initiatives put forward both by the workers and the Office and its Director-General, to slow action they consider hasty, or which would work against the perceived interests of business. Albert Thomas used this metaphor in a speech to the German employers in 1928, and a recent history of the International Organization of Employers, the international umbrella organization for employers, comments that this is "not necessarily unflattering, since a locomotive without brakes has little chance of arriving at its destination".[18] Tensions between employers and the Office have been common. Employers vigorously attacked Albert Thomas in the late 1920s and early 1930s,[19] for instance, and many more recent examples could also be cited. At the same time, employers' representatives in the ILO tend to represent progressive currents of business opinion, and accommodations are usually found. Ultimately the ILO is valuable for both workers and employers because of the voice and influence that it offers them. One author aptly characterizes the importance of tripartism, when discussing the ILO's remarkable survival through the Second World War, as having been both a straitjacket and a lifejacket.[20]

---

[18] J.-J. Oechslin: *The International Organization of Employers: Three-quarters of a century in the service of the enterprise* (Geneva, IOE, 2001), p. 36.

[19] B.W. Schaper: *Albert Thomas: Trente ans de réformisme social* (Paris-Assen, Presses Universitaires de France-van Gorcum, 1959), Chapter 10 (forthcoming in English under the ILO Century Project).

[20] G. Van Goethem: "Phelan's War. The International Labour Organization in limbo, 1941–48", paper presented to the Conference "The ILO: Past and Present" (Brussels, 5–6 Oct. 2007), organized by the International Institute of Social History, Amsterdam, Ghent University and others.

All participants in the ILO have felt that promoting and protecting tripartism has benefits far beyond the ILO itself. There is an intimate relation between workers' and employers' rights and civil liberties more generally, which also places obligations on governments. As the ILO's Committee on Freedom of Association (discussed further in Chapter 2) put it, "the rights conferred upon workers' and employers' organizations must be based on respect for those civil liberties which have been enunciated in particular in the Universal Declaration of Human Rights and in the International Covenant on Civil and Political Rights ... the absence of these civil liberties removes all meaning from the concept of trade union rights".[21] It has also said that: "A free trade union movement can develop only under a regime which guarantees fundamental rights ...."[22] In this way, tripartism promotes not only industrial democracy, but also political and civil democracy at the national level. It is in this sense that tripartism is a form of participatory democracy.

There are, however, weaknesses here. Even if tripartism makes the ILO far more representative of civil society than any other intergovernmental organization, employers' and workers' organizations necessarily represent the formal economy rather than the huge – and growing – informal economy, especially in developing nations. In addition, with membership of trade unions shrinking in many industrialized states, the representativeness of these organizations even in the formal sector is often questioned. Another factor is that the very strength of tripartite structures in the ILO has kept the Organization from following developments in other intergovernmental organizations, which are making a greater place for "civil society" generally, and thereby representing a wider cross-section of views about social responsibilities and priorities.

This issue is regularly debated, and there are arguments on both sides. Workers' and employers' groups view the possible participation of non-occupational, non-governmental organizations (NGOs) in the ILO with deep concern, arguing that most have no democratic or representative credentials. They are very sensitive to any suggestion that NGOs might acquire a formal role in ILO decision-making. Trade unions in particular usually have a far greater claim to being representative than do almost all NGOs. At the same time, even though they espouse many of the same causes as these NGOs, they are usually less able to represent directly the interests of child labourers, indigenous and tribal peoples, and workers in unorganized sectors of the economy or where free organization is not permitted.

---

[21] ILO: *Freedom of Association: Digest of decisions of the Committee on Freedom of Association of the Governing Body of the ILO*, fifth (revised) edition (Geneva, 2006), para. 31.

[22] Ibid., para. 37.

Employers' groups in the ILO have a similar problem with the small and family enterprises that account for the bulk of employment in most countries.

A second element is that globalization has changed the original model upon which tripartism was based: representation at the international level of national economic interests. This early twentieth-century model, based on the then-industrializing world, has developed some gaps. Trade unions have searched for – but not yet found – satisfactory global models for international member-ship. And nationally based employers' organizations cannot adequately represent huge multinational corporations; nor can they effectively exercise pressure upon them to conform to international labour standards.[23] Indeed, even the concept of national sovereignty is changing with institutions such as the European Union, weakening direct government control over the workplace policies that they are bound to implement.

While there are now unions and employers' organizations in virtually all countries (and where they did not exist before the ILO has often helped in their development), these bodies sometimes coexist uneasily with other governing insti-tutions at the national level. Most of Western Europe and the Americas are sol-idly behind freedom of association for workers and employers in the ILO sense, but elsewhere some countries resist the idea of workers in particular being able to organize how and as they like – in part because independent trade unions may be perceived as a threat to insecure or undemocratic governments.

Tripartism has proved to be a resilient institution over the last 90 years. The challenge for the ILO and its constituents is to adapt the tripartite model to a globalizing world, where there are new actors operating outside national frame-works and increasingly diverse forms of voice and representation. Some measures of accommodation have been found, for instance involving cooperation with NGOs in action against child labour, and dialogue with parliamentarians and other important actors. The broader challenge remains.

---

[23] In fact, the International Organization of Employers was created entirely to represent its mem-bers in the ILO, unlike the trade union movement which added representation in the ILO to an existing international vocation.

## The system of international labour standards

The ILO is different from other international organizations in another important respect – in the standards that it adopts and the way it supervises their implementation, a system often described as the cornerstone of the Organization.[24] These standards lay down actions to be taken, or principles to be respected, by governments and others, in the ILO's main fields of action.

### Conventions and Recommendations

The basic standards system was included in the original design offered by the British delegation to the Labour Commission of the Peace Conference. It was generally accepted that the new ILO was to continue the standard-setting work on labour and social matters already undertaken before the First World War by European states and the IALL, commented on above. The system has evolved in the course of the ILO's history, but the basic principles remain.

The original British design proposed the adoption of only Conventions, that would be binding once ratified, in accordance with accepted international law and with the earlier efforts of the IALL.[25] The United States took the opposite position, maintaining that the instruments adopted by the Conference should be merely Recommendations: if no action were taken to enact them into national law, there would be no obligation to pursue the matter further.

Negotiations in the Labour Commission eventually resulted in an agreement to allow the adoption of both Conventions and Recommendations, which would be submitted to the competent national authority for action (and in the case of Conventions, for ratification). While far from assuring implementation, since ratification is optional, the agreement does require consideration in every state of each new instrument.

Like other international treaties, these standards are negotiated in a multinational forum. In the case of the ILO, of course, this forum is tripartite, and the active participation of workers and employers is essential if they are to be adopted.

---

[24] A selection from among the numerous publications on the ILO's standards system is given in Appendix III.

[25] See generally J. Shotwell (ed.): *The origins of the International Labor Organisation* (New York, Columbia University Press, 1934), Vol. 1.

The 188 Conventions and 199 Recommendations adopted since 1919[26] cover virtually all aspects of labour law and labour relations, some of them in considerable detail, and they are very widely reproduced or followed at the national level. There are ILO standards on rights at work, on many aspects of conditions of work, on safety and health, on social security, on labour administration and inspection, on employment and training, on wages, migration, and on particular categories of workers such as seamen, agricultural workers, indigenous peoples or migrants. Together they form a comprehensive corpus of international law.

There had been over 7,500 ratifications of ILO Conventions by 2008. Conventions vary greatly in their success, and many fall into disuse or become out-of-date and need to be replaced. But some 14 Conventions have registered more than 100 ratifications among the 182 member States (including all eight of the fundamental Conventions concerned with basic rights at work); and a further 28 have been ratified by more than 50 countries. In recent years, effort has concentrated on ratification of the fundamental Conventions, but ratifications of other Conventions also continue to be registered, albeit at a slower pace.

### The supervision of standards

Ratification would have little value without follow-up, and here the ILO has a number of distinctive mechanisms, which no other international organization shares.

Governments are obliged to report to an independent Committee of Experts on ratified Conventions (some 3,000 reports are now due per year). Employers' and workers' organizations have the right to receive copies of these reports and practice has evolved to allow them to make their own comments on these reports. This is the only international system in which NGOs have a statutory role in the supervision of international obligations. This system makes it much more difficult (but not impossible) for governments to supply false or limited information to the ILO, as they are wont to do in other international organizations.

A remarkable provision in the ILO's Constitution (article 19) permits the Governing Body also to require reports from all member States on their practice concerning *unratified* Conventions and on Recommendations. This allows pressure to be put on states which fail to pursue widely agreed goals and, notably,

---

[26] Some are now obsolete and others are out-of-date, so the number of operational standards is lower. As of the end of 2008, 30 Conventions have been withdrawn and only 76 are considered fully up-to-date.

basic human rights in the world of work. It has been used in several procedures to expand both the promotion and monitoring of standards.

The ILO's *complaints mechanisms* are also unique. Complaints can be made that a state is not respecting a Convention that it has ratified by:

- another state that has ratified the same Convention;
- delegates to the International Labour Conference (both under article 26 of the Constitution); or
- employers' and workers' organizations, which may make "representations" under article 24 of the Constitution, a form of complaint unique to the ILO.

In 1951, the ILO added an entirely original complaints mechanism, which authorized employers' or workers' organizations to submit complaints alleging violations of the basic principle of freedom of association contained in the Constitution, *even when the relevant Conventions had not been ratified by the member State concerned*. The Governing Body Committee on Freedom of Association, which considers these complaints, thus evolved into a full-blown complaints mechanism itself.

This system of reporting and review deals with both legislative compliance with instruments, and with their implementation in practice – though information on the latter aspect is harder to obtain. Some countries tend to believe that they are unfairly targeted by harsh criticisms from ILO supervisory bodies, consider that "Western" values are applied, or feel that there should be more flexibility and understanding of the obstacles to strict conformity. During the Cold War, for example, there were marked differences of opinion on the meaning of freedom of association and the proper uses of forced labour, which have not entirely disappeared. The supervisory system has been adjusted at intervals to take account of such criticisms, though no fundamental changes have ever been made. In addition, the reporting burden on states, and the administrative burden on the Office, have grown steadily, and several times have had to be trimmed back.

Follow-up to the various complaints mechanisms include a number of procedures, including, in extreme cases, Commissions of Inquiry to investigate allegations in depth. (Examples of such Commissions are given in Chapter 2.)

## Other instruments

Conventions and Recommendations are not the only ILO instruments. The Organization has also adopted a small number of declarations, on particularly important issues. The 1944 Declaration of Philadelphia, which we have discussed above, was the first such instrument, subsequently incorporated into the Constitution. There have been Declarations on Apartheid (1964, revised several times), on Equality of Opportunity and Treatment for Women Workers (1975), on Multinational Enterprises and Social Policy (1977, revised 2000 and 2006) and on Fundamental Principles and Rights at Work (1998). And in 2008, the Conference adopted a Declaration on Social Justice for a Fair Globalization, which consolidated the Decent Work Agenda as the integrated framework for the ILO's action. Appendix II gives the website references to these texts.

Codes of practice are also a long tradition in the ILO,[27] especially as concerns occupational safety and health (OSH). They are not legally binding, but rather serve as practical guides for public authorities and agencies, enterprises and trade unions. The influence they exert on national law and practice is variable, but can be considerable, even without any formal follow-up mechanisms. Many resolutions have also been adopted at the International Labour Conference, some of which have been used as the basis for subsequent policy work.

## The impact of ILO standards

While some high-profile examples can be identified, a systematic assessment of the impact of ILO standards and their supervision has proven difficult to devise. Apart from anything else, while it is possible to decide whether a country is in compliance with the Conventions it has ratified, it is often impossible to decide whether it complies because of the standards themselves, because of ILO supervision or for other reasons.[28]

Clearly, ratification alone is not a sufficient indicator of impact. Nevertheless, ratification usually results in at least legislative conformity with

---

[27] See also Chapter 3. Texts of ILO codes of practice can be found on the ILO website: http://www. ilo.org

[28] However, the reports of the Committee of Experts on progress in national legislation provide some indirect evidence. See I. Boivin and A. Odero: "The Committee of Experts on the Application of Conventions and Recommendations: Progress achieved in national labour legislation", in *International Labour Review* (Geneva, ILO, 2006), Vol. 145, No. 3, which considers 208 cases of progress in the period 2001–05.

Conventions; enables the ILO to exercise supervision; and, over time, creates movement towards practical conformity. In some countries, ratified international Conventions become an integral part of national legislation; in others, they are binding in international but not in national law. A growing number of national courts cite ILO Conventions to interpret national legislation.[29] The majority of labour codes around the world by and large conform to ILO standards, in their main thrust if not always in detail. While generally valid indicators of success have yet to be devised,[30] the accumulated evidence indicates significant and positive impact, though rarely full compliance with Conventions.[31] The major *deliberate* deviations occur because of economic factors such as a belief that standards reduce labour market flexibility, or the desire to attract investment – for instance to export-processing zones with lower standards – and such factors often create resistance to regulation. But, in fact, most failures to comply with ratified standards can be traced to a lack of capacity to implement them because of low levels of economic and institutional development or an underdeveloped commitment to the rule of law. This casts light on the reasons why many countries make requests to the ILO for technical assistance specifically to help implement standards.

The role of labour standards in development remains controversial in some quarters. Standard economic theory would maintain that there is a trade-off between increased regulation and economic performance, but this is too simple a notion where labour protection is concerned. Even though some parts of, for instance, the World Bank discourage the adoption of standards as holding back economic development,[32] there is a growing body of evidence that development is not sustainable if it ignores workers' rights – and this is one of the driving impulses behind the decent work approach.[33] Naturally, the standards a country

---

[29] A database of such citations is maintained by the ILO training centre in Turin, and may be found at http://training.itcilo.org

[30] See, inter alia, E.A. Landy: *The effectiveness of international supervision: Thirty years of ILO experience* (London, Stevens and Sons, 1966). There was also a series of articles in the *International Labour Review* detailing the influence of international labour standards on the law and practice in various member States – now unfortunately discontinued in spite of its obvious value – beginning with Switzerland in 1958 and ending with Australia in 1987.

[31] See, for instance, the description of a project conducted by the International Labour Standards Department on the economic dynamics of international labour standards, in ILO Governing Body document GB.300/LILS/10, 300th Session, Geneva, November 2007.

[32] The World Bank's *Doing Business* reports rank countries for ease of doing business based, in part, on an "employing workers" index that classifies countries in terms of the ease of hiring and firing workers and the laxity of labour standards. See, for instance, the rankings in the 2008 report at: http://www.doingbusiness.org/economyrankings/

[33] See: *International Labour Review* (Geneva, ILO, 2003), Vol. 142, No. 2: Special issue on measuring decent work.

observes should be appropriate to the existing level of development in order for them to exercise this positive impact; but denying these standards altogether is even worse. Research conducted jointly by the ILO and the Asian Development Bank in 2001 came to the firm conclusion that there was a measurable negative cost to development if standards are ignored, even if an individual employer might reap temporary benefit from undercutting conditions of work and pay.[34]

This debate has also taken place within the ILO itself, as concerns the degree to which ILO standards should be observed in providing technical assistance. To date, the most successful approach to this issue has been to place particular emphasis, in development cooperation, on the small number of standards dealing with fundamental rights at work (Chapters 2 and 6). Respect for these standards is increasingly referred to as a condition for favourable tariff rates in international trade,[35] and for loans from multilateral banks.[36] In recent times, more than half the ILO's total technical cooperation expenditure has been related directly to the implementation of core standards. Other standards then provide a frame of reference on which countries can draw to promote social goals, depending on national objectives and development level. These issues are considered further in following chapters.

## Concluding comments

Although the ILO's standards system often appears to be much like other international standards systems, it has unique features that distinguish the ILO sharply from other intergovernmental organizations, and give it a distinctive role.

Nevertheless, the system devised in 1919 has its critics, even inside the Organization, where employers and some governments are increasingly reticent to accept new standards. The need for some degree of regulation is not seriously contested; but there is considerable resistance in some quarters to the idea of a systematic framework of regulation around all aspects of work. That, of course, is the stuff of social dialogue, which can be quite complex at times within the

---

[34] Asian Development Bank: Regional Technical Workshop on Labor Standards (Manila, Philippines, September 2002). See, inter alia, ILO presentation at: http://www.adb.org/Documents/Events/2002/Core_Labor_Standards/agenda.asp

[35] The "Generalized System of Preferences" of both the United States and the European Union are conditioned on compliance with specified ILO standards.

[36] See, for example, Performance Standards adopted in 2006 by the International Finance Corporation; and Environmental and Social Standards adopted in 2008 by the European Bank for Reconstruction and Development.

ILO. Accommodations are usually found, although often at the cost of weaker instruments.

A quite different criticism of the ILO standards system is that it does not have sufficient "teeth" to force implementation of even basic principles when governments fail, or refuse, to comply. While it is true that the ILO cannot apply sanctions or force implementation,[37] the same criticism is equally applicable to other international organizations. It is a fundamental fact that states will not renounce sovereignty to the extent of allowing themselves to be forced to apply international decisions except in extremely limited circumstances. Because of that fact, it is hard to better a system based on the voluntary acceptance of obligations, peer pressure to respect those obligations and, where needed, assistance to countries to help them to do so.

## The ILO in a changing world

The ILO has essentially retained the same institutional design and purpose since its foundation in 1919. Yet the political, economic and social environment today is vastly different from what it was then. Globally, there has been tremendous progress in average levels of wages and incomes, life expectancy, education, health and other key measures of welfare. The world today is also vastly different in terms of the level of technology and productivity, economic structure and the composition of output, occupational patterns and the organization of production, both nationally and globally. The political environment has undergone major upheavals, and many societies have changed dramatically, with the disappearance of traditional ways of life, new class structures and a rise to power of new groups. Virtually every country has adopted laws to protect working people and to regulate the labour market. These changes have necessarily had their impact over time on the methods, scope and effectiveness of the Organization, even though the fundamental issues the ILO was designed to address with respect to labour and social policy in the world remain just as pertinent today as when it was created. While its core rationale remains unchanged, its action has been largely conditioned by changing economic and social circumstances.

---

[37] Although the Constitution (article 33) provides an open-ended authority for the Conference to take "such action as it may deem wise and expedient to secure compliance". In practice, this is, of course, subordinated to wider political considerations. It has only been invoked for the case of forced labour in Myanmar (see Chapter 2).

The ILO exerts some influence on economic and social change, and the nature and extent of that influence are considered in the following chapters. At the same time, it is clear that fundamental forces outside the Organization are the main drivers of global trends. Some of them have had a particularly strong impact on the ILO.

A basic one has been shifts in the predominant view on the correct balance between the market and the state. This often coincides with shifts in the relative importance given to economic or social considerations in policy discourse, and to political views as to the desirability of public regulation.

A second set of factors concerns the global economic situation: the state of prosperity, or otherwise, in the global economy; the extent to which globalization prevails, and the pace of technological change and of the organizational and institutional changes that follow in its train.

A third condition is the extent to which the prevailing political environment is conducive to the idea of universal individual and collective rights, and – connected with this – the prevalence of democratic or authoritarian governments.

A fourth condition, of particular importance to the ILO, concerns changing patterns of work, and of the organization and representation of workers and enterprises at both national and international levels.

And a fifth, broad group of factors concerns key social changes such as the move towards equality for woman, the rise of the middle class and the worldwide process of urbanization.

In the following paragraphs, we shall highlight, very selectively, how some of these factors have impacted on the ILO during its existence, as an introduction to the review of its work in following chapters.

### A changing workforce

There have been dramatic demographic changes since the ILO was created. From 1919 to 2008 the global population grew from 1.8 to 6.7 billion. Improved living conditions, health care and technological advance in industry and agriculture led to a decrease in mortality and rising life expectancy. Fertility declined more slowly, and unevenly. Demographic changes have also been associated, both as cause and as consequence, with increasing labour force participation by women. These patterns were regionally differentiated, so that one part of the world – Japan, for example – would be facing a problem of ageing and a decline in the labour force, while another – much of sub-Saharan Africa – would be faced with an explosion of new labour market entrants. Creating an enormous number of new jobs for young people, of a quality which meets rising expectations, has become a central preoccupation of policy-makers in many developing countries, along with the associated questions of training, mobility and enterprise development. Child labour, seen by many poor families as a solution to income shortfalls, is now recognized as a serious societal problem.

There were equally diverse movements of population, both within countries, as urbanization proceeded apace, and internationally. The greatest voluntary migration in history had taken place between 1900 and 1914, when over 13 million people left Europe to settle in the United States. After the Second World War there were again enormous population movements. Wide gaps between countries in terms of income and opportunities continue to provide enormous pressure for migration, legal and illegal, both within and between regions. However, labour migration from poor to rich countries in the twentieth century became increasingly hard to separate from a constant flood of refugees who fled from, or were uprooted by, famine, political or ethnic persecution, war or civil conflict.

The effect on the ILO's agenda was as diverse at the changes themselves. The ILO's efforts to become the main international agency to manage international migration after the Second World War failed (Chapter 2), but migrants and migration remain a major ILO concern, perhaps even more so as globalization has changed the functioning of global labour markets. The labour market and employment consequences of changing population patterns were an important consideration in the development strategies elaborated by the World Employment Programme. And a major effort to reduce child labour started at the beginning of the 1990s, and has yielded some encouraging results (Chapter 2).

## The economic and political environment up to 1950

The economic and political changes were no less dramatic. The very fact of the ILO's foundation attests to the fact that in 1919 the climate of opinion in the founding states was at the "state" end of the "state or market" spectrum. Apprehension over the prospects of maintaining social peace in war-ravaged economies in the shadow of the Bolshevik Revolution was an important conditioning factor. Social-democratic or coalition governments were formed in many countries in the 1920s, which were favourable to more effective regulation. This initial impetus was sustained by the realization that cooperative international action was important for tackling the monetary and economic imbalances and instability in the global economy.

The First World War not only transformed the international political order. It also shook the international economy to the core. Both businessmen and governments had originally expected that after the temporary disruptions of the world war somehow the world economy would quickly return to the halcyon days before 1914. But readjustment proved more difficult than expected. Economic recovery was uneven, unemployment remained high and the resumption of growth was accompanied by a rapid increase in income inequality. Only by the second half of the 1920s did world trade recover from the disruptions of war and post-war crisis and again reach the level of 1913. But this renewal of globalization came to grief in the crash of 1929 that triggered the Great Depression.

During the 1920s, despite both political and economic instability the underlying environment remained favourable to an international organization dedicated to promoting both economic and social progress. The ILO was able to put in place a series of international standards, establish a basic statistical information system and build up its capability for research in social insurance, OSH and other aspects of the quality of work (see Chapters 3 and 4). In the early 1930s, however, the environment changed with the rapid spread of the economic crisis, the breakdown of the global trading and financial system and the rush to protectionism. Between 1929 and 1935 the volume of world trade diminished by two-thirds. The incapacity of the traditional political parties to respond adequately to the mass unemployment caused by the depression plunged political democracy into a structural crisis. Parliamentary democracy was weak in the successor states to the old European empires as well as in most of the Mediterranean and in Latin America, where military coups installed dictatorships. All were authoritarian and hostile to liberal political institutions. In the search for solutions, the temptation to look at alternative, more radical political models was great. Some turned to communism, others to fascism.

There were multiple effects on the ILO. Fascist regimes were clearly incompatible with the ILO's model of tripartism, in that workers' and employers' delegates were not free of government control. The workers' group had unsuccessfully challenged the credentials of the delegates of fascist Italian trade unions in the 1920s, and the issue also arose with the workers' delegates from the other fascist nations. When the USSR joined in 1934 their workers' and employers' delegates were challenged on the same grounds. But the European countries with Nazi and fascist regimes left the ILO in the mid-1930s, as, in practice, did the USSR in 1939.

In the United States, which joined the ILO in 1934, the crisis led to the election of Franklin Roosevelt and the introduction of the New Deal. The latter reflected the ascendancy of Keynesian ideas in the economics profession, and was based on the premise that the market needed to operate within a framework of public planning and economic management. This was clearly in line with the ILO's vision, and provided ample space for the ILO to address issues of international economic policy and employment (see Chapter 5). On the other hand, the value of international regulation was contested in many quarters, and the ILO's priorities shifted away from standards towards the design of national and regional policy, on social insurance in Latin America, for example (Chapter 4). Other parts of the non-European world remained largely subject to colonial domination, and this was reflected in a very tentative approach by the ILO to extending labour standards in those regions (Chapter 2), which became a truly universal approach only after the war.

The Second World War spelled the demise of the League of Nations, and could easily have done the same for the ILO. As the opening paragraphs of this chapter illustrate, the support of the United States was central to its survival, but the support of workers' and employers' organizations through its tripartite structure also gave the ILO a crucial advantage over the League of Nations. Although the action of the ILO and of its constituents was necessarily reduced during the war, reflection on the role it should play in the construction of the post-war world led in 1944 to the adoption of the Declaration of Philadelphia, discussed at various points in this book and reproduced in Appendix II.

After the war, one of the principal problems faced by the ILO in establishing itself as a specialized agency of the United Nations was hostility from the Soviet Union, which had other plans for dealing with international labour and social policies (see Chapter 2). But this was not the only difficulty. In the new framework, international institutions were created which occupied a good deal of the space the ILO had claimed between the wars (Chapters 5 and 6). The net outcome of the process was an ILO with a very broad mandate, but in practice a reduced political space for action. However, there was one space in which new opportunities for the ILO emerged. The priority which was given to human rights in the wake of the war, enshrined in particular in the Universal Declaration of Human Rights, provided an impetus for progress on fundamental rights at work in the ILO, leading to the adoption of a series of Conventions (Chapter 2).

## The Golden Age and its aftermath

The climate of opinion in the 1950s and 1960s was broadly favourable to ILO values. This was the "Golden Age" of rapid economic growth in the global economy and full employment in the industrialized countries. Many developing countries also experienced higher growth during this period. In terms of political ideology, Western Europe was consolidating the development of welfare states, which in many cases also included significant elements of social partnership. Trade unions were strong, labour markets were being increasingly regulated and the quality of work improved (Chapter 3). The fact that these social developments coincided with rapid growth and full employment left little room for "laissez-faire" ideas to thrive. Another significant feature of this period was the relative stability of the governance of the global economy. The unchallenged hegemony of the United States, the Bretton Woods system of fixed exchange rates (anchored on a fixed parity of the US dollar to gold) and closed capital accounts worked reasonably well in ensuring orderly adjustments and preventing major crises in the global economy.

Three major developments affected the ability of the ILO to take advantage of this favourable environment. The first was the Cold War. The second was decolonization. And the third was the process of change in occupational and industrial structures.

The confrontation between the two superpowers in the decades after the war meant that there were two competing models of social and economic organization, and once the Soviet Union had rejoined the ILO in 1954 the ideological debate clearly limited the ILO's sphere of action. As in the 1930s, there were unsuccessful protests by employers of the Western countries against employer representatives being included in national delegations from the Socialist countries. Behind this issue of representation, however, was a question of the policy positions and advice that the ILO could advocate. Although a social market model continued to predominate in the ILO, much of its work lay uneasily between the more extreme views of East and West, the political environment restricted the ability of the Organization to play a global role, and much energy was wasted in taking and defending political positions in the ILO's governing organs. This was, for instance, one of the reasons why the ILO played a relatively modest role in the development of a social dimension for European integration. It was also one of the factors which led to a temporaray withdrawal of the United States from the Organization in the 1970s (the other being the issue of Palestine – Chapter 2).

Decolonization gave rise to a more positive reorientation. The rise of a Third World of post-colonial states helped move the ILO towards a more global, universal vision, and changed the pattern of debate. These new states shared a number of common interests, especially the need to overcome their underdevelopment, the efforts to organize non-aligned solidarity and the demand for foreign aid. But for some newly independent countries, one kind of repression was replaced by another. Authoritarian regimes spread during the era of decolonization and Cold War.

Partly because of this spread of authoritarian and populist regimes, there were problems in some new member States with ILO issues such as freedom of association and forced labour. But, on the other hand, decolonization reinforced a universalistic vision and ended the ambiguity of dual standards that had characterized the colonial period. Most of the developing world in this period was under the sway of socialist or social-democratic models of development and hence quite at ease with notions of labour market regulation and a strong role of the state in development. Intellectually, however, it required the ILO to generate new knowledge on the clearly different nature of economic, social and labour problems in developing countries and on the types of policies and technical assistance that would work in this context.

This had both substantive and political implications for the ILO. The new developing countries in the ILO's governing organs were able to press for a refocusing of ILO work on their concerns. This led to an expansion of technical cooperation programmes and a reorientation of research towards development issues. Politically, the highest profile action concerned action against apartheid, discussed in Chapter 2, which exemplified the post-colonial frame for much of the ILO's work.

As will be discussed in Chapter 5, the ILO successfully engaged with the new development agenda through the World Employment Programme (WEP). Among other themes, the work of the WEP highlighted the awkward, almost existentialist issue of the informal sector that still bedevils the ILO today. What is the optimal response of the ILO to the fact that in low-income countries its labour standards and the key labour market institutions reach only a minority of the labour force? Contrary to earlier expectations this is not a problem that will go away in the course of development, it may, in fact, be intensifying in some countries because of accelerating globalization. How this issue is ultimately resolved will depend not only on a better understanding of the causes and consequences of informality but also on what view as to the appropriate balance between the state and markets holds sway within the ILO.

Meanwhile, radical changes in occupational and industrial structures were modifying the nature and the spatial pattern of work. The industrial patterns which characterized the world of the early ILO changed in the decades after the

Second World War. Employment in manufacturing and mining in countries which were once accurately described as industrialized started to decline, first as a result of labour-saving technology, and in due course because of a restructuring of production in the global economy. The traditional industries did not disappear but shifted from old to new industrial countries. Textiles, clothing and footwear migrated massively. Iron, steel and ship-building virtually disappeared from the countries of early industrialization in the second half of the twentieth century, but surfaced in Brazil, Korea, Poland and Romania, and later on in China and India. Meanwhile, in high-income countries, but increasingly in poorer countries, employment in services has grown rapidly to take the place of industrial jobs, with implications for the organization of both workers and firms.

The world of the 1920s was also essentially agrarian, save in a few of the most industrialized countries, and this too has changed dramatically. Only two regions of the globe retain a rural majority today: sub-Saharan Africa and parts of South and East Asia, notably with the enormous rural populations of China and India. Over the years, the agricultural workforce, of which women formed a large part, has been reduced through the mechanization of agriculture and the introduction of improved crops, and this process too accelerated in the post-war decades. As the land emptied, the cities filled up. The world of the second half of the twentieth century became urbanized as never before. The multi-million city mushroomed. By far the most gigantic urban agglomerations were to be found in the Third World (in places like Mexico City and Mumbai).

The importance of these changes for the ILO is evident. They have modified the size and geographical distribution of what can still be called the working class, and changed its pattern of organization. The sense of a cohesive working class, which aimed to improve living and working conditions through collective action, was clearly stronger in the early ILO than today. It has not, of course, disappeared, but working class lives and interests have been transformed. Together with the growth of the tertiary sector and the rising proportion of skilled and white-collar workers, this has weakened the traditional labour movements. It is true that a strong labour movement has developed around the industrial sector in some middle-income countries – Brazil, Republic of Korea – but in many lower-income developing countries formal organization covers only a small minority of workers. Beyond the question of organization and representation, these changes affect the quality and security of jobs, the skills needed to undertake them, their distribution among different groups of workers, the extent to which rights are respected, incomes and productivity, in short the whole of the ILO's agenda.

The 1970s marked the end of the relative stability of the "Golden Age". The first oil shock in 1973 triggered rising inflation, economic turbulence and social tensions across the world. The oil shock itself was symbolic of a broader claim by the Third World for a New International Economic Order that would finally redress the economic injustice of centuries of colonial pillage and exploitation. The naive hopes that political emancipation would soon yield economic take-off were rapidly dashed. Yet popular expectations remained high and the modest gains from development efforts fuelled social unrest. In the industrialized countries, the aftermath of the first oil shock placed great strains on the welfare state and the commitment to full employment. Inflation driven by rising costs was a major problem as trade unions used their bargaining power to protect the real incomes of their members. Incomes policies based on social dialogue failed to provide the solution and industrial unrest increased.

The 1970s also marked the end of the Bretton Woods fixed exchange rate system based on the dollar and the beginning of a period of increased exchange rate instability. The seeds of the debt crisis that hit the developing world in the early 1980s were also being sown as increased balance of payments difficulties and the availability of recycled petro-dollars lead to increasing foreign indebtedness in many developing countries. At the same time, this period marked the growth of economic differentiation in the developing world as a minority of high-growth countries, mainly in East Asia, pulled away from the rest on the back of export-led industrialization. The trend has since continued with the more recent rise of China and India. The rise of the "Newly Industrializing Countries" was also important from an ideological standpoint, since neo-liberal economists selectively depicted their experience as a powerful demonstration of the benefits of trade liberalization for development. This was an important contribution to the triumph of neo-classical economics that was soon to come.

## A global market economy

In the 1980s, neo-liberal thought became dominant in international economic policy. As will be discussed in Chapter 5, this placed severe restraints on the ILO's room for manoeuvre and left it marginalized from the great economic and social issues of the decade such as privatization, labour market deregulation, the rolling back of the welfare state in the industrialized countries and structural adjustment in the developing world. The ILO model of tripartite dialogue was contested, and trade unions in particular faced an unfriendly economic and political environment.

During the 1980s, these fundamental developments in the economic and social sphere also affected the political world order. Growth in the market economies in the 1980s was uneven – it was the "lost decade" in Latin America – but the expansion of international trade and the rise of the "tiger" economies in Asia highlighted the economic and technological shortcomings of the Soviet bloc. Increasing dissent during the decade culminated in the fall of the Eastern European socialist regimes and the disintegration of the Soviet Union. The ILO's constituents in the countries concerned were of course involved in this process, and the ILO itself played a significant role, notably in Poland (Chapter 2). These political changes in Eastern Europe naturally created new demands for the ILO, notably to strengthen independent workers' and employers' organizations in the countries concerned.

But the economic impact was at least as important as the political. For during the 1980s the foundations for a new wave of globalization were being laid. The significant economic liberalization that occurred in the industrialized and many developing countries meant that policy obstacles to the growth of trade, investment and financial flows were being lowered. At the end of the decade the collapse of the Soviet bloc accelerated the move towards the dominance of the global market economy. This, together with the implementation of economic reforms in China, and to a lesser extent in India, meant that the stage was set for the rapid globalization that was to occur from the 1990s onwards.

The early 1990s saw a continuation of the neo-liberal hegemony of the 1980s. The action was centred on the former communist countries where "big bang" programmes of economic liberalization were implemented at high social cost. Although there were considerable implications for ILO goals and constituents, the Organization had little influence over these events. By the mid-1990s, however, there were more hopeful signs. As will be discussed in Chapter 6, there was a growing reaction to the excessive social costs of neo-liberal policies and this found political expression both in efforts to promote a social clause in international trade and in a series of global UN summits, which reasserted the importance of social concerns. At the same time financial globalization also began to take off and financial crises increased in frequency and intensity in its wake. The devastating social costs of these crises created an obvious need for a social response to globalization, to which the ILO has attempted to respond.

The 2000s have seen an accelerated broadening and deepening of globalization. The global economy is now a far more complex entity than even a decade or two ago. A new global production system has grown rapidly, creating complex multi-country and multi-tiered economic relationships among governments, multinational companies, local firms and workers. The scope of cross-border transactions has expanded greatly and now includes the off-shoring of many service activities. Financial globalization has grown exponentially while the global reach and market power of MNCs in the real economy has increased greatly. These developments have weakened the power of governments to control and regulate national economies while instruments for global governance remain underdeveloped. Civil society groups active on labour and social issues have also proliferated. Access to knowledge and the flow of information and communication is now virtually instantaneous. How intelligently and how quickly the ILO can respond to the challenges posed by this new complex global economy will be a crucial determinant of its future effectiveness and relevance (Chapter 6).

## A changing social environment

These developments formed part of a broader process of social and economic change which has impinged on the ILO's work in many ways. Partly as a result of shifts in industrial patterns, there has been a rather fundamental change in the conceptualization of the employment relationship in industrialized countries. From a model of the regular, full-time, waged, male breadwinner in industrial work – never the most abundant type of work but the dominant frame of reference from the beginnings of the ILO, in part because this group was easiest to organize – the concept of work and employment has widened, reflecting improved understanding, but also changes in labour markets towards more fragmented and differentiated statuses (Chapter 3). There has also been some movement towards gender equality in employment, or at least the recognition of this goal, which has affected the way ILO policies are conceived – for example, on night work for women (Chapters 2 and 3). Of course, part of the change in approach results from the expansion of ILO work on employment in developing countries, where the "standard" employment relationship remains very far from standard in reality.

These changes in patterns of work and production are mirrored in trends in poverty and exclusion, and it is clear that progress is highly uneven. Despite economic growth, the absolute numbers of poor people are falling little, indeed outside China and India they are rising – a process which is no doubt exacerbated by the global economic crisis under way as we write. Polarization shows up in a widening gap between the top and bottom of the income scale both within and between countries, and informality and the persistence of precarious and fragmented work intensify patterns of exclusion. Overcoming these failures is a central policy concern in much of the world – and this highlights the space and need for ILO action in favour of employment and decent work (Chapter 5).

There are aspects of a wider social transformation, which also includes the emergence of the consumer society and the rise of the middle class. The new middle class may have more common interests across borders than with other groups within countries. New movements – religious, political, interest-based – are developing as existing political, social and economic institutions are questioned. There is a state of flux and great global diversity, which resists the imposition of oversimplified universal solutions. The ILO has responded with greater or lesser agility to these developments in its various domains of work. To these we now turn.

# Human rights and rights at work[1]

2

## Introduction

On 18 June 1998, the International Labour Conference was poised to adopt the Organization's first explicit and comprehensive statement of a commitment to human rights since the Declaration of Philadelphia in 1944. It had taken days of heated discussions to reach this point. Although the Declaration on Fundamental Principles and Rights at Work now enjoys universal support, it was a matter of considerable controversy at the time. The committee room had been filled with what was called the greatest assembly of trade ambassadors ever gathered in Geneva to discuss labour issues – and they were afraid that the adoption of an ILO commitment to human rights would be used to undermine the ability of developing countries to take advantage of cheap labour to maintain their export markets. Indeed, the trade representatives had been caught totally unawares when they had lost a vote in committee because the employers and workers had combined to defeat a proposal they supported.

In the plenary, the President of the Conference was about to bring the gavel down for unanimous adoption of the new Declaration when suddenly the Egyptian Minister of Labour called for a vote. The leader of the Workers' group, Bill Brett, immediately came to the podium to call for a record vote – seeing only after he had done so that the hall was far from full, putting adoption in danger because of the quorum rules of the Conference. The Officers of the Conference took advantage

---

[1] The principal author of this chapter is Lee Swepston.

of a very convenient failure of the electronic voting system to scour the coffee bars and bathrooms of the Palais des Nations to summon delegates, weary at the end of a difficult Conference, back to the Assembly Hall. When the vote was finally concluded, there were no voices against the Declaration, but a large number of abstentions – and the new commitment of the ILO to fundamental human rights was adopted by a margin of only 9 votes above the quorum needed.

Why were the ILO constituents in two minds about adopting a full-blown commitment to human rights? And why did the opposition to the Declaration come above all from the government benches? The answer lies in a long and complex history. From its very beginning, the ILO has played a key role in anchoring the concept of social and economic human rights in the international discourse of the twentieth century.

A few words are necessary about the term "human rights". In popular parlance, this is understood to refer to basic rights and freedom to which all human beings are entitled, such as those covered in the 1948 Universal Declaration of Human Rights and the ILO's own 1998 Declaration on Fundamental Principles and Rights at Work. The 1998 Declaration covers four categories of principles and rights: freedom of association and collective bargaining, forced labour, child labour and discrimination at work. When it was being discussed, some advocated extending this list to include subjects such as occupational safety and health; but, in the end, it was decided to include only these four categories as being "enabling" rights that would allow others to be achieved over time. In a broader sense, however, the term "human rights" incorporates all the notions that make up what the ILO terms "decent work". It is now firmly established in international human rights law that everyone has the right to a decent working life, including many aspects that are dealt with in subsequent chapters of this book. One powerful argument for considering that most ILO standard-setting falls into the human rights category is that Articles 6 to 10 of the United Nations International Covenant on Economic, Social and Cultural Rights, adopted in 1966, are a brief restatement of ILO standards adopted up until that time. Indeed, they refer to a range of subjects relevant to labour, including rights related to the quality of life and work – such as occupational safety and health, wages, rest and protection of the family. The Covenant accords the designation of rights to all these subjects.

The commitment of international organizations to the international human rights movement is largely a post-Second World War phenomenon. The Covenant of the League of Nations did not contain the commitment to human rights that is found in the United Nations Charter. And the word "right" used in the Treaty of Versailles refers almost entirely to territorial and other sovereign rights of states, the only exception being a reference to the right of workers and employers to organize in the chapter of the Treaty which established the ILO. Certainly there was no deficit of rights notions available, including the French Declaration of the Rights of Man of 1789, and the 1776 United States Declaration of Independence and its Constitution. The drafters of the Covenant of the League of Nations had lengthy discussions on whether to include references to other categories of rights, including women's rights and minority rights, but they decided that the political risks of doing so were too high.[2]

The situation changed with the Second World War, in reaction to the horrors of the concentration camps and the brutalities committed against civilians and soldiers alike. President Franklin Roosevelt in his "Four Freedoms" speech to Congress in 1941 looked forward to a world in which human rights would be recognized and protected. The 1945 United Nations Charter followed the lead of the ILO's 1944 Declaration of Philadelphia in containing rights language, and the Universal Declaration of Human Rights, adopted in 1948, remains today the broadest and most fundamental international expression of human rights. But for nearly 50 years after the establishment of the United Nations, there were debates – which arose with the Cold War – on classifying and interpreting human rights, based on a politically-inspired distinction between different categories of rights. As a result, the United Nations adopted two Covenants in 1966: the International Covenant on Economic, Social and Cultural Rights and the International Covenant on Civil and Political Rights. The ILO took an active part in drafting the Covenants – and both contain provisions closely related to ILO standards. However, they were treated in very different ways by many member States until the mid-1990s, with the "western" states maintaining that only civil and political rights were really important, and the Communist states and their allies supporting the fundamental importance of economic, social and cultural rights. To some extent, this debate continued even after the end of the Cold War had removed the ideological reasons for considering them to be separate categories. The ILO, unlike the rest of the "human rights community", never made any such distinction.

One reason for this may be that, although the labour instruments adopted before the ILO's establishment, and by the ILO itself after 1919, resulted in the protection of workers' rights, they were almost never framed in the same rights terms as those the UN began to adopt after the Second World War. Instead

---

[2] For a recent survey, see D. Bromley: *Human rights and the League of Nations: How ideas about human rights came to be included in the Charter and work of the League of Nations*, paper prepared for the annual meeting of the Western Political Science Association, San Diego, CA, 20 Mar. 2008. See also R. Normand and S. Zaidi: *Human rights at the UN: The political history of universal justice* (Bloomington, Indiana University Press, 2007), United Nations Intellectual History Project Series, available at: http://www.unhistory.org

they speak in terms of governments' obligations to ensure certain outcomes or processes. The fact that they result in increased human rights protection is rarely expressed in the instruments themselves, including the ILO's fundamental Conventions on human rights.

The ILO itself does not distinguish between different kinds of workers' protection standards for most purposes, though it does ensure that no ILO action runs counter to basic rights notions. All ILO standards are set, and supervised, with the involvement of the same tripartite participants, according to the same methods and with the same attention to detail. While there are some differences in the structures created internally to deal with the "rights" subjects – such as the 1998 Declaration and the Committee on Freedom of Association (see Chapter 1) – and in the frequency of reporting on some subjects, the social security and safety and health standards in the ILO are dealt with in the regular ILO supervisory system in the same way as those on forced labour or discrimination.

The UN has classified eight of its Conventions as comprising the International Bill of Human Rights, and most of them cover labour rights, among other subjects. Some are based directly on earlier ILO standards, as are the relevant parts of the two International Covenants of 1966 in particular, and there are references to ILO standards or the notions found in them in others. The UN has consistently accepted, without attempting to modify them, the rights recognized for workers in international labour standards, and expanded their applicability to a broader context on the basis of earlier ILO provisions. Neither ILO nor UN Conventions take legal precedence, although as a part of the United Nations system the ILO must remain consistent with the parameters of UN standards. In practical terms, the ILO has often led the way in setting basic standards – and ILO standards are usually narrower but considerably more detailed than the general principles laid down by the United Nations. By way of example, the general principle that children shall not be subject to economic exploitation expressed in Article 32 of the United Nations Convention on the Rights of the Child, adopted in 1989, has been the subject of more than a dozen detailed ILO Conventions. In addition, ILO and UN secretariats have always taken an active part in each other's standard-setting when the subjects under discussion have overlapped the responsibilities of both organizations – for instance when the UN adopted standards on migrant workers, the rights of persons with disabilities and indigenous peoples. Finally, the supervisory systems of the two organizations maintain close contact, referring to each other's conclusions, drawing on facts available to both organizations, and ensuring consistency of judgements. Thus, ILO standards protecting workers' and employers' rights are firmly embedded in the canon of human rights adopted by the international system.

## Human rights and ILO history

Until the end of the Second World War, the history of human rights in the ILO was entirely one of standard-setting and promotion. During the first 15 years after the war, the ILO adopted or updated almost all its own fundamental human rights standards, and also laid the foundation for United Nations human rights standard-setting, while introducing practical work on the ground through technical cooperation; and, in the last 30 years, it has put in place a more thorough partnership between legal and practical action.

### The League of Nations

The first phase of ILO standard-setting lasted from the ILO's founding until the Second World War, during which time the Organization had two main orientations. The first was to take up the work of the International Association for Labour Legislation that had been established in the early twentieth century (see Chapter 1), laying down standards on minimum age, hours of work and other subjects for member States. This utilitarian approach to workers' protection took place in the light of section I of Part XIII of the Treaty of Versailles which became the original ILO Constitution, quoted in Chapter 1. And Article 427, section II of this Part of the Treaty, which became article 41 of the ILO Constitution, listed "General Principles" concerning labour; article 41 was later replaced by the Declaration of Philadelphia adopted in 1944 (both texts are reproduced in Appendix II of this book).

With the exception of the right to association, the general principles and the ILO's mandate were expressed as a matter of welfare and not of rights – even though they included subjects such as equal treatment for men and women and child labour which have since been considered as fundamental human rights.

### Lower rights for indigenous colonial workers

The ILO's membership at the time it was established was dominated by industrialized European states, and the Organization therefore essentially produced standards aimed at industrial and European workers. For instance, article 41 of its original Constitution referred to policies to be "adopted by the industrial communities", and assumed that some parts of the world could not be expected to adopt such high standards immediately. The ILO's first standards on hours of work, night work for women, minimum age and protection of young persons, safety and health, and other technical questions, were aimed at the populations of independent states, and were not intended to cover people in colonies and other dependent territories.

However, the Treaty of Versailles also laid down the basis for treating colonies – or "non-metropolitan territories" – differently and for applying lower standards to the workers who lived there. Based on the "differences of climate, habits, and customs, of economic opportunity and industrial tradition" (cited in article 41), article 35 of the Constitution provided that states could decide the degree to which the Conventions they ratified should be applied to non-metropolitan territories, and with what modifications – a facility denied them when ratifying Conventions to be applied to the metropolitan areas of these states. Article 35 regulated the application of international Conventions to "colonies, protectorates, and possessions that are not fully self-governing" depending on "local conditions".[3] In addition, some of the early ILO standards provided for lower standards for countries including China, India, Japan, Persia and Siam, where it was felt that they could not be expected to apply the higher standards applicable to what would later be termed "developed" countries.

Between 1930 and 1939, the Conference went a step further towards differentiating between the rights of workers in developed and "underdeveloped" regions when it adopted the so-called "Native Labour Code", consisting of instruments on forced labour and the conditions of work of "indigenous workers" – an expression which at the time referred to workers in colonial territories. These Conventions and Recommendations were the first attempt to regulate the conditions under which the labour of the populations of European colonies in Africa and Asia was exploited. The first of these instruments was the Forced Labour Convention, 1930 (No. 29), which established limits on the kinds of forced labour that were permissible in any state. It is, in fact, the oldest of what later came to be considered the ILO's fundamental human rights Conventions. Although Convention No. 29 accepted the continuing existence of forced labour in the dependent territories where it still existed, it also declared forced and compulsory labour to be unacceptable generally, restricted its use to the public sector and declared its use by the private sector illegitimate, and laid the foundation for its gradual elimination. This is dealt with in more detail below.

In the colonies, the interwar period was characterized by the imposition of European styles of employment on colonies that had little experience of wage

---

[3] See L. Rodríguez-Piñero: *The ILO and indigenous peoples: A historical anomaly*, paper submitted to the ILO Century Project Workshop, Geneva, 27–28 Aug. 2007.

labour, resulting in systematic forced labour imposed by the colonial authorities to compensate for manpower shortages. By adopting the series of Conventions and Recommendations that made up this colonial legislation, the ILO faced up to the notion that the colonial powers would not accept that workers in their colonies should enjoy the same rights as workers in independent countries. As Maul has stated, "Basically, all colonial philosophies distinguished between a European and a 'native' economic and labour sector and bridged manpower gaps in the first using methods of coercion. The result was pre-programmed social and political stagnation, and the often unscrupulous temporary poaching of manpower from the indigenous communities."[4] At the same time, the Native Labour Code instruments laid down a set of rights – albeit lower than for other workers – that for the first time placed restrictions on the abuses being practised in the colonies and began a transition to full recognition of these workers' rights.[5] Fifteen years after the adoption of Convention No. 29 in 1930, the transitional measures contained in it helped lead to a radical shift in favour of equal protection as the post-war system began to create the conditions for the end of the colonial system and the launching of the decolonization movement. By shifting its position during the Second World War, when it moved from accepting and providing a legal basis for colonial regimes to proclaiming equal rights for all in the Declaration of Philadelphia, the ILO marked a definitive break with its colonialist past and helped usher in the post-colonial world that emerged after 1945.

## The Second World War and the Declaration of Philadelphia

Discussions during the Second World War, after the League of Nations had collapsed and the Allies were designing the new international architecture, had a strong influence on the ILO. It was the first international organization that took a global view of human rights as a legitimate subject for international concern. When the International Labour Conference met in Philadelphia in 1944 to

---

[4] For an account of the colonial forced labour situation in the interwar period, see ILO: *Social policy in dependent territories* (Montreal, 1944), pp. 20–38. For Africa, see F. Cooper: *Decolonization and African society: The labour question in British and French Africa* (Cambridge University Press, 1996), pp. 25–107. More specifically, for French West Africa, see B. Fall: *Le travail forcé en Afrique Occidentale Française, 1900–1946* (Paris, 1993).

[5] L. Rodríguez-Piñero: *Indigenous people, postcolonialism and international law: The ILO regime (1919–1989)* (Oxford, Oxford University Press, 2005); D.R. Maul: "The International Labour Organization and the struggle against forced labour from 1919 to the present," in *Labor History* (2007), Vol. 48, No. 4, Nov., pp. 477–500.

consider its future, a turning point was reached both in the ILO's thinking and in the international paradigms for human rights and social development. Doubts had already been expressed in the ILO secretariat itself about the Organization's explicit support for colonial regimes, and the expropriation of manpower for the colonial powers this implied. The lower set of standards in the Native Labour Code was unsustainable in a world moving towards decolonization and the recognition of equal rights for all people.

In addition, during the early part of the war, the ILO constituents and the Allied powers had been shaping the post-war architecture of international governance. As the war ended, the solutions seemed to lie in international organizations that could promote parallel development across the world, and alleviate the exploitation that was one of the roots of conflict. Article 5 of the Atlantic Charter, negotiated by Churchill and Roosevelt in August 1941,[6] which pleaded for "economic cooperation between all countries in order to guarantee improved working conditions, economic progress and social security for all", was specifically seen as a guideline for the development of a new ILO, which took shape at the International Labour Conference in Philadelphia three years later.

The colonial reform programme expressed in Philadelphia was the context in which the connection was made for the first time between economic and social development and basic human rights principles. In it, the ILO laid down the cornerstones of a future peacetime order, and put forward for the first time in an international document the concept of universal social rights of the individual. It then made this the basis of its demand that member States commit to implementing economic policies governed by an overriding social objective – and this has been one of the main characteristics of the ILO contribution to the development debate ever since. The inextricability of rights and development was made particularly clear in those passages of the Declaration of Philadelphia which made freedom from discrimination and forced labour preconditions of "true" development. The prime example of this approach was the endorsement of the principle of freedom of association, highlighting the fact that development measures would succeed only if those concerned had the opportunity to participate fully and create local structures "from the bottom up" which would represent their interests.

With the adoption of the Declaration of Philadelphia in 1944, and its incorporation into the ILO Constitution in 1946, the next phase of standard-setting was launched. Today, we can recognize that the instruments adopted in

---

[6] A.C. Brinkley and D. Facey-Crowther (eds): *The Atlantic Charter* (New York, St Martin's Press, 1994).

the decade following the Second World War laid down the intellectual foundation of much of the subsequent human rights standard-setting in the UN and in various regional instruments, as well as in the ILO. These standards have exercised a major influence in setting a floor under workplace policies, and human rights more generally, in the emerging post-colonial world.

## Major themes of the ILO's human rights work

It soon became apparent after the war that the ILO was adopting human rights instruments, although many years were to pass before it had an acknowledged human rights framework. The core themes of the ILO's human rights focus today are the four subjects taken up in the 1998 Declaration – freedom of association, and freedom from forced labour, discrimination and child labour. Generally speaking, this aspect of the ILO's work on human rights is aimed at removing obstacles to access to work, through its attempt to eliminate discrimination on the basis of sex, ethnicity and otherwise; and to provide a basis for decent conditions of work. As it did earlier with the Native Labour Code – and later with its standards on women, children and indigenous and tribal peoples in independent countries – this has meant laying down minimum conditions of work for those who are most exploited because of their exclusion from the levers of economic power, and even from the monetary economy. And, of course, the ILO's standards on freedom of association and collective bargaining aim to ensure that working people and employers can participate in setting the conditions under which work is carried out.

### *Freedom of association and the right to collective bargaining*

As already mentioned, the Treaty of Versailles and the original Constitution recognized "the principle of freedom of association for all lawful purposes" among the principles on which the ILO was founded. Organizing for the protection of economic interests was already well established by the time the ILO was created in 1919.[7] From about 1750 onwards, workers had started to associate in Europe.

---

[7] For an excellent background, see H. Dunning: "The origins of Convention No. 87 on freedom of association and the right to organize", in *International Labour Review* (Geneva, ILO, 1998), Vol. 137, No. 2, pp. 149 et seq. Much of the information on the origin of Convention No. 87 is drawn from this article.

Governments and employers reacted quickly, and laws and regulations were adopted to restrict such activities. In Great Britain, for example, the Combination Acts of 1799 remained in force for 25 years, regulating and even prohibiting workers' organizations among others.

In time, the recognition of the right to "combine" gained ground. By the mid-nineteenth century, workers' organizations had developed throughout Western Europe, composed in particular of workers in the skilled trades; it was to be another quarter-century before unskilled workers began to enter the trade union movement. In part, this was because of restrictions in many countries on, or prohibition of, the formation of trade unions in agriculture and among certain occupations – and still today workers in agriculture are often explicitly denied the right to organize. International trade unions began to be established in the second half of the nineteenth century, leading to the establishment of the International Trade Secretariats.

In 1913, the secular national trade union centres formed the International Federation of Trade Unions. Members of the international trade union movement managed to keep in touch across warring lines between 1914 and 1918, and trade union leaders on both sides of the conflict were quick to see the advantages in a situation where governments had to appeal to workers to support the war effort, in this new form of industrialized warfare. In spite of wartime restrictions, workers held national or international conferences at which they were able to voice their plans for post-war settlement. The trade union conference in Leeds, England, in July 1916, adopted a long list of demands, including freedom of association, limited working hours, a minimum working age of 14 years, the abolition of night work for women, comprehensive social security and factory inspectorates, and called for an international labour office. And within a few years of the end of the war, every one of these demands had been taken up by the ILO, or was well on the way to being addressed.

Although there was disagreement among workers' organizations about the new organization, the majority of them agreed to try to make the ILO a useful instrument for protecting their rights, while complaining that the Peace Treaty fell short of the targets workers had set for themselves. In relation to freedom of association, for example, "whereas the Treaty only recognized the right of association 'for all lawful purposes' (a wording which might give governments the possibility of declaring illegal the right to strike) the workers had wanted all laws against the right of association suppressed".[8]

---

[8] A. Alcock: *History of the International Labour Organization* (London and Basingstoke, Macmillan, 1971).

The new Organization was not immediately successful in adopting standards to give substance to this right. At its third session in 1921, the Conference had before it a series of reports relating to work in agriculture, one of which dealt with freedom of association for the workers of that sector. Despite objections – in particular by the Government of France – to dealing with this subject at the international level, the Conference in due course adopted the Right of Association (Agriculture) Convention, 1921 (No. 11). Article 1 stated:

> Each Member ... which ratifies this Convention undertakes to secure to all those engaged in agriculture the same rights of association and combination as to industrial workers...

The obvious flaw in this new instrument was that the ILO had not yet defined the substance of the right to freedom of association. An attempt to deal with the subject at the Conference in 1927 failed when severe disagreement broke out over whether employers and workers should also have the right *not* to combine. Another subject of disagreement was the meaning of the phrase "for all lawful purposes", as the workers in particular did not want any Convention to specify exactly what trade unions were permitted to do, lest this be interpreted as rendering any other action beyond their rights. Finally, the committee recommended that this item should not be included in a future Conference agenda, and the subject was dropped until after the Second World War.

In 1944, the Declaration of Philadelphia reaffirmed that:

> ... the war against want requires to be carried on with unrelenting vigour within each nation, and by continuous and concerted international effort in which the representatives of workers and employers, enjoying equal status with those of governments, join with them in free discussion and democratic decision with a view to the promotion of the common welfare.[9]

This declaration omitted any reference to "for all lawful purposes". The door was thus finally opened for a new ILO Convention on the right to organize.

However, in January 1947, the World Federation of Trade Unions (WFTU), which had increasingly become allied to the "socialist" countries, addressed a letter to the Secretary-General of the United Nations, requesting that the Economic and Social Council (ECOSOC) examine trade union rights. Shortly

---

[9] Declaration of Philadelphia, section I (d).

afterwards, the American Federation of Labor countered with a recommendation to the UN that the problem of trade union rights be referred to the ILO. As Harold Dunning points out,

> Representatives of the socialist countries, led by the USSR, expressed their full support for WFTU and for direct action by ECOSOC .... It was clear that in the view of some members, the ILO could not be trusted to give the workers a fair deal, largely because of the participation of representatives of employers. The spokesmen from 'non-socialist countries', on the other hand, declared their full support of the ILO, basing their arguments on the record of ILO achievements since 1919, and the relevant articles of the United Nations Charter and the United Nations/ILO agreement.[10]

The subject was referred to the ILO. In the first discussion in 1947, the Employers' group once again moved that after the words "the right to join" should be inserted "or not to join". However, this amendment was rejected, and the item was placed on the agenda of the Conference in 1948. The Government delegates from two Eastern European states proposed that the word "employers" be deleted from the text so that the Convention would provide only for the rights of workers. The majority of the Employer members disagreed, and were supported by the Worker members as well as by most Government members – and the proposed deletion was rejected. Possibly as a *quid pro quo*, the Employers did not reintroduce the 1947 amendment to add "or not to join", and the Freedom of Association and Protection of the Right to Organise Convention (No. 87) was adopted with a large majority in 1948. The same year, the Universal Declaration of Human Rights was adopted by the UN and included the phrase: "Everyone has the right to form and to join trade unions for the protection of his interests." This is obviously derived from Convention No. 87, even though it does not include the right of employers to organize, due to the greater influence of Eastern European states in the UN as compared to the ILO. In 1948, the Conference placed on its next session's agenda an item entitled "Right to organize and collective bargaining" which in 1949 produced the Right to Organise and Collective Bargaining Convention (No. 98) to supplement Convention No. 87.

The importance of the inclusion of employers' rights in these Conventions needs to be underlined. A limited but important number of cases before ILO

---

[10] Dunning, op. cit., p. 160.

supervisory bodies have defended them vigorously.[11] The ILO has been conscientious in ensuring that UN references to "fundamental workers' rights", as in the final statement of the Copenhagen Social Summit in 1995, be enlarged to include employers. For instance, the 1998 Declaration opted for the expression "principles and rights at work" to recognize employers' rights as well as those of workers.

In addition to adopting these standards, in 1951 the Governing Body established the Fact-Finding and Conciliation Commission and the Committee on Freedom of Association to examine complaints of violations of this principle – even by states which had not ratified the relevant Conventions. These bodies were intended to supplement the regular supervisory procedures applying to the new Conventions Nos. 87 and 98, especially in the case of non-ratifying states.

Conventions Nos. 87 and 98 form the basic international law on this subject. Over the years, the ILO has adopted a certain number of other instruments on freedom of association and collective bargaining, but these are in fact merely elaborations of the basic principles laid down in the Constitution and Conventions Nos. 87 and 98. In 1998, freedom of association and collective bargaining was listed first among the fundamental rights enunciated in the Declaration on Fundamental Principles and Rights at Work. One measure of the importance given to Convention No. 87 in international law is that the two covenants on human rights adopted by the UN in 1966 refer directly to only one other international convention: both of them provide that nothing in the covenant shall authorize States Parties to ILO Convention No. 87 to prejudice the guarantees provided for therein.

The ILO's supervisory bodies – especially the Committee of Experts on the Application of Conventions and Recommendations and the Committee on Freedom of Association – have elaborated the basic rights expressed in the Conventions and in the Constitution over the years,[12] and it is now probably the most thoroughly examined human right in the international sphere.

The basic principle in these instruments is an elaboration of the general right to associate, which is recognized in virtually all States. It is simply that all employers and workers have the right to organize to defend their interests, and that the organizations thus formed have the right to operate independently to do so.

---

[11] See, for instance, ILO: Observation by the Committee of Experts concerning the application by the Bolivarian Republic Venezuela of Convention No. 87, in *Report of the Committee of Experts on the Application of Conventions and Recommendations*, Report III (Part 1A), International Labour Conference, 97th Session, Geneva, 2008.

[12] See, especially, ILO: *Freedom of association: Digest of decisions and principles on the Freedom of Association Committee of the Governing Body of the ILO*, fifth (revised) edition (Geneva, 2006).

This right is deeply rooted in political democracy, which cannot function fully unless freedom of association is recognized. Protection of the right to freedom of association has therefore been critical for the ILO and its member States over the years. While it is always difficult to attribute too much credit to a single instrument, the outcome of a number of national crises has been an increase in the legal and practical impact of the right of workers and employers to organize, accompanying a greater degree of democracy, even if these crises have on occasion taken years to resolve.[13] The major violations of the Conventions are based on the fear of governments – especially, but not only, totalitarian governments – that independent trade unions, and sometimes employers' organizations, are a threat to government power. And indeed, in situations of crisis or political change, trade unions (and sometimes employers' organizations) are often the only organized independent non-governmental entities.

Trade union leaders are often in the front line of political change in favour of greater democracy, and in many cases are assassinated, imprisoned or exiled for their beliefs and their actions. There have been a number of Commissions of Inquiry dealing with such situations based on complaints under article 26 of the Constitution, or Fact-Finding and Conciliation Commissions when governments have agreed to this procedure. All these cases have been undertaken in response to governments' attempts to restrict the freedom of action of trade unions. And they have all resulted in real improvements in the freedom of trade unions to take part in economic governance – and sometimes in greater political freedom as well. The most prominent such case concerned Poland (see box 2).

The ILO's successful intervention in Poland was not unique. After the coup d'état in Chile in September 1973 that overthrew President Salvador Allende, the Pinochet Government was accused of grave violations of both human rights generally and of trade union rights in particular, and a Commission of Inquiry was active in 1974–75. The ILO was the only international organization allowed into the country to investigate a human rights complaint. Once the complaint was examined, and after a time during which the situation was followed up by the Committee on Freedom of Association, the worst of the restrictions on freedom of association were removed in 1979, though the restoration of democracy took much longer.

South Africa left the ILO in 1966, in response to international pressure against apartheid (see also under "Equality" below). Much later, a complaint of grave violations of trade union rights was submitted by the Congress of South

---

[13] For more details, see G. von Potobsky: "Freedom of association: The impact of Convention No. 87 and ILO action", in *International Labour Review* (Geneva, ILO, 1988), Vol. 137, No. 2, pp. 195 et seq.

## Box 2  Poland, Solidarność and the ILO

When a complaint on violation of freedom of association rights in Poland was received in 1978, the Committee on Freedom of Association proposed a mission of direct contacts, which was carried out in May 1980 by Nicolas Valticos, Assistant Director-General of the ILO and Director of the Standards Department. This visit eased the way for the adoption of the Gdansk Agreements in August of that year, recognizing the principles of Conventions Nos. 87 and 98. When the new trade union Solidarność encountered difficulties in being registered, Valticos again went to Poland in October 1980, and the following month Solidarność was recognized. This was followed up in May 1981 by the personal intervention of Director-General Francis Blanchard, who urged the Government to complete drafting a new law on trade union matters, and helped secure the recognition of Rural Solidarność. The Government, made nervous by the growth in strength of Solidarność and by other challenges to the Communist regime, cracked down in December 1981, proclaiming martial law and the suspension of trade union activities, and soon jailed Lech Wałęsa, who headed Solidarność. A further visit by Valticos took place in May 1982, and an Article 26 complaint was filed by Workers' delegates at the Conference in June 1982. After further attempts to mediate a solution, a Commission of Inquiry was established in March 1983. The Government announced that it was suspending its cooperation with the ILO, and refused to furnish documentation or to allow the Commission to visit. When the findings were announced in May 1984, the Government of Poland filed notice of withdrawal from the ILO – although it later changed its mind and remained a Member. Discussions in the ILO Committee of Experts and the Committee on Freedom of Association continued, and in 1987 the Director-General again visited Poland. The findings of the Commission of Inquiry were used as a basis of the round-table discussions on democratization in Poland in the late 1980s. Finally, in 1990, ILO bodies were able to note the reinstatement of striking workers, the lifting of sentences for strike action and the establishment of trade union pluralism in all sectors. The Prime Minister of the new democratic Government of Poland, Tadeusz Mazowiecki, addressed the 77th Session of the Conference in June 1990, 10 years after Lech Wałęsa's speech as Workers' delegate had drawn a packed audience to the Palais des Nations Assembly Hall. The pressure and the mediation from the ILO were critical factors in these changes, the first in a Communist country.

African Trade Unions in 1988, and was referred to the United Nations' ECOSOC, as the procedure provided for non-member States of the ILO. The Government agreed to the establishment of an ILO Fact-Finding and Conciliation Commission in 1991, and the Commission visited South Africa for hearings and investigations under a mandate that had been made wider with a view to examining the emerging changes in the political system, already evident at the time. The Commission's report in May 1992 contained a detailed examination of the trade union situation and of collective labour relations, as well as of the situation of workers and territories excluded from the Labour Relations Act under apartheid. In April

1994, the first multiracial elections were held in the country, and South Africa rejoined the ILO the following month. The ILO launched a programme of technical cooperation and training, based to a very large degree on the findings of the Fact Finding and Conciliation Commission. In 1995 the Government adopted a new Labour Relations Act, and in 1996 ratified Conventions Nos. 87 and 98, implementing most of the recommendations made by the ILO.

Colombia was another kind of case. For some years there had been a situation in which there were "acts of violence against trade union leaders and trade unionists which include murders, kidnappings, attempted assassinations and disappearances, and ... the grave impunity which surrounds such acts". There were also allegations of

> the use of various types of contractual arrangements, such as associated work cooperatives and service, civil or commercial contracts to carry out functions and work that are within the normal activities of the establishment and which result in it being impossible for the workers to establish or join trade unions ... [and of the] restructuring of public bodies, which are then closed down so as to be re-established without a trade union ... the arbitrary refusal to register new trade union organizations or new rules or the executive committee of a trade union; the acceptance of challenges by employers against the registration of new unions; and the prohibition of the right to strike in certain services which are not essential services.[14]

Although the Government maintained that it had taken significant measures to combat these problems, under sustained pressure from the ILO and international trade unions, these problems continued to be noted at almost every session of the Governing Body, the Committee of Experts and the Conference over many years. In the end, a Tripartite Agreement on Freedom of Association and Democracy was signed by the representatives of the Government, employers and trade unions of Colombia in Geneva on 1 June 2006, during the Conference.

> Its stated aim was, among other things, to promote decent work and to strengthen the defence of the fundamental rights of workers, their organizations and trade union leaders, especially as regards respect for human life, trade union freedom, freedom of association and speech, collective bargaining and free enterprise for

---

[14] This is a selection of the allegations, all well substantiated, enumerated in ILO: Observation by the Committee of Experts concerning the application of Convention No. 87, in *Report of the Committee of Experts on the Application of Conventions and Recommendations*, Report III (Part 1A), International Labour Conference, 95th Session, Geneva, 2006.

employers. In order to facilitate the implementation of this Agreement, the ILO has established a permanent representation in Colombia and a technical cooperation programme is being carried out.[15]

Other measures continued – as this was written in 2008 – to implement and reinforce this Agreement. Although violence continues against trade unions in that country, it has been greatly reduced, and this Agreement shows the potential for governments, employers and workers to find means of cooperation through the ILO, and in response to the ILO's continuing attention to such situations.

## Equality

The original Constitution of the ILO contained no general statement on equality of treatment, though it did have a phrase concerning equal remuneration for men and women and called on States to ensure "the equitable economic treatment of all workers lawfully resident therein". This put the achievement of equal treatment resolutely on a pragmatic basis as a means to achieve social harmony and peace. Nor did any of the pre-Second World War Conventions make any general statement in favour of equality other than concerning equality between men and women; indeed, as indicated above, the Conference adopted a series of standards allowing *unequal* treatment of workers in colonies. It did adopt a series of instruments providing special protection for women, children and migrants, which later became part of its approach to equal treatment, but which did not seem to be situated in a mind-set of equality.

There was a radical change after the redefinition of the ILO's mandate in the Declaration of Philadelphia, which included the new statement that "all human beings, irrespective of race, creed or sex, have the right to pursue both their material well-being and their spiritual development in conditions of freedom and dignity, of economic security and equal opportunity".[16] The Preamble of the amended Constitution now also referred to "recognition of the principle of equal remuneration for work of equal value".[17]

---

[15] ILO: Governing Body, 301st Session, Geneva, Mar. 2008, GB.301/17/2, para. 1.

[16] ILO: Declaration of Philadelphia, II(a), Annex to the Constitution of the ILO, 1946.

[17] Which was confusingly rendered in French, equally authoritative, as "a travail égale, salaire égale", a different and lower standard requiring equal pay only for equal work – but still referring to equal treatment in this limited respect. This deviated from the French version of Article 437 of the Treaty of Versailles, which was much closer to the English – and the later Convention No. 100 – in declaring "Le principe du salaire égal, sans distinction de sexe, pour un travail de valeur égale".

The ILO soon began to adopt standards on equality, beginning with the Equal Remuneration Convention, 1951 (No. 100), examined more fully below. In 1958, the ILO adopted the Discrimination (Employment and Occupation) Convention (No. 111), which has been the foundation for ILO action in this domain ever since. Both instruments preceded the adoption of the more general equality standards by other international organizations, and are broadly reflected in them. Convention No. 111, a subtle and flexible instrument, requires ratifying countries "to declare and pursue a national policy designed to promote, by methods appropriate to national conditions and practice, equality of opportunity and treatment in respect of employment and occupation, with a view to eliminating any discrimination in respect thereof" (Article 2). It covers "any distinction, exclusion or preference made on the basis of race, colour, sex, religion, political opinion, national extraction or social origin, which has the effect of nullifying or impairing equality of opportunity or treatment in employment or occupation" (Article 1(1)(a)) and allows countries to expand the grounds covered after consultation with employers' and workers' organizations. The Convention has had a significant impact – not only in providing a basis for standard-setting elsewhere in the international system, but more directly because its requirements are found in the Constitutions and Labour Codes of nearly all member States. Even if equality in fact remains a dream in many countries, the legal basis for it is in place everywhere.

### Apartheid and the ILO [18]

The ILO took concerted and increasingly effective action against apartheid over many years, in the first major test of its policies in favour of equality. Beginning with the 1948 election victory of the National Party, which launched an epoch of intensified legislative discrimination in South Africa, the ILO had joined the rest of the international community in focusing attention on apartheid – at first through the findings of ILO supervisory bodies and at various meetings. The international organizations hardened their position after the 1960 Sharpesville massacre of workers protesting against pass laws, and the Government's declaration of a state of emergency. The International Labour Conference adopted a first resolution condemning the racial policies of the South African Government in 1961, also calling upon it to withdraw from the ILO. In this respect, both the

---

[18] This brief description of a long and complex reaction to apartheid is based on ILO: *Special Report of the Director-General on the application of the Declaration concerning action against apartheid*, International Labour Conference, Geneva, 81st Session, 1994; the subject is dealt with in more detail in N. Rubin: *From pressure principle to measured militancy: The ILO in the campaign against apartheid*, paper prepared for the ILO Century Project, 2008, available at: http://www.ilocentury.org

ILO's tripartite bodies and the Office were pushed into more direct action than, for instance, the UN, because of the emerging alliance between the new post-colonial African States and the Workers' group. An ILO programme for the elimination of apartheid in labour matters in the Republic of South Africa, and the Declaration concerning the Policy of Apartheid of the Republic of South Africa, were unanimously adopted at the Conference in 1964, but in March of that year the Government had already filed notice of its intention to withdraw from the ILO, which became effective two years later.

Action intensified from this point on. The declaration requested the Director-General to submit a special report on its implementation every year to the Conference, which was put before a special committee until 1994. These reports [19] demonstrate how international pressure against apartheid evolved over more than a quarter of a century from initial recommendations to the Government to a second phase of mobilization of opinion, and to a third phase of recommending disinvestment, boycotts and isolation of apartheid South Africa – coupled with increased material and political support for the national liberation movements and trade unions fighting apartheid. The reports later expanded to cover Namibia, suffering under an apartheid regime of its own, and began to focus on subjects such as the work of employers' and workers' organizations in combating apartheid, and the special situation of women. They analysed the effects of apartheid's violations of basic human rights – equality, freedom of association and freedom from forced labour – and the damage they did both to workers and to the economy. The ILO also began to provide assistance to opposition groups through funding, training and political recognition. Similarly, the work of the Fact-Finding and Conciliation Commission (that the Government finally accepted in 1991 – see above) led to detailed recommendations that were implemented by post-apartheid South Africa. And in 1990, a newly freed Nelson Mandela addressed the Conference during his first visit abroad, where he thanked the ILO for the support and practical action it had levied against apartheid. Over the years the ILO's Apartheid Declaration was regularly revised and updated, until it was rescinded in 1994 after the adoption of a plan of action to support the social and economic needs of post-apartheid South Africa. A free South Africa rejoined the ILO in 1994.

What lessons can be learned from this campaign? First, it showed that the ILO can mobilize effectively to defend and promote the human rights which lie at its core, especially in the face of such massive violations, with the support of all its constituents. It can do so most effectively, as in this case, as part of a broader

---

[19] Ibid.

international effort and as a part of the UN system. In this particular case, it demonstrated a willingness to explore practical and effective measures to put real pressure on South Africa. Second, the ILO's work during this 30-year period demonstrated the disastrous effect of apartheid on both the economy and individuals, with massive violations of rights – and revealed how continued pressure can be adapted over time to provide support and guidance as countries move into new phases of their existence. Since then, securing rights as a condition of continued development has been a vital component of ILO action, and has helped to form the responses the Organization has made to rights violations in Chile, Poland, Myanmar and others. Finally, this experience demonstrated once again that industrial democracy lies at the heart of political democracy and freedom – and that there can be neither lasting peace nor economic development without social justice and the support of workers and employers.

## Occupied Arab territories

The ILO's action against apartheid provided a partial model for its attempts to protect workers in the occupied Arab territories under the general banner of equal treatment, although efforts there have proven much less successful. A 1974 Conference resolution condemning Israel for its treatment of workers in the occupied Arab territories resulted in the United States filing a letter of notice of withdrawal in 1975, citing the ILO's condemnation of Israel without investigation as one of two major reasons (the other being an over-lax attitude towards the Soviet Union and its allies with respect to compliance with labour standards). By the time this withdrawal came into effect in 1977, the Director-General had sent the first in a long series of missions to Israel and the occupied territories, which continue up to the time this book was completed in 2008. When the United States returned to the Organization in 1980, the Director-General's annual report on the situation of workers in the occupied Arab territories had become an established fact. Each report is based on an on-the-ground mission to Israel and the occupied territories, and in the early years of this process they were discussed by the Conference at a special sitting; later these discussions were incorporated in the general discussion of the Director-General's report at the Conference. The Arab States and their allies have from time to time proposed a procedure similar to that adopted on apartheid, urging that a special Conference committee be established to discuss these reports. But in the face of a divided membership – and resistance from the United States in particular – this has never materialized, and the amount of time and attention the Conference devotes to these reports continues to decrease.

The reports have consistently been both concrete and detailed, bringing to light in an objective way the economic costs of the occupation and severe violations of human rights, and making recommendations for improving the situation. The ILO has been the only body in the UN system to be allowed regular access by the Israeli authorities to examine conditions in the territories. On the basis of these reports, and of discussions of the situation in the Governing Body, special programmes of assistance have been formulated at times when tensions have calmed sufficiently to make them seem worthwhile. Sadly, however, the promised stability and reforms have never materialized, and the action programmes have had little effect – in sharp contrast to the apartheid campaign. This clearly shows that despite all efforts by the ILO to review a particular situation and recommend action, there can be no improvements unless the membership itself exerts concerted pressure for change. In time, the Organization's persistence may bear fruit once the situation is more stable, as with apartheid, and provide a sound basis for future action.

## Gender[20]

The ILO had an ambivalent attitude towards the situation of women in the workforce in its earlier days, but has gradually evolved towards "gender mainstreaming" – taking gender into account in all the Organization's activities. Although the new Organization did adopt progressive ideas such as equal remuneration for work of equal value, its first standards in this area were highly protective and followed the temper of the times in assigning women a secondary role in the economy – conferring international legitimacy on women's economic straitjacket that it took decades to unfasten. One of the two pre-ILO standards adopted in Europe had provided for restrictions on night work for women,[21] and women's interest groups felt that this excluded women from important areas of the labour market. They did not want the new ILO to continue with this approach; but their wishes were ignored.

Nevertheless, the Treaty of Versailles clearly stated that "men and women should receive equal remuneration for work of equal value";[22] and the first ILO

---

[20] Based in part on a submission by Lin Lim Lean for the ILO Century Project, Aug. 2007. Another significant document used is M. Gaudier: *The development of the women's question at the ILO, 1919–1994 – 75 years of progress towards equality* (Geneva, ILO, International Institute for Labour Studies, 1996).

[21] International Convention respecting the Prohibition of Night Work for Women in Industrial Employment, Berne, 26 Sep. 1906.

[22] *Treaty of Versailles*, Article 427.

Constitution of 1919 stated in its Preamble that one of the Organization's aims would be "the protection of children, young persons and women". The Constitution also provided that "when questions specially affecting women are to be considered by the Conference, at least one of the advisers [on national delegations] shall be a woman". This obligation has been ignored by most nations, despite some very minor improvements recently.

The Conference displayed something of a split personality in its early years when adopting standards on women at work. The Maternity Protection Convention, 1919 (No. 3), and the Night Work (Women) Convention, 1919 (No. 4) were the ILO's earliest forays into this field, followed by instruments on night work, underground work and other questions which tended to class women among the groups to be protected rather than promoted. These protective standards provoked intense debate. Many women's organizations feared that they would further weaken the already unfavourable position of women in the labour market. Others realized the need for special protection for women but preferred this to be limited to the specific question of pregnancy and maternity. It is this second view to which the ILO subscribed, at least in principle.[23] Some of these questions are discussed further in Chapter 3.

When the Conference did adopt instruments in the early years providing for greater access for women to the economy, they took the form of Recommendations, which removed a good deal of their force. The Constitution specifically stated that: "Each State should make provision for a system of inspection in which women should take part, in order to ensure the enforcement of the laws and regulations for the protection of the employed." The Labour Inspection Recommendation, 1923 (No. 20), thus provided that the labour inspectorate "should include women as well as men inspectors ... [who] ... should in general have the same powers and duties and exercise the same authority as the men inspectors, ... and should have equal opportunity of promotion to the higher ranks". The Minimum Wage-Fixing Machinery Recommendation, 1928 (No. 30) stipulated "that men and women should receive equal remuneration for work of equal value". And one of the last instruments adopted before the Second World War, the Vocational Training Recommendation, 1939 (No. 57), provided that "Workers of both sexes should have equal rights of admission to all technical and vocational schools". But none of these provisions were included in Conventions at the time, and even the

---

[23] When the ILO revised the 1919 night work instruments in 1949 with the Night Work Convention (Revised) (No. 89), it retained the prohibition on women working at night. It was not until 1990 that the Conference eventually adopted a more balanced position with the Night Work Convention (No. 171), and its accompanying Recommendation, and a Protocol to Convention No. 89 allowing more equal treatment.

principle of equal remuneration for work of equal value had to wait until 1951 to be put into Convention form.

By the time of the Great Depression in the 1930s, a concern for women's equality and non-discrimination in employment based on sex began to be evident in ILO publications that criticized legislation restricting the employment of women as the solution for alleviating the unemployment of men – despite the Conference's reticence to adopt standards in this sense. Albert Thomas created a section responsible for women's questions and appointed a woman (Marguerite Thibert, a specialist in the French women's movement) as its head. The increasing concern for the promotion of women's equality reflected not only the increasing activism of women's organizations but also the changes that had taken place in women's participation in the workforce. A turning point in the ILO's attitude was reached with the American Regional Conference in Havana in 1939, which helped prepare the way for a different attitude post-war with a series of resolutions concerning women's right to representation; the right of married women to work; statistics on women's work; domestic work; and other matters.[24]

With the growing numbers of women entering the workforce during and after the Second World War, the ILO began to reformulate the "women's problem", along with others, as one of human rights and a demand for equality. The ILO's approach to women's issues was henceforth guided by the call in the Declaration of Philadelphia that "all human beings, irrespective of race, creed or sex, have the right to pursue both their material well-being and their spiritual development in conditions of freedom and dignity, of economic security and equal opportunity". This was the first time that any international organization had proclaimed the general right to equality, and it established the basis for the remarkable period of affirmation that was to follow. At the same time, the external context was marked by the reorganization of employment in the period of transition from war to peace. Numbers of economically active women were increasing, and they were forming and joining trade unions and professional associations. The objective was therefore redefined: to ensure to all, men and women alike, a just share in the fruits of progress, in terms of wages and earnings, hours and other conditions of work; to provide child welfare and maternity protection; and to guarantee equality of educational and vocational opportunity.

The way was now open for the Equal Remuneration Convention (No. 100), which was adopted in 1951. As mentioned above, it consecrated the Constitutional requirement of equal remuneration for work of equal value for men and

---

[24] See complete list in M. Gaudier, op. cit.

women, and went well beyond the "equal pay for equal work" provision of the Universal Declaration of Human Rights adopted three years earlier. Convention No. 111 of 1958 broadened the field by including sex as a prohibited ground of discrimination, and Conventions Nos. 100 and 111 were the first ratifiable international instruments with the specific aim of promoting equality and elimination of discrimination. They are among the most widely ratified of international labour Conventions, and they influenced the drafting of subsequent and related UN Conventions, including in particular the Convention on the Elimination of All Forms of Discrimination Against Women (CEDAW). In addition, they made it clear that equality of opportunity and treatment did not mean only the same or equal treatment but also substantive equality of opportunity, results and human dignity, and that the concept included affirmative or positive action to deal with the consequences of past discrimination.

This period also witnessed the increasing realization that women's full participation was essential to development. Even if attitudes continued to lag behind at the national level, the Office began to carry out missions and to produce studies on the participation of women in the workforce in Africa and Asia as well as in Latin America, and there was a marked increase in activities designed to encourage women to work – such as the provision of childcare facilities and equal access to training.

In the 1960s, the pattern continued to broaden with the realization that equality at work could only be achieved through attainment of equality and empowerment in all aspects of life. The Employment Policy Convention, 1964 (No. 122) emphasized "freedom of choice of employment and the fullest opportunity for each worker to qualify for, and to use his skills and endowments in, a job for which he is well suited, irrespective of race, colour, sex, religion, political opinion, national extraction or social origin". The Workers with Family Responsibilities Convention, 1981 (No. 156), emphasized the joint responsibility of women and men for the family, and superseded Recommendation No. 123 (1965), in which responsibilities for home and family had been assigned only to women. In 1985, the Conference adopted a resolution on equal opportunities and equal treatment for men and women in employment, which called for measures at the national level to review all protective legislation, and emphasized the need to strengthen rather than review maternity protection. And in 1990 the Conference finally adopted a gender-neutral night work instrument in Convention No. 171, coupled with a Protocol allowing countries to make the earlier Convention No. 89 on the same subject more gender-neutral. The 1998 Declaration on Fundamental Principles and Rights at Work recognized Conventions Nos. 100 and 111 as being fundamental instruments, and the Global Reports under its follow-up have been invaluable sources of information on progress in achieving equality, with a certain emphasis on gender equality.[25]

In the 1970s, increased attention to poverty and basic needs led to greater advocacy on the issue of women in development, and the Second United Nations Development Decade (1971–80) included the integration of women in development as an objective. Based on the premise that women's contribution to development had been under-valued, the policy evolved towards using development resources for improving women's conditions and making their contributions visible. The title of the responsible unit created in the ILO – the Office of the Special Adviser on Women Workers' Questions – was indicative of the focus (it is now the Gender Bureau). But the realization that the programmes did not address the existing social structure of inequality in the relationships between women and men led to the adoption of a gender and development (GAD) approach by the 1980s.

The 1980s and 1990s were marked by high profile international women's conferences, the United Nations Decade for the Advancement of Women and the establishment of women's ministries by national governments. ILO programmes began to focus on gender analysis and planning, as well as on gender relations and the restructuring of social institutions. However, gender issues were not prominent in the work of the Organization during this period, despite efforts by a number of committed individuals on the staff.

Gender mainstreaming was first formulated as the "transformative strategy" to achieve gender equality at the Fourth World Conference on Women in Beijing in 1995. In 1999, the newly elected ILO Director-General, Juan Somavia, announced a Policy on Gender Equality and Mainstreaming, made operational through an action plan, which consists of a gender perspective in the design and implementation of all programmes and projects. The action plan has been successful in introducing participatory gender audits – the first exercise of its kind in the UN system; and in emphasizing the importance of labour market statistics disaggregated by sex. The focus on specific groups of women workers such as domestic workers, homeworkers, migrant workers and victims of trafficking, as well as the girl child, has drawn attention to vulnerability linked to multiple forms of discrimination.

Yet, while there have been many improvements in the understanding of gender, true gender equality in the workplace and in society remains a distant

---

[25] ILO: *Time for equality at work*, Global Report under the Follow-up to the ILO Declaration on Fundamental Principles and Rights at Work, International Labour Conference, 91st Session, Geneva, 2003; ILO: *Equality at work: Tackling the challenges*, Global Report, International Labour Conference, 96th Session, Geneva, 2007.

goal, even in the countries that have taken it most seriously. Much of the ILO activity on this issue has been generated by the Office, and with a few exceptions[26] has not originated in the membership. The 2006 Global Report under the follow-up to the ILO's 1998 Declaration[27] concludes that despite advances, in particular the considerable progress in women's educational attainments, women still earn less than men everywhere, and the unequal burden of family responsibilities continues to place them at a disadvantage in finding full-time, formal employment. There are also new and multiple forms of discrimination, for instance against the increasing numbers of women migrant workers. There is growing concern that progress has stalled. The energy of global women's movements appears to be waning, gender mainstreaming initiatives have not lived up to their expectations, and donor and government funding for gender equality remains static or, in some cases, is even in decline, despite the fact that many countries will not be able to meet the United Nations Millennium Development Goal on gender equality.

## Forced and compulsory labour[28]

Forced labour was the first human rights subject dealt with at the international level. In 1815 the Congress of Vienna expressed its desire, in the name of the universal principles of morality and humanity, to put an end to a scourge that had desolated Africa, degraded Europe and the Americas and afflicted humanity for so long.[29] Great Britain was a leader in this effort internationally. Following the Congress of Vienna, national laws were adopted and bilateral treaties concluded which gave effect to the commitment to prohibit the slave trade and enforce its

---

[26] A notable exception is the Pay Equity campaign being led by Public Service International. See International Trade Union Confederation (ITUC): *The global gender pay gap* (Brussels, 2008). A summary is given at: http://www.ituc-csi.org/IMG/pdf/gap-1.pdf

[27] ILO: *Equality at work*, op. cit.

[28] See history and background of forced labour and slavery in ILO: *Forced labour in Myanmar (Burma)*, Report of the Commission of Inquiry appointed under article 26 of the Constitution of the International Labour Organization to examine the observance by Myanmar of the Forced Labour Convention, 1930 (No. 29), Geneva, 1998, paras. 199 et seq. Much of the following background is taken from this report. The detailed references to the treaties and other acts listed here can also be found therein.

[29] Final Act of the Congress of Vienna, reproduced in G. de Martens: *Nouveau recueil général de traités et autres actes relatifs aux rapports de droit international, 1814–1815*, Tome II, p. 433. Austria, France, Great Britain, Prussia and Russia, meeting in Verona in 1822, reaffirmed their commitment to seeking the most effective means of preventing a trade which had already been declared illegal and repugnant by almost all civilized countries and to rigorously punish those who continued in breach of these laws. See also G. de Martens: *Nouveau recueil général de traités et autres actes relatifs aux rapports de droit international, 1822–1823*, Tome VI.1, pp. 136–137.

prohibition with penal sanctions, and a number of other multilateral instruments were signed under the auspices of the Great Powers for the purposes of prohibiting the practice and coordinating action to suppress it.

After the First World War, slavery and slavery-like practices were among the first issues addressed by the League of Nations. Under its impetus, nearly all states adopted legislation to prevent slavery internally and the importation of slaves. The Slavery Convention, concluded by the League on 25 September 1926,[30] defined slavery for the first time as, "the status or condition of a person over whom any or all of the powers attaching to the right of ownership are exercised",[31] and required ratifying states to prevent and suppress the slave trade; to bring about, progressively and as soon as possible, the complete abolition of slavery in all its forms; and to adopt the necessary measures in order to ensure that breaches of laws and regulations are punished by severe penalties.[32] It was against this background that the Forced Labour Convention (No. 29) was adopted by the ILO in 1930.

Daniel Maul identifies three distinct phases in the ILO's treatment of forced labour: (1) the period between the wars, when forced labour was treated mainly as a colonial phenomenon; (2) the post-1945 period, during which a new international human rights discourse, the move towards "welfare colonialism" in the European colonial territories and, above all, the East–West conflict, restructured the ILO debates on forced labour; and (3) the 1960s and beyond, when, mainly as a consequence of decolonization in Africa and Asia, the question of the appropriate balance between the development demands of the new nations and the justified use of coercion came to the fore. Now that almost all government-sanctioned systems of forced labour for development have come to an end, a fourth phase may be identified – one that is characterized by debate on the thorny subject of privatized prison labour, and the forced labour aspects of the growing problem of trafficking.

ILO Convention No. 29 requires states to abolish all forms of forced and compulsory labour, while identifying certain acceptable exceptions such as compulsory military service, prison labour under certain conditions, and minor

---

[30] Reproduced in League of Nations Treaty Series (Geneva, 1927), Vol. LX, No. 1414, pp. 253–270. The Convention was amended in 1953 (reproduced in United Nations Treaty Series, 1953, Vol. CLII, No. 2422, pp. 51–72).

[31] Art. 1(1).

[32] Arts. 2 and 6. Thirty years later, the Supplementary Convention on the Abolition of Slavery, the Slave Trade, and Institutions and Practices Similar to Slavery, was adopted at the initiative of ECOSOC on 7 September 1956, including subjects that are also covered by various ILO standards. While the UN convention is not subject to reporting and supervision, the ILO standards are.

## Box 3  Myanmar – A special situation

Myanmar's gross violations of the Forced Labour Convention, 1930 (No. 29), have been criticized by the ILO for more than 30 years. It is the only case in which all the procedures for reviewing and correcting violations of ILO Conventions have ever been used. It represents slow progress, but also shows that international supervision alone can go only so far in getting countries to eliminate abuses.

Myanmar ratified Convention No. 29 in 1955. It was not long before allegations of forced labour were received, and the Committee of Experts began raising increasingly urgent questions, to which the Government failed to respond. In November 1994, a committee convened to examine a representation filed against Myanmar by the International Confederation of Free Trade Unions (ICFTU). When the Government still failed to act, a "complaint" under article 26 of the Constitution was submitted by a group of Workers' delegates to the Conference in June 1996, and a Commission of Inquiry was established. Although the Government refused to cooperate with the Commission, extensive hearings were held and the Commission visited refugee camps in Myanmar and other sites in the region. It concluded that the Convention was violated in national law and practice in a widespread and systematic manner.* The abuses noted were horrendous, involving the requisition of entire villages by the military, forced prostitution, a practice called "porterage" in which villagers were forced to transport military supplies without compensation and under constraint, and even the forcing of villagers to walk into minefields to clear them for the military.

The Government remained unmoved, and the Governing Body took the unprecedented step, in March 2000, of using article 33 of the Constitution which provides that, if a government does not implement the recommendations of a Commission of Inquiry (or the International Court of Justice) within the time specified, "the Governing Body may recommend to the Conference such action as it may deem wise

civic obligations.[33] It states, in Article 25, that "the illegal exaction of forced or compulsory labour shall be punishable as a penal offence" and that the penalties imposed must be "really adequate" and "strictly enforced".

By today's standards, Convention No. 29 is a rather strange human rights instrument, and most of it is no longer considered applicable. Articles 3 to 24 allowed for the continuation of forced labour in European colonies for a transitional period pending its eventual abolition, and aimed to impose limits on the ways in which these powers exploited the "native populations" of Africa and Asia. However, the Committee of Experts remarked in its 2007 General

---

[33] For a full explication of the requirements of the Convention, including the very complex situation of these exceptions, see, in particular, ILO: *Eradication of forced labour*, General Survey concerning the Forced Labour Convention, 1930 (No. 29), and the Abolition of Forced Labour Convention, 1957 (No. 105), International Labour Conference, 96th Session, Geneva, Committee of Experts on the Application of Conventions and Recommendations, Report III (Part IA), 2007.

*Cont'd*

and expedient to secure compliance therewith". From that time on, the continued pressure – combined with growing criticism of the Government's denial of political freedoms – began to force a slow and intermittent response. The ILO Conference called on all member States, employers' and workers' organizations, as well as other international organizations, to review their relations with Myanmar to ensure that they were not supporting forced labour in that country. Myanmar's participation in all ILO activities was forbidden, unless they contributed directly to halting forced labour. The Conference Committee on the Application of Standards now holds a special sitting at each session on the situation in Myanmar, and there are discussions at every session of the Governing Body, in which the Government has never failed to take part.

The Government has slowly responded, including accepting an ILO Liaison Officer in the country who works on the elimination of forced labour – the only international human rights official with regular access to the country. Under pressure from its neighbours to make some progress and remove the stain on the region's reputation, the military Government has accepted repeated missions by senior ILO officials, which have extended even to a rare meeting in 2008 with the reclusive Head of State.

While all of this has not yet, as of the writing of this book in 2008, persuaded Myanmar to end forced labour, it has given rise to the only regular cooperation the Government has with any international organization on human rights issues. ILO interventions have on several occasions led to the freeing of people jailed for protesting against forced labour, and to the publishing of orders banning it. Limited as these successes are, they represent movement that would not have been achieved without ILO action.

* See ILO: *Report of the Commission of Inquiry, 1998*. Available on the ILO website: http://www.ilo.org. This report is one of the best examples of human rights investigation anywhere, and is well worth reading.

Survey that "it is important to ensure that there is no room for misinterpretation of Articles 3 to 24 of Convention No. 29, which contain provisions that were applicable during a transitional period. The Committee notes that this period expired long ago, and that the provisions in question are therefore no longer applicable".[34]

The practices covered in Convention No. 29 are far from abolished in practice, although the colonialist attitudes it was intended to address at the time have nearly disappeared.[35] The ILO supervisory bodies have in more recent years noted

---

[34] Ibid., para. 196.

[35] Except in a few scattered instances. For instance, it can be argued that the massive use of forced labour by the Government of Myanmar which occupied much attention in the ILO throughout the early 2000s was internal colonialism based on the same assumptions of absolute control as the colonial powers assumed 70 years earlier.

the continued existence of this fundamental violation of human rights, being manifested in slavery in out-of-the-way corners of countries which have banned it by law – but where law enforcement does not reach. The Committee of Experts noted in its 2007 General Survey: "At the time of the adoption of Convention No. 29, there were far more instances of slavery and slave-like practices worldwide than exist today. In this respect, there have been improvements in many countries in relation to the gross and more obvious forms of forced labour. However, some of these practices regrettably still exist in a number of countries in various forms, including debt bondage."[36] Forced labour thrives where governments have failed to exercise police power, and where traditional systems such as debt bondage have not yet been the target of effective national action. Some of the worst abuses of child labour were dealt with under Convention No. 29 until the Worst Forms of Child Labour Convention, 1999 (No. 182), began to take effect in a growing number of countries.

Forced and compulsory labour also continues to take new forms, even as the older ones persist in some places. The 2005 Global Report on the abolition of forced labour estimated the size and distribution of various kinds of forced labour in today's world: "This year for the first time we have estimated that there are at least 12.3 million victims of forced labour around the world. Of these, 9.8 million are exploited by private agents, including more than 2.4 million in forced labour as a result of human trafficking. The remaining 2.5 million are forced to work by the State or by rebel groups."[37]

One of the most difficult questions arising in recent times under Convention No. 29 is the acceptable limits on labour imposed in prisons, especially privatized prisons or prisons where private enterprise has established programmes. Other questions are related in particular to the spectacular rise in trafficking in persons for the purposes of labour exploitation – whether for sexual exploitation or for other forms of imposed labour; and to the conditions of work of domestic workers, who are almost always out of sight of the authorities and who are abused by their employers with depressing frequency.[38]

Convention No. 29 was complemented by the Abolition of Forced Labour Convention (No. 105), adopted in 1957 to address practices that had emerged during the Second World War and in the Soviet Gulags. This instrument forbids

---

[36] ILO: *Eradication of forced labour*, op. cit., para. 195.

[37] ILO: *Director-General's introduction to the International Labour Conference: Consolidating progress and moving ahead*, Report I(A) International Labour Conference, 93rd Session, Geneva, 2003.

[38] Trends in modern forced labour are explored thoroughly in the Global Reports prepared under the follow-up to the ILO Declaration on Fundamental Principles and Rights at Work. See *A global alliance against forced labour*, Report 1(B), International Labour Conference, 93rd Session, Geneva, 2005.

forced labour as a punishment for political crimes, for participation in strikes, as a means of racial or other discrimination, or as labour discipline. It finds its main application in situations which are in themselves beyond the ILO's immediate human rights mandate – such as the exercise of free speech – but which are punished by imposing forced labour, bringing it within the ILO's purview.

Conventions Nos. 29 and 105 are the most widely ratified ILO standards, with 170 and 166 ratifications, respectively, in mid-2008. For far too long, neither the ILO nor any other international organization had field programmes in place to combat slavery and forced labour, perhaps because they assumed that these practices were gradually dying out. But after the adoption of the Declaration on Fundamental Principles and Rights at Work in 1998, a Special Action Programme against forced labour was created in the Declaration secretariat. This Programme has revealed a need for much research and practical assistance in this area, on account of the unexpectedly high number of people suffering from forced labour in a number of countries.[39] This has resulted in practical action, with the help of the ILO, to bring these practices to light and to move towards their abolition.

### Child labour

The original Constitution provided that "the abolition of child labour and the imposition of such limitations on the labour of young persons as shall permit the continuation of their education and assure their proper physical development" were to be among the ILO's basic concerns, and at the first session of the Conference in 1919 it adopted the Minimum Age (Industry) Convention (No. 5). This was the first in a long series of instruments on minimum age and the conditions under which young persons were allowed to work, including hours of work, night work and medical examinations. The minimum age Conventions adopted between 1919 and 1921 were the very first international instruments concerning children's rights, and among the earliest concerning human rights in general. Until the 1980s, the ILO's concern on this issue was expressed entirely through standard-setting, which evolved over the years.[40]

---

[39] See website for Special Action Programme: http://www.ilo.org/sapfl/lang--en/index.htm

[40] For a detailed examination of this evolution, see in particular, M. Dahlén: *The ILO and child labour*, paper prepared for the ILO Century Project, 2008, available at: http://www.ilocentury.org; A. Fyfe: *The worldwide movement against child labour: Progress and future directions* (Geneva, ILO, 2007).

At the national level, the earliest labour legislation concerned the regulation of child labour, as it was easier to achieve consensus about the protection of children than for the protection of adult workers. Traditionally most children had worked in agriculture and in the trades, but the Industrial Revolution changed this pattern. The mass employment of children in the factory towns made the grim exploitation only too visible to the public. With the ideological, political, economic and social changes in Western societies brought about by the American and French Revolutions, and later by the Industrial Revolution, attention was focused on children in a way that it had never been before.

The earliest legal expressions of this concern for children and childhood were the child labour laws passed during the nineteenth century in the leading industrial nations. Great Britain was a forerunner in this respect and it introduced the so-called Factory Acts as early as 1802. France and Prussia were quick to follow the example. Most European countries and the North American States adopted more or less similar legislation during the later decades of the nineteenth century. The factory legislation provided for standard minimum ages that were adjusted to school-leaving age and the conditions of production in the different economic sectors; it also established maximum hours of work – but only for industrial work. These laws allowed various and generous exceptions.

The labour movement supported the demands for international regulation of child labour, building on plans by the International Association for Labour Legislation that had been shelved on the eve of the First World War. For example, the Berne Manifesto, adopted by the International Trade Union Conference at Berne in 1919, demanded regulation of the work of children in the form of minimum age, limited hours of work and compulsory education for all. But the reason for this was not only to protect children. The main concern of the trade unions after the First World War was to secure employment for the hundreds of thousands of demobilized soldiers who had returned home to unemployment. Women and children had successfully replaced the male workforce during the war – so successfully that production increased – but after the war, they were unwanted competitors in a restricted employment market.[41]

In addition, employers in the industrialized countries had come to consider child labour as unacceptable, partly because it did not promote production in the long run. A consensus evolved that better working conditions, including a decrease in child labour, were necessary for the sustainable development of industry, and for the stability of the nation state, though, sadly, many have not yet shared this

---

[41] M. Dahlén, op. cit.

epiphany. The converging interests of the labour movement, the women's movement, employers and governments therefore coincided on the matter of children's protection. As a result, the regulation of child labour was proposed as an agenda item in all the various proposals to the Peace Conference from the British, French and American governmental delegations.[42] According to figures in the American proposal, twenty-three countries in Europe had already enacted minimum age legislation by 1918, and thirteen of them had made 13 or 14 years the minimum age for employment.[43] The Labour Commission at the Peace Conference proposed the employment of children – minimum age, employment during the night and in unhealthy processes – as the third item on the agenda of the first session of the International Labour Conference in Washington in 1919.

Two Conventions on child labour were adopted at the Conference in 1919: the Minimum Age (Industry) Convention (No. 5); and the Night Work of Young Persons (Industry) Convention (No. 6). The ILO subsequently adopted three more Conventions in quick succession setting a minimum age at sea, in agriculture and for "trimmers and stokers" (working on steam engines). The minimum age was the same in all the Conventions – 14 years – except for work during the night and for work as a trimmer or stoker, for which the minimum age was set at 18 years. This was based on existing factory legislation and the educational systems in the industrialized member States. There was general concern about leaving a gap between the school-leaving age and the minimum age for employment. "Idle children" were seen as a threat not only to childhood but also to society. The minimum age of 14 years in agriculture was severely undercut by the fact that all agricultural work outside school hours and some work during school hours was permitted in these early standards.[44] With the adoption of the Minimum Age (Non-Industrial Employment) Convention (No. 33) in 1932, which completed the first cycle of standards, it was intended that all work should now be covered by the same minimum age provisions to prevent the risk of children moving from a regulated sector to a less regulated one. Convention No. 33 set the pattern for future standards when it added exceptions for harmful occupations and consideration of the consequences of such work for the health, morals, development and

---

[42] J.T. Shotwell: *The origins of the International Labour Organization*, Carnegie Endowment for International Peace (New York, Columbia University Press, 1934), two volumes. See for example: "Note from the French Minister of Labor to the Premier and the Minister for Foreign Affairs, January 20, 1919", Vol. II, doc. 28; "Recommendations relative to legislation in regard to international labor, submitted by James T. Shotwell to the American Delegation at the Peace Conference, January 21, 1919", Vol. II, doc. 29; and "Draft Convention creating a permanent organisation for the promotion of international regulation of labour conditions, prepared by the British Delegation, January 21, 1919", Vol. II.

[43] Ibid.

[44] Convention No. 10, Article 1.

education of the child. It also introduced a greater differentiation in the age levels; for instance, light work was allowed, provided that it did not prejudice children's attendance at school or their capacity to benefit from the instruction dispensed therein (Article 3 (1)(b)). It was, however, left to the national authorities – after consultation with the workers' and the employers' organizations – to decide the forms of employment that should be classified as light work and dangerous work (Article 3 (3)), thereby extending tripartite involvement.

These instruments all provided for some exceptions, many of which are reproduced in some fashion throughout the history of ILO standards. Family undertakings were excluded in most instances because, as one of the delegates at the Conference stated, "family sentiment" would automatically protect the child from being exploited.[45] The Office cautioned that there was "considerable danger of abuse" even when parents were employers. The fact that children's work contributed substantially to the family economy and that their withdrawal from the labour market might cause financial hardship, was not discussed at that stage by the Office or at the Conference.

In addition, several of the pre-war Conventions had separate provisions with lower requirements for China, India and Japan, which varied according to the instrument. During the discussions on Convention No. 33, for example, the Workers' group demanded that Indian children should have the same protection as other children, but the Employers' group and some Governments argued for "a principle of gradualness". The colonial Indian Government attributed the lack of compulsory school legislation and child protection in India to the "imperfect conditions of India" and the "backwardness" of the Indian people. The "imperfect conditions" were defined as tropical climate, habits and customs, economic opportunity, industrial tradition, the lack of compulsory schooling, poor laws, social insurance and insufficient education of parents.[46] The same arguments were repeated when these Conventions were revised in 1936 and 1937, and it was argued that India's developing industrialism should not be "stifled and hampered" by regulations developed for entirely different conditions by countries that were competitors to India.[47] The argument that some countries are insufficiently developed to eliminate child labour has continued into the twenty-first century, and has changed little – although some of the terminology has evolved.

---

[45] ILO: *Record of Proceedings*, International Labour Conference, 1st session, Washington, 1919.

[46] ILO: *Record of Proceedings*, International Labour Conference, 16th Session, Geneva, 1932, pp. 402–404, 406–414, 474–477.

[47] Speech by India's Employer adviser, in ILO: *Record of Proceedings*, International Labour Conference, 23rd Session, Geneva, 1937, p. 338.

In the early years of the ILO, the greatest evils were attributed to the industrial world. In 1919, the majority of the European population still lived in rural areas, and it seemed neither realistic nor desirable to many to abolish child labour in agriculture. As the French Government declared in its answer to the Office's questionnaire concerning minimum age in agriculture: "Agricultural work is not comparable with industrial labour; the former is rather a healthy sport graduated according to the strength of the child."[48]

No sooner had the "circle" of regulation on minimum ages in the various sectors been completed, than a number of revisions were made to the relevant Conventions. A major reason for this appears to have been the Depression. Once again, there was a need to cope with widespread unemployment, and many believed that fewer young people should take on jobs that should go to adults. This led to a series of instruments being adopted with a higher minimum age (15 years), stricter enforcement provisions and narrower exceptions – with regard to family undertakings, inter alia. These were ratified by a number of states, but widespread ratification of the ILO's child labour Conventions was to come only later. The motivations behind the adoption of certain instruments, subsequently considered as promoting fundamental human rights, were not therefore as elevated as they might have seemed.

When the ILO resumed operations after the Second World War, perceptions about children and young persons had begun to change. Children suffered terribly in the war, not least because there had been a considerable increase in the employment of young people. The ILO adopted a resolution concerning the protection of children and young workers in 1945, which drew attention to a number of interrelated problems concerning the education, employment, protection and general welfare of children and young persons. It identified three main points of action for the ILO: (1) the long-term objective of a minimum age of 16 years; (2) the bridging of any gap between the school-leaving age and the minimum age for employment; and (3) the standardization of the minimum age in all economic sectors.[49]

In the report on children and young workers to the Conference in 1945,[50] much emphasis was laid on the need to guarantee a basic income for families. The Introduction stated that material aid to the family was a fundamental factor in any social programme for child welfare. For the first time, the connection

---

[48] ILO: *Record of Proceedings*, International Labour Conference, 3rd Session, Geneva, 1921, p. 48.

[49] Ibid.

[50] ILO: *Protection of children and young workers*, Report III, International Labour Conference, 27th Session, Paris, 1945.

between the abolition of child labour and children's need of maintenance was recognized and a complete scheme of social security and family allowances was proposed. This was in line with developments in the European industrial nations, which had already introduced family and children's allowances as part of national policies to deal with the decreasing populations.

In 1973, with the adoption of the Minimum Age Convention (No. 138), the sector-by-sector approach to standard-setting on child labour was abandoned in favour of a comprehensive instrument that would cover all children in employment or work. Dahlén attributes the reason for adopting this Convention as "part of the strategies to defeat or mitigate unemployment and 'social unrest' in times of economic and political crisis", as had been the case for some of the earliest minimum age Conventions.[51] However, it was also part of a wider Office strategy to update and consolidate Conventions applying only to given sectors of the economy. Convention No. 138 referred for the first time to a minimum age of admission to employment "or work", compared to previous instruments which had focused only on employment. This Convention contained exceptions as earlier ones had, but they were framed so as to ensure that children would not be able to do dangerous work even under the exceptions allowed. Nevertheless, it is a highly technical instrument, and attracted few ratifications for over 25 years, both because many countries considered it too detailed, and because they were not ready to make a commitment to tackling child labour on a comprehensive basis. When the ratification campaign for human rights instruments was launched in 1995, Convention No. 138 was included but few governments responded with ratifications at first. But a new era was about to begin.

The situation began to evolve in the 1990s. The Social Summit in 1995 included child labour among the human rights subjects of the ILO, and the Conference adopted a resolution underlining a new consensus on action against child labour in 1996.[52] The following year, the Governing Body placed the discussion of the worst forms of child labour on the Conference agenda. And in 1998, the elimination of all forms of child labour was included among the fundamental human rights enunciated in the Declaration of Fundamental Principles and Rights at Work. The adoption of the Worst Forms of Child Labour Convention (No. 182) in 1999 marked a significant departure for the ILO. While retaining the basic idea that the abolition of child labour was the primary objective, this Convention prioritized certain forms of child labour as being particularly reprehensible. It also

---

[51] M. Dahlén, op. cit.

[52] ILO: Resolution concerning the elimination of child labour, International Labour Conference, 83rd Session, Geneva, 1996.

departed from the ILO's traditional acceptance of gradualism as being necessary in the elimination of child labour, and took the approach that certain manifestations of this problem were so abhorrent that no delay and no excuse could be accepted. The Convention quickly became the most rapidly ratified Convention in ILO history – and it began to pull ratifications of Convention No. 138 along with it.[53] By mid-2008, Convention No. 138 had 149 ratifications, and Convention No. 182 had 167.

## The establishment of IPEC and the launching of practical action

Until well after the Second World War, ILO action against child labour mainly took the form of standard-setting, with almost no field work. The ILO did undertake a few technical missions (to India) in the early 1980s, and held tripartite workshops in Asia and Africa. In 1989, with support from the Government of the Netherlands, the ILO launched its first dedicated technical assistance project on child labour – the so-called "Smoky Mountain" project at a dump site in Manila. While not entirely successful, it taught the Office lessons that have influenced its approach to the question ever since. In particular, it learned that improving the working conditions of children does not contribute to eliminating child labour.

This situation changed radically in 1992, when the Government of Germany allocated 50 million DM to the ILO over a five-year period to launch the International Programme on the Elimination of Child Labour (IPEC), which now has become by far the ILO's largest and most successful technical cooperation programme. It has attracted funding from a growing number of countries, and works in some 90 target countries. Using the basic idea of Convention No. 182 that programmes for the elimination of child labour should be "time-bound" – that is, have defined goals to be achieved within stated periods – IPEC has combined with other international efforts on child labour to have a significant effect. While these efforts generally pursue compatible goals, there have been instances when the ILO's objective of eliminating child labour has not been fully supported by others, in particular UNICEF, whose major goal is increasing children's welfare. This has sometimes led UNICEF to advocate the right of children to work – one of the rare instances when human rights and humanitarian goals are not in agreement.

---

[53] The United States, which has ratified fewer ILO Conventions than any other developed state, was one of the first to ratify Convention No. 182.

The IPEC website and the Committee of Experts cite a number of instances in which countries have taken concrete and effective measures to eliminate child labour. The 2006 Global Report on child labour,[54] issued under the 1998 Declaration follow-up, stated that over a four-year period between 2000 and 2004 child labour around the world had fallen by a remarkable 11 per cent, from 245 million worldwide to 218 million – still far too many, but it showed that progress was being made. And it demonstrated once again that standards often need to be supplemented by practical action and supported by a broad consensus in favour of that action.

## Protecting and promoting particular categories of workers

Since its earliest days, the ILO has adopted measures for particular categories of workers. In addition to the situation of children, much attention has been paid to such groups as disabled persons, as well as to occupational categories including, inter alia, merchant seafarers. Two of these special groups are migrant workers and indigenous and tribal peoples, for which the ILO has done groundbreaking work.

### Migrant workers

The story of the ILO and migrant workers[55] is one of lost opportunities and divided priorities among the ILO's constituents. Although the ILO was able to adopt the basic international standards on the subject, its periodic attempts to exercise a real influence on international policies have fallen on deaf ears.

At the Paris Peace Conference in 1919, the trade unions from the major industrialized countries urged the new ILO to accord very high priority to migrant workers. The United States and British Governments, however, were against bringing up migration questions in the context of the ILO,[56] as neither wanted "outside interference" in their management of migrant workers. The French Government and trade unions, on the other hand, maintained that the demand for equality of wages

---

[54] ILO: *The end of child labour: Within reach*, Global Report under the Follow-up to the ILO Declaration on Fundamental Principles and Rights at Work, International Labour Conference, 95th Session, Geneva, 2006.

[55] This subject is dealt with in much greater detail in W.R. Böhning: *A brief account of the ILO and policies on international migration*, paper prepared for the ILO Century Project, 2008, available at: http://www.ilocentury.org

[56] See Shotwell, op. cit., 1934, Vol. II, doc. 16 of Sep. 1918 regarding the United States, together with doc. 37 of Feb. 1919, and doc. 17 of Nov. 1918 regarding Great Britain.

and working conditions between national and foreign workers was a basic tenet.[57] Experiencing labour shortages, France had concluded the first-ever international migration agreement with Italy shortly before the First World War, and after the war France feared a "demographic deficit" compared to Germany and a lack of manpower for the reconstruction of its own devastated departments and economy. France and Italy therefore submitted proposals to the Labour Commission that foresaw, among other things, the adoption of "Conventions providing for equality of wages and working conditions ... between foreign and native workers" and the examination of "freedom of migration of workers who of their own free will desire to proceed abroad and the regulation of collective migration". But the British proposals, on which the discussions were based, contained the far more limited idea of "protection of the interests of workers when employed in countries other than their own" in the draft Preamble to the proposed ILO Constitution. The British text was adopted almost without discussion. Böhning points out that:

> the basic negotiation pattern has been repeated over and over again: Immigration countries dominate outcomes at the international level; the stronger delegations among them ... secure their interests more easily than the weaker ... As emigration countries stand cap in hand before the countries they want to admit their surplus population, they are in the weakest position of all, as demonstrated by Italy's vain attempts at influencing the Labour Charter.

Nevertheless, in spite of the lack of detail, this was the first time in history that a global organization had been endowed with functions in an area that states had always jealously defended as a core part of their sovereignty.

Despite the Constitution's weak wording, over the years the Organization has adopted a fairly large number of Conventions and Recommendations on, or affecting, migrant workers. (A few standards have also dealt with internal migrants – that is, workers who move within their own country – but this chapter deals only with international migrants for work.) The Organization has had a twofold aim when adopting these instruments: to regulate the conditions in which the migration process takes place; and to provide specific protection for a very vulnerable category of workers. The ILO's standard-setting activities in this area have therefore been concentrated in two main areas.

First, the Organization has endeavoured to establish the right to equality of treatment between nationals and non-nationals in the field of social security, and

---

[57] Ibid., Vol. II, doc. 3, pp. 19–22, 25, 28.

to institute an international system for the maintenance of acquired rights and rights for workers who move from one country to another. The first Conference in 1919 adopted the Unemployment Convention (No. 2), which provided that member States "shall, upon terms being agreed between the Members concerned, make arrangements whereby workers belonging to one Member and working in the territory of another shall be admitted to the same rates of benefit [of established systems of insurance against unemployment] as those which obtain for the workers belonging to the latter" (Article 3). The Organization went on in time to adopt four Conventions and two Recommendations on these lines, all designed to limit progressively the scope of certain restrictive clauses based on the method of financing social security.[58]

Second, the Conference has tried to find comprehensive solutions to the problems facing migrant workers and to regulate the conditions under which they migrate, and has adopted a number of instruments to this end – including some containing only a few provisions relating to migrant workers.[59] These were consolidated in 1949 with the adoption of the Migration for Employment Convention (Revised) (No. 97) and its accompanying Recommendation (No. 86). In 1975, the Conference supplemented the 1949 instruments by adopting the Migrant Workers (Supplementary Provisions) Convention (No. 143) and the Migrant Workers Recommendation (No. 151) which, among other things, expanded coverage to undocumented migrants.

To return to the ILO's early work on this subject, on the proposal of the Italian and French Governments an International Emigration Commission was established in the new ILO, supported by a special technical section on migrant workers in the Office, "to consider and report what measures can be adopted to regulate the migration of workers out of their own States and to protect the interests of wage earners residing in States other than their own". When, in early 1923, the Governing Body considered the Commission's proposal to put the subject of equality of treatment on the agenda of the Conference, the immigration/emigration fault lines and certain racial overtones among the colonial powers manifested themselves – and not for the last time. The 1925 Conference nevertheless adopted both a Convention and a Recommendation concerning equality of treatment for national and foreign workers with respect to accident compensation. Convention

---

[58] The Equality of Treatment (Accident Compensation) Convention, 1925 (No. 19), and its accompanying Recommendation (No. 25); the Maintenance of Migrants' Pension Rights Convention, 1935 (No. 48); the Equality of Treatment (Social Security) Convention, 1962 (No. 118); and the Maintenance of Social Security Rights Convention, 1982 (No. 157), and its accompanying Recommendation, 1983 (No. 167).

[59] For a more comprehensive listing, see Böhning, op. cit.

No. 19 has been one of the most successful international Conventions on migrant workers, with 121 ratifications by mid-2008. It broke new ground by associating international reciprocity with its ratification: "Each Member of the International Labour Organisation which ratifies this Convention undertakes to grant to the nationals of any other Member which shall have ratified the Convention ... the same treatment ... as it grants to its own nationals" (Article 1 (1)).

The mid-1920s was a comparatively optimistic period for Europeans and Americans, and even in the migration field the ILO was beginning to move along purposefully. The League of Nations transferred its refugee operations to the Office in 1925 without much ado. A World Migration Congress, convened by the International Federation of Trade Unions and the Labour and Socialist International in London in June 1926, sought to push the Office more broadly and deeply into this field – also suggesting that a separate international migration body be established "if the Office proved unable to move forward". Unfortunately, confidence in the future was soon sapped by continued challenges to the ILO's migration competence and by fascist movements, as when Mussolini stopped Italian emigration. The League of Nations, reversing its earlier cession of competence to the ILO, made plans to hold an International Conference on the Treatment of Foreigners in late 1929 with the possibility of drafting an international Convention.

In the summer of 1929, the Conference underscored the topicality of international migration by adopting two resolutions on that subject, submitted respectively by the Chinese Government and its Workers' delegation. The second of these requested the "Governing Body ... to consider the desirability of placing on the agenda of a very early Session of the Conference ... the question of equality of treatment between national workers and coloured foreign workers employed in the territories of States Members or in their possessions and colonies". The fact that it went no further highlighted the racist attitudes inherent in the reticence of some countries to accept migrants without restriction.

Then the crash in Wall Street changed the economic and political parameters. International economic migration came to a halt. Nevertheless, a few years later, the Conference managed to adopt the Migration for Employment Convention (No. 66) in 1939, less than three months before the outbreak of the Second World War. This never entered into force because of lack of ratifications but it provided the basis for the standards adopted in the aftermath of the war. This Convention reflected the concern of a number of Latin American countries about the restrictions on emigration by several central and eastern European Governments – and, of course, by the fascist Governments of Germany and Italy; and they wanted to mobilize the ILO to get the movement of settlers towards Latin America going again.

With the outbreak of the Second World War, large numbers of refugees were left stranded throughout Europe. The 1944 Declaration of Philadelphia renewed the call for attention to migration with its provision that the Organization should:

> further among the nations of the world programmes which will achieve: (a) full employment and the raising of standards of living; ... (c) the provision, as a means to the attainment of this end and under adequate guarantees for all concerned, of facilities for training and the transfer of labour, including migration for employment and settlement.

The Migration for Employment Convention (No. 97), adopted in 1949, was an early manifestation of European social-democratic views of the way in which societies should handle migrant workers. Its Article 6 prohibits "discrimination in respect of nationality, race, religion, or sex" in the case of lawfully resident foreign workers in most situations. The accompanying Recommendation (No. 86) stipulates in Paragraph 4 (1) that:

> it should be the general policy of Members to develop and utilise all possibilities of employment and for this purpose to facilitate the international distribution of manpower and in particular the movement of manpower from countries which have a surplus of manpower to those countries that have a deficiency.

Annexed to the Recommendation is a Model Agreement on Temporary and Permanent Migration for Employment, including Migration of Refugees and Displaced Persons, which has inspired many countries at both ends of the migration chain. The Convention has not, however, been very widely ratified, especially by countries of immigration, like other international instruments on the subject.[60]

Most Western European economies began to experience sustained growth during the 1950s. Switzerland, with an economy undamaged by the war, had already begun to import foreign workers. Pressed by unions, the equal pay for equal work principle was accepted and generally applied in practice. The "rotation" principle was also applied – foreigners would come without their families, work and eventually return home for good, endowed with new skills and hard currency savings, and this model was replicated by several other European countries at the time. Most

---

[60] By the end of 2008, Convention No. 97 had acquired 48 ratifications, and the later Convention No. 143 had 23. The United Nations Convention on the Rights of all Migrant Workers and Members of their Families had acquired 40 ratifications.

European flows to traditional settlement destinations had dried up by the early 1970s, while new migrants from Asia, Haiti, Latin America, Lebanon and elsewhere started to knock at North American and Australian doors. The United States and Canada were driven by a combination of economic forces and the principle of equality to modify their discriminatory admission policies in 1965 and 1967, respectively, and Australia dropped its racially-based selection criteria in 1975. In addition, with the end of many colonial regimes after the Second World War, some previously intra-colonial movements turned into international migration. A similar effect would be produced with the collapse of the USSR in the early 1990s.

David Morse, who had been elected Director-General in June 1948, instructed the Office to elaborate an ambitious technical cooperation programme encompassing manpower planning, vocational training and international migration. What was missing was a central body to organize movements and funds to pay for transport and training, inter alia. Morse convened a Preliminary Conference on Migration in April–May 1950. The Preliminary Conference adopted a general conclusion that stressed the "outstanding role which falls to the International Labour Organisation in this matter" and recommended that it should draw up, after consultation with the governments concerned, appropriate proposals for submission to them at a subsequent meeting.

But it was not to be. Already during the summer of 1951, it became clear that there were hesitations, particularly on the part of the Governments of Australia, Canada, Great Britain and the United States. Some governments were simply not willing to accord powers to an international organization that might impinge on their sovereign right to admit and refuse entry to non-nationals – and in the case of some states which would later drop such requirements, notably Australia, this was influenced by a fear that international control of migration would eliminate racial barriers.[61] More decisively, the Cold War and fear of communist infiltrators made the United States House of Representatives in August 1951 attach language to financial provisions destined to move refugees and migrants out of Europe according to which "none of the funds made available ... should be allocated to any international organization which has in its membership any communist, communist-dominated or communist-controlled country, to any subsidiary thereof or to any agency created by or stemming from such organization".[62] Although the USSR was not at that time a member State of the ILO (it joined in

---

[61] Alcock, op. cit., p. 231.

[62] The wording is that of the Conference Committee of both Houses of Congress of October 1951, quoted without comment in a footnote to an article on the Naples Conference, in *International Labour Review* (Geneva, ILO, 1952), Vol. LXV, No. 2, p. 178.

1954), countries such as Czechoslovakia and Poland were, and it was feared that they could place agitators among the displaced persons or unemployed candidates for migration who might not be weeded out by the Office or its Migration Administration.

By the time the Office convened its Migration Conference at Naples in October 1951, the rug had already been pulled from under its feet, and the ILO's plans went nowhere. The United States Government convened a meeting in Brussels one month after the Naples Conference. Almost all the countries that had participated in Naples attended the Brussels meeting, plus a few others. And the United States submitted many of the Office's earlier plans in all but name. Brussels established an intergovernmental organization that was first called the Intergovernmental Committee for European Migration (ICEM), which has now matured into the International Organization for Migration (IOM). All its directors have been United States citizens to date.

For a while after this, the Office continued providing advisory services to European and Latin American countries, turning out migration publications[63] and issuing articles in the *International Labour Review*.[64] But soon the Office's migration activities withered away, except for the supervision of the basic migration Convention No. 97 and the elaboration of some new standards. Among them was the Equality of Treatment (Social Security) Convention, 1962 (No. 118), which put nationals and non-nationals on the same footing with respect to social security. The specific problems of workers who move between countries and might not qualify for any benefits were regulated in the 1982 Maintenance of Social Security Rights Convention (No. 157). Neither Convention No. 118 nor Convention No. 157 has attracted many ratifications, but both have exerted an influence on countries' practices, especially in Europe.

Towards the end of colonial times and up until the 1980s, South–South migration expanded enormously. This form of migration also prevailed in long-decolonized Latin America and in the Caribbean, sometimes under very abusive conditions. In one of the worst cases, migrants from the Dominican Republic had to pay some 10 US dollars for the privilege of working in Haiti, which went straight into the private coffers of Haiti's President-for-Life, François Duvalier ("Baby Doc"). This prompted several delegates to the 1981 Conference to lodge

---

[63] On advisory services and publications, see ILO: *Survey of migration activities*, Governing Body 122nd Session, Geneva, May–June 1953, pp. 111 ff. *Migration*, a technical news summary, was issued at two-monthly intervals throughout 1952 and became a monthly supplement to *Industry and Labour* in 1953.

[64] Articles and reports kept appearing until the mid-1960s; then there was a lull. After the adoption of several resolutions by the Conference at the beginning of the 1970s, the *International Labour Review* again published articles on international migration questions in different parts of the world.

a complaint, leading to the establishment of a commission of inquiry[65] and, among other things, the cessation of these poor-to-rich payments. The large oil-price increases of October 1973 and 1979–80 permitted oil-exporting countries to launch vast infrastructure projects, allowing many private households to enjoy previously unheard-of incomes. Both effects induced growing and increasingly diversified flows of workers to the Arab countries of the Gulf region, plus a sprinkling of engineers, technicians, managers and traders from advanced industrial countries. When the real price of oil dropped substantially during the second half of the 1980s, the inflow of construction workers slowed in Arab countries, but the demand for housemaids from Sri Lanka, the Philippines and elsewhere continued unabated.

In 1975, the ILO returned to standard-setting with the Migrant Workers (Supplementary Provisions) Convention (No. 143). The Conference in 1975 elaborated a complex new Convention consisting of two parts that could be ratified independently of each other. The objective of part I is to suppress illegal migration and employment, while part II aims not only at equality before the law but also at equal treatment in practice. The accompanying Recommendation (No. 151) deals at length with questions of equality and social policies, including family reunification.

However, a number of developing emigration countries were unhappy with the ban on clandestine migration and illegal employment as formulated in part I of Convention No. 143. Led by Mexico and Morocco,[66] ECOSOC and the UN General Assembly adopted several resolutions at the end of the 1970s that resulted in the establishment, in October 1980, of an open-ended General Assembly working group entrusted with drafting a Convention on migrant workers – in which the Office took part, despite a fear of encroachment on the ILO's competence. When the first Mexican–Moroccan draft was on the table, many European and other representatives were shocked because it appeared to go too far in the opposite direction and to open the doors wide to illegal migration and employment. A group of small or medium-sized emigration and immigration countries from the northern rim of the Mediterranean and from Scandinavia, whose governments were headed by social-democratic parties at the beginning of the 1980s, asked the Office for technical assistance in preparing a

---

[65] "ILO: Report of the Commission of Inquiry appointed under article 26 of the Constitution of the International Labour Organisation to examine the observance of certain International Labour Conventions by the Dominican Republic and Haiti", in *Official Bulletin* (Geneva, ILO, 1983), Vol. LXVI, Series B.

[66] Whose Ministry of Labour and non-governmental representatives had voted in favour of Convention No. 143 in 1975. In New York, the Ministry of Foreign Affairs delegates displayed a different perspective.

counter proposal – on the understanding that the draft could contain provisions of the UN Covenants and the ILO's standards but should not go beyond them. In the end, the General Assembly adopted the International Convention on the Protection of Rights of all Migrant Workers and Members of their Families in 1990. The UN Convention is more comprehensive and detailed than the ILO's existing standards, and in some ways it updates and modernizes them, but it broadly offers the same level of protection except in the field of social security. The Office must, under the terms of the Convention, be consulted on the committee that monitors the application of this instrument.

The number of economically-active foreigners in migrant-receiving countries has been constantly growing. For example, Western Europe hosted about 7 million economically-active foreigners, plus 6.5 million dependents, in 1975; but by 1995 it counted about 9 million economically-active foreigners plus 13 million dependents; and there were probably as many as 11 million economically-active foreigners and 14 million dependents, by the end of 2007. The Office calculated that the number of major migrant-receiving countries had grown from 39 to 53 between 1970 and 1990, the number of major sending countries went from 29 to 46, and the number of countries qualifying simultaneously as major receivers and major senders from 4 to 15.[67] One manifestation of the growing complexity of international economic migration is the fact that many more women migrate independently of men than in the past, that is, not as dependents. Another is the apparently increasing number of foreigners who are economically active without the requisite authorizations – including those who are smuggled across borders and still others who are trafficked, sometimes under conditions of forced labour.

For all of this, there is still no coherent international regulation of the phenomenon. Governments of immigration countries in particular have continued to struggle to find appropriate responses, and the end of the last century and the beginning of this one have witnessed an upsurge in initiatives on questions of international migration. In 1999, for example, a mandate was created for a Special Rapporteur on the Human Rights of Migrants by the United Nations Commission on Human Rights (resolution 1999/44). In June 2001, Japan sponsored the establishment of an Independent Global Commission on Human Security.[68] And in the same month, the Swiss Federal Department of Justice and Police launched

---

[67] W.R. Böhning and N. Oishi: "Is international economic migration spreading?", in *International Migration Review* (New York, Centre for Migration Studies, 1995), Vol. XXIX, No. 3 (Fall), pp. 794–799. All figures exclude the USSR and Yugoslavia as well as their successor States.

[68] For its 2003 report, see http://www.humansecurity-chs.org/finalreport/English/FinalReport. pdf

the so-called Berne Initiative, which aims at achieving better management of migration at regional and global levels through enhanced interstate coopera-tion.[69] In December 2003, UN Secretary-General Kofi Annan convened a Global Commission on International Migration.[70] Also in December 2003, the General Assembly decided to devote a high-level dialogue to international migration and development during its 61st Session in 2006.[71] The Office was involved in some of these discussions, worked closely with regional partners[72] and, as will be seen, took initiatives of its own.

In 1999, the ILO carried out a General Survey by the Committee of Experts with respect to Conventions Nos. 97 and 143 and their accompanying Recom-mendations. The Experts' report concluded that the Organization's standards, even though they contained a few outdated provisions and had a few gaps, were "still valid today".[73] It saw two options: to retain the existing instruments and to cover gaps through protocols; or to revise them in various ways. Instead, it was decided to hold a broad discussion on the subject of migrant workers generally, and the item was put on the agenda of the 2004 Conference.

Shortly before the general discussion on migration took place, and amidst an upsurge of interest in various parts of the world, another independent body made its voice heard in this field – the World Commission on the Social Dimension of Globalization, which was established by the Organization in 2002. Its report of February 2004 included an examination of questions of international economic migration, and called for the initiation of a

> preparatory process towards a more general institutional framework for the move-ment of people across national borders. This means a transparent and uniform system, based on rules rather than discretion, for those who wish to move across borders. The ultimate objective would be to create a multilateral framework for immigration laws and consular practices, to be negotiated by governments, that

---

[69] See the International Agenda for Migration Management at http://www.bfm.admin.ch

[70] For its 2005 report, see http://www.gcim.org/

[71] For the Secretary-General's input report to the high-level dialogue, see UN: *International migra-tion and development*, Report of the Secretary-General, United Nations, General Assembly, 60th Session, New York, 2006.

[72] ILO: *Towards a fair deal for migrant workers in the global economy*, Report VI, International Labour Conference, 92nd Session, Geneva, p. 105.

[73] ILO: *Migrant workers*, General Survey on the reports on the Migration for Employment Con-vention (Revised) (No. 97), and Recommendation (Revised) (No. 86), 1949, and the Migrant Workers (Supplementary Provisions) Convention (No. 143), and Recommendation (No. 151), 1975, Report III (1B), International Labour Conference, 87th Session, Geneva, 1999, p. 246.

would govern cross-border movements of people. This would be similar to multi-lateral frameworks that already exist, or are currently under discussion, concerning the cross-border movement of goods, services, technology, investment and information.[74]

The report submitted to the 2004 Conference for general discussion [75] referred to the World Commission's views on migration. It mentioned the "need for an international regime based on the rule of law, that establishes common parameters for all, clear accountabilities, and mechanisms for reporting and monitoring";[76] but it was otherwise unspecific. Its most detailed proposals actually related to standard-setting, where questions of the revision of existing instruments or the elaboration of new ones were again raised.[77] At the 2004 Conference, the Employers' group did not want Governments to ratify Conventions Nos. 97 and 143; it did not want the ILO to promote them, let alone revise them or elaborate new standards; and it wanted them replaced by a non-binding multilateral framework which took account of national labour market needs. In the end, the main outcome of the Conference's discussions was a plan of action that included the "development of a non-binding multilateral framework for a rights-based approach to labour migration which takes account of labour market needs, proposing guidelines and principles for policies based on best practices and international standards". A Meeting of Experts was convened in 2005 to flesh out the non-binding principles and guidelines. The Experts drafted an ILO Multilateral Framework on Labour Migration: Non-binding principles and guidelines for a rights-based approach to labour migration; and the Governing Body decided in March 2006 that this "Framework" should be published and disseminated. As of this writing, the proposal has gone no further.

This complex story shows that the ILO has attempted since its beginning to help impose sensible and humane rules for international migration. While the ILO has adopted good – if sometimes over-complicated – standards, the approaches it has supported have come up against the reluctance of governments, of immigration countries in particular, to accept any restrictions on their actions. At crucial moments, the constituents have turned away from the ILO for other initiatives; the creation of the IOM and the UN preoccupation with the issue

---

[74] ILO: *A fair globalization: Creating opportunities for all*, World Commission on the Social Dimension of Globalization, Geneva, 2004, p. 98.

[75] ILO: *Towards a fair deal for migrant workers in the global economy*, op. cit., p. 129.

[76] Ibid., p. 127.

[77] Ibid., p. 96.

are two cases in point. But, in the final analysis, the solutions proposed do not essentially differ from those advocated by the ILO. And there is still no generally-accepted framework at the international level to manage migration for work. This remains one of the major failings of the international system, resulting in a great deal of hardship and exploitation, and urgently needs to be taken more seriously by the world community.

### Indigenous and tribal peoples[78]

All contemporary discussion about the rights of indigenous peoples in international law is based on the ILO's work on this issue. The ILO has adopted the only two international Conventions dealing with indigenous and tribal peoples – in the modern sense of "indigenous", as compared to the pre-Second World War meaning of the term when applied to "native" workers in colonial settings: Convention No. 107 (1957) and Convention No. 169 (1989). These norms reflect two conflicting paradigms in the approach to indigenous policies during the last century: the first is based on the principle of assimilation; while Convention No. 169 presents a human rights-based approach to indigenous policies from the standpoint of multiculturalism.

A concern with the rights of indigenous and tribal peoples by the ILO is far from evident at first glance. As stated by Virginia Leary, "[t]he ILO's adoption of Conventions on indigenous peoples ..., Conventions which are not limited to labour issues, might be interpreted as an anomaly".[79] Nearly all the reservations that have been expressed about the ILO's role in this area – not only by outside observers but at important junctures also by parts of the ILO constituency as well – overlook the fact that many indigenous and tribal peoples are the very model of the informal economy with which the ILO has become concerned in more recent years. These instruments have provided guidance on what needs to be done to allow groups who are either outside or at the margins of national societies and economies to survive when faced with other economic and social models. In addition, both Conventions deal with the fact that when these groups do enter the workforce they are almost always at the bottom of the scale, and uniquely vulnerable to abuses that are tied closely to their social situation and within the

---

[78] This section draws on the writings and experience of the author, as well as on the excellent study by L. Rodríguez-Piñero: *Indigenous peoples, post-colonialism and international law: The ILO regime (1919–1989)* (Oxford, Oxford University Press, 2005). It will be noted that this author and Mr Rodríguez-Piñero differ on important details of motivation for the ILO's involvement, but on none of the facts.

[79] V. Leary: *La utilización del Convenio No. 169 de la OIT para proteger los derechos de los pueblos indígenas* (San José de Costa Rica, Instituto Interamericano de Derechos Humanos, 1999).

ILO's area of responsibility. And these peoples are found in most parts of the world – some 350 million in all.

The ILO's initial concern with indigenous peoples was a manifestation of its work in the pre-Second World War colonial context. Rodríguez-Piñero notes that "the notion of 'native labour' was a translation of the notion of 'trust of civilization' into the ILO's realm of activity, referring widely to the duty of protection over 'indigenous workers' living in a 'lower scale of civilization', both in formerly colonial territories and in post-colonial states".[80] After the Second World War, the international trust doctrine evolved to cover indigenous peoples in independent countries.

Another path into this subject came from the Americas, and corresponds more closely to present-day concerns. The First American Regional Labour Conference, which was part of a wider attempt to shift the focus of the ILO away from Europe and make it more universal, took place in 1936. When the Office asked American States which issues should be prioritized in the region, they pointed to the working and living conditions of "indigenous populations" – which, in their case, did not refer to populations of dependent territories but to the relevant populations of their own countries. For two decades, the "living and working conditions of indigenous populations" was a distinct item on the agenda of the periodic American regional conferences, leading to the first international expert missions and the first reports ever published by an international organization concerning indigenous peoples. This period is marked by the influence of "indigenism", a transnational community linking academics and policy-makers in the search for a "scientific" solution to the so-called "Indian problem". The ILO assumed the main tenets of the movement, including the objective of social and cultural integration, recourse to cultural anthropology and the emphasis on development intervention, and turned them into international law.

Two important developments occurred in the early 1950s. The first was the transition from a regional to an international policy, as reflected in the publication of the 1953 book, *Indigenous peoples*,[81] and the establishment of the short-lived ILO Committee of Experts on Indigenous Labour. The second was the passage from theoretical studies to specific action, with the launching in 1952 of an historic milestone – the Andean Indian Programme (AIP).

The AIP was an ambitious macro-development project, led by the ILO and involving several other parts of the new UN system. It lasted for nearly two decades

---

[80] L. Rodríguez-Piñero, paper submitted to the ILO Century Project Workshop, op. cit.

[81] ILO: *Indigenous peoples: Living and working conditions of aboriginal populations in independent countries* (Geneva, ILO, 1953).

and covered six countries, and its explicit objective was to promote the integration of indigenous populations in the Andean region. Despite the shortcomings of this first generation of international development projects, the AIP had two important effects for the ILO's future work in indigenous issues. It had an undeniable demonstration effect for other states with indigenous and tribal populations, showing the benefits – in terms of "development" – of the ILO's further involvement in these issues. And it consolidated the ILO's leadership role on this issue vis-à-vis other international organizations and agencies, including the UN.

One of the recommendations of the second session of the ILO Committee of Experts on Indigenous Labour in 1954 was the adoption of a "comprehensive recommendation" formulating "general standards of social policy" in relation to indigenous groups. At the peak of the AIP, the Conference adopted the Indigenous and Tribal Populations Convention (No. 107) and its accompanying Recommendation (No. 104) in 1957. These were the first international standards dealing with the rights of indigenous and tribal populations in independent countries, and aimed well beyond the Americas. The rest of the UN system took part in the deliberations, and was to participate in supervision of the Convention, though in fact they never did so. The Convention is conceived as an applied anthropology handbook to lead states' development policies towards indigenous groups. Under the general objective of integration – a notion that incorporated simultaneously notions of development, cultural change and nation-building – the Convention and its accompanying Recommendation contain practical guidance on a wide range of issues, including land reform, education, health, professional training and micro-industry. Some of these subjects go beyond the ILO's usual fields of action. Convention No. 107 was eventually ratified by only 27 countries, 14 of them in Latin America, but also included an interesting selection of other countries, including Bangladesh (on separation from Pakistan), Egypt, India, Iraq, Malawi and Pakistan.

The implementation of Convention No. 107 was not supervised seriously for over a decade. The end of the AIP in 1972 meant, in practice, the end of the Organization's indigenous policy and the dismantling of internal structures that were responsible for the subject, and the 1957 instruments on indigenous and tribal peoples were very close to being consigned to history. In addition, the integrationist focus of Convention No. 107 ran afoul of other developments.

The emergence of the international indigenous movement in the mid-1970s, and the first institutional moves in this realm by the United Nations Centre for Human Rights, suddenly reawakened the ILO's indigenous policy from its state of lethargy. Convention No. 107 was rediscovered as being the only international instrument dealing with indigenous and tribal peoples, and started being targeted by newly established indigenous groups and activists as the embodiment of the assimilation policies they sought to reverse. The Office began to review this Convention, and to take an active part in the emerging discussions at the international level.

Rodríguez-Piñero, who is practically alone in researching this period of the ILO involvement with the subject, has written that the Office was essentially reacting to a perceived threat to its primacy from the sudden interest of the UN in the subject, and that subsequent ILO work was intended to pre-empt UN action on it. The recollection of the author of this chapter (who as a junior official was the only ILO staff member working on the subject from the early 1970s until the mid-1980s) is that the revival of the ILO's interest paralleled that of the UN in reacting to a change in the international climate and to the criticism of Convention No. 107. The Convention was recognized as having the wrong focus, and even as being destructive to the aspirations of the emerging indigenous movement. There was also a concern that the UN's intention to adopt new standards could encounter political obstacles with which the ILO's tripartite processes might be able to deal better – which proved prescient. Francis Blanchard, Director-General throughout this period, had been closely involved with the AIP, and allowed the work to proceed. That being said, inter-organizational rivalry might have played a role.

Reacting to severe criticism from the emerging indigenous movement and from other observers of the integrationist and colonialist orientation of Convention No. 107, as well as to pressure on Director-General Blanchard from Jef Rens, the former ILO Deputy Director-General, who had been responsible for much of the ILO's work on this subject during the 1950s and 1960s, the Office proposed to the Governing Body a Meeting of Experts to consider revising the Convention. This colourful meeting in 1986 was the first exposure of the emerging international indigenous community to the ILO, as the usual tripartite participants were supplemented by indigenous members of trade unions, employers' organizations and government ministries, and by a selection of concerned NGOs. The Meeting of Experts concluded that the Convention should be revised to remove its integrationist tone – although positions differed on how far the revision should go. The Governing Body decided to place the item on the Conference agenda for 1988 and 1989, and, after a decidedly unusual ILO Conference discussion that included delegates on all benches who had never encountered the ILO before, the Indigenous and Tribal Peoples Convention (No. 169) was adopted.

Two points of vocabulary in Convention No. 169 are crucial. With regard to coverage, the ILO position has been to look beyond the notion of "first nations" prevalent in the Americas – and later in the United Nations – and to focus on the social situation of the people concerned, rather than on descent alone. Conventions Nos. 107 and 169 therefore cover indigenous and tribal populations/peoples – or what might be described as tribal populations, whether or not they are indigenous in the anthropological sense of the term. In the rest of the international system, the term "indigenous" is now being used to refer to the same peoples covered by Convention No. 169. However, the rejection by countries such as India – which has some 80 million "tribal" people – of the notion that any population group in the country precedes any other, has allowed a number of countries to claim that standards using the term "indigenous" alone do not apply to them. Politically, its importance is that the UN discussions beginning in the mid-1970s reflected a bottom-up initiative from groups who considered themselves "first nations", with claims built on prior occupancy rather than the ILO's "social policy" focus. For instance, the ILO standards apply to groups such as the "garifuna" in Central America, descendants of escaped slaves who live in a way similar to Amerindians but who clearly are not indigenous.

The second point is the word "peoples" in Convention No. 169 – which replaces "populations" in Convention No. 107. The adoption of this term has marked discussions in international forums since the mid-1980s. It is important in law because both the UN international covenants on human rights provide that "All peoples have the right to self-determination". The use of the term "peoples" therefore carries potentially heavy consequences. The ILO was the first to be able to adopt the term "peoples" – although in so doing Convention No. 169 provided that the use of this term did not determine its meaning in international law.

Convention No. 169 rejected the notion of integration as the basis for national policy, and replaced it with respect, consultation and participation, and recognition of the continued right of these peoples to exist. At the end of 2008, the Convention has been ratified by only 20 countries, but its influence on both national and international policies has far exceeded the expectations that this low number might imply. The development policies adopted by the World Bank, the Asian and American Development Banks, the UNDP and a number of governments, have taken the Convention as the indisputable floor for action. Countries including Denmark, the Netherlands and Spain have ratified it as a guide for their international development policies. It has had a significant effect on the countries that have ratified it, and has provided a model for action in a number of other countries.

Finally, ILO action on fundamental rights at work has also been influenced. It is no coincidence that indigenous and tribal peoples suffer more from workplace abuses than any other identifiable ethnic group. Denmark and, later, the European Union and others have funded an ILO project to promote Convention

No. 169, which has carried out studies and offered practical assistance to communities and to countries.[82] Surveys by the ILO's Special Action Programme on forced labour have identified problems affecting these peoples in particular. And both the Global Reports under the Declaration and the Committee of Experts have frequently remarked on discrimination against them.

The ILO was not acting in a vacuum by the time it began to review Convention No. 107. The UN had completed a study on indigenous peoples in 1981, and in the same year established the Working Group on Indigenous Populations as an organ of the Sub-Commission on Prevention of Discrimination and Protection of Minorities of the Commission on Human Rights. The Working Group's efforts to produce UN standards on indigenous peoples finally yielded the Declaration on the Rights of Indigenous Peoples in 2007 – but it looks unlikely that the United Nations will draft a Convention on the subject. In addition, after proposals agreed upon at the World Conference on Human Rights in 1993, the Permanent Forum on Indigenous Issues was established in 2000 as an organ of ECOSOC, composed jointly of members of indigenous peoples and of governments; while the new Human Rights Council has established a "mechanism" on indigenous rights. The titles of these bodies reflect a continuing lack of comfort with the term "peoples". The ILO and the UN together established in 1989 what evolved into an Inter-Agency Support Group on Indigenous Affairs, a coordinating body at the secretariat level that has exercised a considerable influence on UN-system deliberations.

## Concluding remarks

The ILO's concern with human rights has been wide and varied. Its reluctance to use the "rights" concept in its instruments has gradually changed, and labour is now an increasingly important aspect of international human rights law and action. There has been a gradual acceptance by the international development community, and the ILO itself, that rights and development are inherently interdependent. In spite of this, ILO human rights work remains unknown to many international rights advocates.

This work has not always been fruitful. But if there is one constant in its action in this area, it is that the Organization has defined the terms of discussion

---

[82] http://www.ilo.org/public/english/standards/egalite/itpp/index.htm

of nearly every human rights subject with which it has been concerned. The analytical contribution of the ILO to this discussion may have been its greatest achievement until recent years.

However, the ILO has also demonstrated that continued attention to a situation, based on its supervisory work, can put it in a position to lend practical assistance once the national situation has evolved. The tripartite nature of the ILO has allowed it go where a purely intergovernmental organization often fears to tread. Its concern with freedom of association, apartheid, Myanmar, migrant workers and indigenous and tribal peoples, inter alia, bears witness to this. On the other hand, the ILO's tripartite character can prevent it from going as far as it should, as when male-dominated trade unions contributed to "protective" legislation for women to keep them from competing with men.

Another aspect of the influence of the ILO's fundamental instruments is that they are increasingly being used as a benchmark in bilateral trade agreements, in the "generalized system of preferences" provisions of both the United States and the European Union, and as the basis for conditions for loans and assistance from a wide range of international financial institutions.

Neither the ILO nor any other part of the international system can force countries to change until they are ready – the desire for "teeth" for international organizations is a misleading distraction. But, when countries move to a desire for help based on democratic and human rights principles, it is often the ILO whose persistence has put it in a position where it can step in and provide assistance.

Finally, to respond to the question posed at the beginning of this chapter, the reluctance of states to approve the Declaration on Fundamental Principles and Rights at Work in 1998 was not a reluctance to proclaim human rights. Instead, it was a reflection of the fear that increased respect for human rights would slow down economic development, by making production more expensive and by imposing restrictions on national freedom of action (see the discussion of the "social clause" in Chapter 6). This has been a constant struggle in the ILO since its very origins. It has affected the denial of real regulatory power to international organizations, in particular the ILO, to manage migration for work. It has been the main reason for the long failure to take effective action against child labour and to continue to impose restrictions on the rights to organize and bargain collectively. But the failure to block the adoption of the Declaration was another step in the long struggle of the ILO to prove that there is no contradiction between workers' rights and economic progress, and that social and economic progress are interdependent.

# The quality of work[1]

# 3

There are able-bodied men here who work from early morning until late at night, in ice-cold cellars with a quarter of an inch of water on the floor – men who for six or seven months in the year never see the sunlight from Sunday afternoon till the next Sunday morning – and who cannot earn three hundred dollars in a year. There are little children here, scarce in their teens, who can hardly see the top of the work benches – whose parents have lied to get them their places ....[2]

## Improving working lives

The drive to create the ILO came in large part from the urgent need to improve the appalling working conditions faced by many workers in the early decades of the Industrial Revolution. Long working hours in unhealthy environments, the unchecked use of dangerous materials and equipment, the widespread employment of children and wages which obliged workers and their families to live in the most squalid conditions, shocked progressive thinkers and mobilized political action throughout the nineteenth century.

The Preamble of the ILO's Constitution made a powerful call for improvement in the conditions of labour:

as, for example, by the regulation of the hours of work, including the establishment of a maximum working day and week, the regulation of the labour supply, the prevention of unemployment, the provision of an adequate living wage, the protection

---

[1] The principal author of this chapter is Gerry Rodgers. Jaci Eisenberg provided research assistance.
[2] From *The Jungle* by Upton Sinclair, 1906. This novel about the United States meat processing industry at the turn of the twentieth century was one of many writings which had an important impact on public opinion.

of the worker against sickness, disease and injury arising out of his employment, the protection of children, young persons and women ....[3]

And the Preamble provided two political arguments as to why action was needed: the first was that if conditions did not improve, there was a risk of "unrest so great that the peace and harmony of the world are imperilled"; and, second, that "the failure of any nation to adopt humane conditions of labour is an obstacle in the way of other nations which desire to improve the conditions in their own countries".

From the start, then, the ILO aimed to improve peoples' working lives. That included making work itself more desirable – in terms of the working environment and the organization of work, protection from disease or injury, and the content and dignity of work itself. A second aspect concerned the balance between work and other aspects of life, and in particular participation in work, and the length and organization of working time. A third referred to the productivity and remuneration of work. And a fourth concerned security of work, especially vulnerability to unemployment and loss of income.

Taken together, these aspects make up what we call "the quality of work" – the subject of this chapter (income security will be dealt with in Chapter 4). They are major issues in all societies. They determine the distribution of time and effort between work, family and other pursuits, and the resources which individuals and families can use for other ends. And beyond these utilitarian notions, the quality of work is also about the value of work in its own right – how far people can realize personal goals in their work, apply and develop their skills, claim a social identity, or, on the contrary, are subject to compulsion and deprivation, to risk, stress or drudgery.

At the same time, these issues are among the most complex in the world of work. They concern both the organization of production and fundamental concerns about the purposes that production serves. They take different forms at high- and low-income levels, in agriculture or in industry, in wage employment or self-employment, for different groups in the population. Safety at work is often a highly technical question concerned with acceptable exposure to chemicals or radiation; but it is also a matter of work culture and habits. The organization of working time may be about protection from exploitation, or about balancing production with consumption. Creativity and fulfilment are understood differently in different societies.

Above all, improving the quality of work runs up against economic considerations. "Remuneration and conditions of work must, of course, improve," commented a 1972 ILO report on the Conditions of Work Programme, "But it must be

---

[3] In full in Appendix II.

noted that increases in remuneration and improvements in conditions of work are not costless in terms of potential growth of output ... or employment".[4] In the dominant economic model of growth and development, rising wages are the result of rising production and productivity, and by extension the same argument applies to all workplace standards, whether of working time, of safety, of security, or of other conditions of work. Social policy therefore cannot get too far ahead of the economic fundamentals. And one enterprise, or one country, it is held, could not apply higher standards of working conditions or wages in a competitive market economy.

But there are a number of counter arguments. First, as David Morse put it, "social progress and the rising levels of employment on which it depends do not automatically emerge from economic progress".[5] In other words, improvements in output and productivity do not necessarily lead to improvements in the quantity and quality of work, so that these goals must be actively promoted in their own right. Second, the social goal is as valid as the economic one, and cannot be subordinated to it. Third, while accepting that economic progress is necessary for at least some aspects of social progress, it is an article of faith in the ILO that "humane conditions of labour" are both possible and desirable in all economic and social environments. There are many possible ways by which this can and has been achieved: by regulating and legislating to ensure that minimum standards are followed by all; making better work more productive, and so eliminating the trade-off, if there is one, between conditions of work and competitiveness; promoting forms of production and management in which better conditions of work are an explicit goal; appealing to social solidarity and ethical principles. Ways to achieve the goal may vary across situations and countries, but the goal of better quality work is common. This is a fundamental "ILO idea".

That is not to say that the idea originated in the ILO. As we saw in Chapter 1, the ILO was born out of ideas on how to achieve social progress that had been circulating for some time. But, in 1919, the ILO was a vastly more powerful instrument than those existing hitherto for pursuing and promoting these ideas. The goal of improved quality of work was a high priority for the young organization. Of the nine principles specified in its original Constitution, which were to guide its work (listed in Appendix II), two were directly concerned with working time, one with wages, one with child labour, while a fifth concerned the enforcement of policies in these areas.

---

[4] ILO: *In-depth review of the general conditions of work programme*, Governing Body, 188th Session, Geneva, Nov. 1972, GB.188/FA/8/9.

[5] D. Morse: "Unemployment in developing countries", in *Political Science Quarterly*, Vol. 85, No. 1 (Mar., 1970), p. 1.

## A changing policy environment

Over the last century there have been important changes in attitudes to and policies aimed at the quality of work, which have conditioned the ILO's work and its impact.

### Between the wars

As we saw in Chapter 1, the period immediately following the First World War was a favourable environment for advance on international social and labour policy. There were two main directions of thinking on the quality of work. The first was to find ways to improve work itself – notably, in the early days of the ILO, by eliminating risks and hazards, and extending various protections. The second was to improve the balance between work and other social goals, by putting limits on working time and setting rules to protect particular groups from the obligation to undertake work of some or all types. ILO research addressed these issues in the 1920s, and a series of Conventions and Recommendations was developed. Much of this agenda reflected the demands of workers, and the willingness of governments to respond to those demands. Despite their many reservations and an insistence that the ILO be "modest, methodical and circumspect",[6] employers also participated constructively in the ILO's work. Mr Olivetti, Italian Employer delegate and Employer Vice-Chairman of the Governing Body, wrote that it was

> certain that the decisions of the Conference, the studies and researches of the Office, and the calm discussions of the Governing Body have served to throw fresh light on social questions, to point the way for the solution of unsolved problems, and to give prominence to new methods and new ideas.[7]

Up to the onset of the Great Depression, the main concern was to promote growth in productivity and improved conditions of work simultaneously. It was

---

[6] In the words of Robert Pinot, a leading figure among employers at the ILO in the early years, cited in J.J. Oechslin: *The International Organisation of Employers: Three-quarters of a century in the service of the enterprise (1920–1998)* (Geneva, IOE, 2001), p. 35.

[7] In ILO: *The International Labour Organisation, 1919–1929* (Geneva, 1930), p. 21. Pierre Waline, another prominent employer for over half a century in the ILO, endorses this same quotation in his book: *Un patron au Bureau International du Travail* (Paris, Editions France-Empire, 1976). Olivetti was close to the fascist regime at the time, but later broke with Mussolini and died in exile (Oechslin, op. cit., p. 45).

the era of Taylorist management methods[8] and the growth of mass production, which continued the process of narrowing of jobs, through the division of labour, and their intensification, which had been underway throughout the Industrial Revolution. But at the same time there was widespread support for an emerging framework of regulation and improved conditions of work. In the 1920s, after the recession of 1919–21, this was combined with recovery in real wages in many industrialized countries,[9] and significant support for a high wage policy, notably in the United States. Industrialists such as Henry Ford believed that high wages were good for business.[10]

The impact of the ILO's work in this period is not easy to measure objectively. Ratification of the early standards, a majority of which concerned some aspect of the quality of work, was distinctly slower than had initially been hoped, as governments were cautious about locking themselves into international obligations, or faced national resistance. The objections by the French Government to the ILO's work extending to conditions of work in agriculture,[11] for example, and the reticence of the British Government to ratify the Convention concerning white lead in paint (see below), or the Hours of Work (Industry) Convention, 1919 (No. 1), reflected this political reaction. Albert Thomas was disappointed that ratification of Convention No. 1 was so slow.[12] Nevertheless, the ILO was clearly a leading actor in efforts to embed social policy objectives in the economic system, at least in Europe. In 1929, over 70 per cent of European countries had ratified 11 or more of the 28 Conventions adopted by then. However, this was true of only two (Cuba and India) of the 16 non-European countries among the original membership of the ILO.

---

[8] Frederick Taylor's "principles of scientific management", published in their fullest form in 1911, were influential in legitimizing an extreme division of labour in the pursuit of higher productivity.

[9] According to Broadberry and Ritschl, in both Germany and Great Britain the rise in real wages outstripped the growth of labour productivity. S.N. Broadberry and A. Ritschl: "Real wages, productivity, and unemployment in Britain and Germany during the 1920s," in S. Eddie and J. Komlos (eds): *Selected cliometric studies on German economic history* (Steiner, 1997), pp. 196–217. Country studies in P. Scholliers and V. Zamagni (eds): *Labour's reward: Real wages and economic change in 19th- and 20th-century Europe* (Aldershot, Edward Elgar, 1995), show an uneven pattern over time and across countries, but the predominant trend was upward.

[10] Henry Ford laid out his philosophy in his 1922 book: *My life and work* (New York, Garden City Publishing Company).

[11] A. Alcock: *History of the International Labour Organisation* (London and Basingstoke, Macmillan, 1971), pp. 53–56.

[12] In his Preface to *The International Labour Organisation: The first decade* (Geneva, ILO, 1931), Albert Thomas complains of the complications and obstacles to ratification, while still claiming considerable progress.

An anecdote which illustrates both the difficulty of publicizing the ILO's work and the imagination of the Office staff in promoting it is told by Edward Phelan – later Director-General of the ILO – in his memoirs. A session of the International Labour Conference was discussing anthrax and lead poisoning, serious concerns for particular groups of workers, but the international press was taking no interest in the ILO's work. Phelan then visited a number of restaurants and bars in Geneva and persuaded them to put up notices advertising "Anthrax and lead cocktails". Journalists were soon sending off reports about these new cocktails on sale in Geneva, followed up, of course, with reports of what was happening at the Conference.[13]

In the 1930s, mass unemployment modified the picture. As Auer has pointed out,[14] policy interest in the quality of work drops off rapidly when unemployment rises, as it did in the early 1930s. The pace of ratifications of ILO standards, which had increased in the latter part of the 1920s (in part as a result of considerable pressure from the Office), dropped in the first half of the 1930s,[15] and while some further labour standards on the protection of workers were adopted, the main focus of attention was elsewhere. Working time, which we consider in more detail below, remained on the agenda – indeed it received more attention than ever, since it was discussed at every International Labour Conference in the 1930s.[16] But the issue was now work sharing, that is, reductions in working time in order to preserve jobs, rather than improved conditions of work. In general, the pressure on working conditions during this period was downwards. Albert Thomas acknowledged this in 1932:

> the atmosphere to which the depression gives rise, the thought that now it might be necessary to restrict social reform and to keep protective legislation down to the limits set by economic possibilities – a suggestion which some of the employers representatives have made to us – all of these I am fully aware ....[17]

---

[13] E. Phelan: "The birth of the ILO: The personal memories of Edward Phelan", in *Edward Phelan and the ILO: The life and views of an international social actor*, ILO Century Project, forthcoming. Phelan does not say which year it was, but it was probably 1925, when a Convention on compensation for occupational diseases, including anthrax and lead poisoning, was adopted.

[14] P. Auer: "Travail et emploi: Un plaidoyer pour l'interdisciplinarité", in *L'Emploi: Dissonances et défis* (Paris, L'Harmattan, 1994). Auer was comparing the 1980s with the 1970s.

[15] Most European countries saw a sharp decline in ratifications in the period 1930 to 1934, picking up again slowly after 1935. New ratifications dropped from 299 in 1919–29 to 107 in 1930–34. These numbers cannot be directly compared, however, because on the one hand the latter period is shorter, whereas on the other there were more Conventions available for ratification.

[16] G.A. Johnston: *The International Labour Organisation* (London, Europa, 1970), p. 165.

[17] Albert Thomas at the 16th Session of the International Labour Conference (Geneva, 1932), excerpted in A. Thomas: *International Social Policy* (Geneva, ILO, 1948), p. 95.

## *The decades after the Second World War*

Reconstruction was the initial priority of governments after the Second World War, along with the establishment of a series of basic human rights and social institutions. Conditions of work improved in parallel with progress towards full employment in industrialized market economies, and were an integral part of the social and political framework in the socialist countries of Central and Eastern Europe. The ILO, taken up with the promotion of rights at work, the development of technical cooperation and the difficulties of dealing with the Cold War, contributed to this process through its research and standard-setting on wages and occupational safety and health but was not a major actor. The main concern of the ILO was the impact on conditions of work of issues such as technological change, raised in the Reports of the Director-General to the Conference in 1957 and again in 1972. There were, however, some significant initiatives during this period. For instance, in 1955 a group of experts led by the well-known Swedish economist Bertil Ohlin prepared a report on the compatibility between labour conditions and expanding trade in the context of European integration.[18] The report argued that, while there was no particular need to harmonize social policies or social conditions among European countries, it was important to deal with abnormally poor conditions (of wages, hours of work and other aspects of working conditions) in the process of integration. But the Ohlin report appears to have had little impact on the design of the Treaty of Rome, the founding document of the European Economic Community,[19] and the European Social Charter only emerged much later.

In the early 1970s, an in-depth review was undertaken by the ILO Governing Body of the Organization's activities relating to conditions of work. It found that:

> activities concerning the industrialised countries have suffered from a failure to appreciate the significance of emerging trends, to see particular issues in their wider context and to respond quickly to the most urgent needs .... New trends in systems of remuneration and other conditions of work have received only cursory attention, and the larger problem of the humanisation of work virtually none.

---

[18] ILO: *Social aspects of European economic co-operation: Report by a group of experts* (Geneva, 1956). Ohlin, in addition to being co-author of the influential Heckscher–Ohlin theorem of comparative advantage in international trade, was a Swedish Government delegate to the ILO.

[19] J. Murray: *Transnational labour regulation: The ILO and EC compared* (The Hague, Kluwer Law International, 2001), pp. 77–82.

In developing countries, the situation was even worse:

> Standards on hours of work, holidays, welfare and minimum wages have little meaning.[20]

The report concluded that ILO work was fragmented, uncoordinated, and only reached a fraction of the working population.

This and subsequent reviews led up to the Director-General's Report to the 1975 International Labour Conference, entitled "Making work more human", which called for work which respected the worker's life and health; left him free time for rest and leisure; and enabled him to serve society and achieve self fulfilment (the original text uses the masculine pronoun). In the wake of this Conference, and encouraged by Scandinavian interest and support, a new programme was launched to address the problems of the working environment – PIACT, the French acronym for the International Programme for the Improvement of Working Conditions and Environment.[21] PIACT was the brainchild of Jean de Givry, a long-serving French official, who had been responsible for ILO work on labour relations and social institutions since the 1950s. It brought together work on working conditions and occupational safety and health (OSH) – but not wages, which were hived off to another department. PIACT stimulated new research and technical cooperation in these fields, raised the profile of the issues involved and helped to build up institutions to deal with them in a number of countries.

But, like the World Employment Programme, discussed in Chapter 5, this embryonic programme faced an unpromising international environment. The oil shocks and their aftermath, and rising unemployment, implied that, just as in the 1930s, the quality of work slid down the priority agenda almost as soon as the programme had been launched. With the shift of economic model in the 1980s, labour market regulation which set high standards for employment security, conditions of work or wages came under attack, especially in the Anglo-Saxon world. An internal evaluation of the programme in 1984[22] reiterated the importance of the issues, but found that the impact of PIACT had been fairly limited. Lack of resources for technical cooperation was an important factor, and although many specific contributions could be identified – creating national institutes, strengthening

---

[20] ILO: Governing Body, 1972, op. cit., paras 109–112.

[21] J. de Givry: "The ILO and the quality of working life. A new international programme: PIACT", in *International Labour Review* (Geneva, ILO, 1978), Vol. 117, No. 3, May–June.

[22] ILO: *Evaluation of the International Programme for the Improvement of Working Conditions and Environment (PIACT)*, Report VII, International Labour Conference, 70th Session, Geneva, 1984.

factory inspectorates, training of managers and policy-makers, dissemination of information – it was not clear that these had made a qualitative difference. A subsequent programme of Work Improvement in Small Enterprises within PIACT tried to overcome the trade-off between conditions of work and employment by treating work improvement as a productive factor. An innovative programme which included a number of successful local projects, it was nevertheless relatively poorly funded and dependent on the energy of a small number of staff members.

## The quality of work and development

PIACT represented a significant shift towards developing countries in the ILO's efforts to improve the quality of work. In the early years of the ILO, the extent to which the Conventions and Recommendations governing conditions of work could be applied to countries such as China, India or Japan was a subject of some controversy, it being generally assumed that such goals were out of reach.[23] The early Conventions had included clauses which defined lower standards for some countries; Convention No. 1 on hours of work, which specified a general limit of 48 hours, offered a standard of 57 hours for Japan, 60 for India and left the situations of China, Persia and Siam for later consideration. Nevertheless, according to Georges Barnes, one of the principal drafters of the ILO's Constitution in the Labour Commission of the Peace Conference, there was progress in the early years of the ILO, at least in terms of national legislation to provide some protection, in China, India, Japan and even Persia, and evidence of government intervention to prevent abuse.[24]

The argument that labour standards were needed to prevent unfair competition was of course valid for these non-metropolitan territories too, but in the early years of the ILO these economies did not present much of a threat to industry in the metropolitan countries, while poor labour conditions helped to keep down commodity prices. Concerns were nevertheless expressed that the expanding production capacity of low-income countries might have adverse effects on industrialized countries, but an ILO-commissioned study on economic development in 1945 provided many arguments as to why such fears were unfounded.[25] External pressure to raise labour standards in low-income countries was thus weak.

---

[23] This issue is discussed further in Chapter 2, in the context of colonial policy.

[24] G. Barnes: *History of the International Labour Office* (London, Williams and Norgate, 1926), pp. 63–70.

[25] E. Staley: *World economic development: Effects on advanced industrial countries* (Montreal, ILO, 1944).

In the early phases of decolonization and development planning after the war, the issue of quality of work took another form. A dualistic model of economic development emerged, built around a process of transfer of labour from a traditional to a modern sector. The notion of the modern sector broadly reflected the predominant production model in industrialized countries at the time – regular wage employment with decent conditions of work, subject to a framework of regulation and organization. Development was thus seen as a process of labour transfer from poor to good quality employment, and at the same time from low productivity to high.

The contribution of the ILO to this process lay partly in the legislative framework for modern employment.[26] Labour codes built up from the corpus of international labour standards proliferated in newly independent countries, and the ILO had a large hand in their drafting. But the growth of good quality employment in the modern sector was dependent on the rate and structure of overall economic growth, which in turn was conditioned by the growth of capital stock and the availability of the skills needed for advanced industrial production, rather than on specific interventions to improve employment quality.

In the early 1970s, this model was modified by the emergence and widespread adoption of the concept of the "informal sector", in part due to its effective use in the 1972 report of the ILO Employment Strategy Mission to Kenya. As is discussed further in Chapter 5, it had become clear that for most developing countries modern sector growth could not solve employment problems in a reasonable time horizon. Outside the modern sector, a heterogeneous informal sector provided income-earning opportunities to much of the labour force. But informal sector jobs were generally of poor quality, often involving long hours of work at low productivity and low incomes, with scant regard for safety and social protection. The traditional labour policies of regulation and inspection were – and remain – ineffective by virtue of this sector's unorganized nature. Moreover, much of the informal sector consisted of self-employment. At the same time, dualism persisted because relatively protected, higher-quality jobs dominated in parts of the economy, especially in the public sector and in larger, more technologically advanced firms, where efficient operation required a secure and skilled workforce with decent working conditions. The problem for the ILO was that it was identified with the formal sector. Its worker and employer constituents represented interests in this sector, and demanded a programme which responded to

---

[26] D. Maul: *Menschenrechte, Sozialpolitik und Dekolonisation: Die Internationale Arbeitsorganisation (IAO), 1940–1970* (Essen, Klartext, 2007). Forthcoming in English under the ILO Century Project as *Human rights, social policy and decolonization: The International Labour Organization (ILO) 1940–1970.*

the interests of their members. The lack of representation of the informal sector among the ILO's constituents therefore made it hard to develop an effective policy response. Yet the problem of informality was in large degree a problem of the quality of work. Indeed, it was in informal employment that the greatest problems of employment quality were to be found.

Of course, the pattern varied in different parts of the world. In much of South Asia and sub-Saharan Africa the modern sector was small, and remains so to this day. A literature developed on the "labour aristocracy" – that is, those with good working conditions and decent wages were seen as a privileged elite and an obstacle to egalitarian development. The ILO's action, it was argued by writers such as Robert Cox and Jeffrey Harrod, merely bolstered the capacity of this elite to defend their vested interests.[27] The labour aristocracy model was less widely accepted in Latin America, where many countries had a relatively large modern industrial sector and extensive social legislation. Moreover, the successful phase of import-substitution-led growth in that region between 1950 and 1980 produced a significant growth in protected urban wage employment, thereby increasing the proportion of good quality jobs.[28] It was the recession in the 1980s, "the lost decade", which brought this model to an end, in ways that paralleled developments in Western Europe, leading to a widespread deterioration in labour market outcomes.

At the same time, however, in East Asia a small number of countries were successfully pursing an export-led growth model, which both created jobs and raised their quality. In the Republic of Korea, for instance, between 1965 and 1991 real wages rose between 5 and 11 per cent annually, weekly hours of work fell from 51.6 (1970) to 48.2, and industrial accidents declined by more than half.[29]

This said, the quality of employment has had far less priority in development policy than its quantity, and the ILO did not succeed in changing that priority. That remains true today. The failure of even rapid development to create enough jobs to absorb a growing labour force and meet increasing expectations remains one of the principal unsolved development problems, and a political priority everywhere. "First let us have jobs, and we can worry about their quality later," is a common refrain in developing countries, and this has weakened efforts

---

[27] This argument was developed by Jeffrey Harrod in: *Power, production and the unprotected worker* (New York, Columbia University Press, 1987).

[28] Discussed further in R. Jolly et al.: *UN contributions to development thinking and practice* (Bloomington, Indiana University Press, 2004).

[29] Y.B. Park: "State regulation, the labour market and economic development: The Republic of Korea", in G. Rodgers (ed.): *Workers, institutions and economic growth in Asia* (Geneva, International Institute for Labour Studies, 1994).

to promote better quality employment. For instance, a recent major effort by a National Commission in India to identify policies which could improve the quality of work in the unorganized sector, including a widened framework of regulation, and an active promotional policy covering wages, hours of work, safety and other matters, has been received poorly at the political level, in contrast to an employment guarantee scheme which has had widespread political support.[30]

### Labour market regulation

In the 1980s and early 1990s, policies to improve the quality of work faced increasing pressures for labour market deregulation, both within countries and at the international level. The World Bank's view was expressed clearly in its 1990 *World Development Report*: "Labour market policies – minimum wages, job security regulations, and social security – are usually intended to raise welfare or reduce exploitation. But they actually work to raise the cost of labour in the formal sector and reduce labour demand ... increase the supply of labour to the rural and urban informal sectors, and thus depress labour incomes where most of the poor are found."[31] The Organisation for Economic Co-operation and Development (OECD) took a similar line in its 1994 *Jobs Study*.[32]

By the end of the 1980s, in industrialized and developing countries alike, a process of flexibilization of labour markets could be observed, with increases in the share of precarious jobs in countries where previous regulation had been relaxed, such as Spain,[33] and a trend towards informalization of formerly regulated labour markets in many parts of the world – particularly well documented in Latin America.[34] Women tended to be overrepresented in part-time, temporary and informal work, and so were disproportionately affected. The collapse of the

---

[30] Government of India, National Commission for Enterprises in the Unorganised Sector (NCEUS): *Report on conditions of work and promotion of livelihoods in the unorganised sector* (New Delhi, 2007). The Government has been unwilling to bring in legislation to implement this aspect of the Commission's proposals, unlike social security measures, where some progress has been made.

[31] World Bank: *World Development Report, 1990* (Washington, DC, 1990), p. 63.

[32] OECD: *The OECD Jobs Study: Facts, analysis, strategies* (Paris, 1994).

[33] On the process in general, see G. Rodgers and J. Rodgers (eds): *Precarious jobs in labour market regulation: The growth of atypical employment in Western Europe* (Geneva, International Institute for Labour Studies, 1989); on the Spanish case in particular, see J. Banyuls et al.: "The transformation of the employment system in Spain: Towards a Mediterranean neoliberalism?", in G. Bosch et al. (eds): *European employment models in flux: A comparison of institutional change in nine European countries* (New York and Basingstoke, Palgrave, 2009).

[34] For Latin America, see V. Tokman: *Una voz en el camino: Empleo y equidad en América Latina: 40 años de búsqueda* (Mexico, Fondo de Cultura Económica, 2004), Chapter IV.

Central and Eastern European socialist regimes at the end of the 1980s and in the early 1990s left many workers vulnerable to a rapid loss of employment security, declining wages and deteriorating conditions of work, from which recovery took many years, especially in the case of countries which had not yet been admitted to the European Union. Again, it was women who bore the brunt, since they had previously been incorporated into the workforce on a large scale, and were vulnerable to the dismantling of systems of recognition and social protection which had supported this process.

The ILO's constituents did not have a unified position on these developments. The position of most employers and some governments was – and still is – that regulation of working conditions is liable to have adverse effects on economic efficiency, growth and employment creation. Workers and most governments, on the other hand, resisted deregulation. They were broadly supported by the Office, which published critiques of labour market flexibility and fragmentation, and undertook research that attempted to highlight the economic benefits of a variety of protective labour institutions.[35] But the diverging views clearly affected the Organization's response, and the Office's research had little impact in the face of strong economic forces. Standard-setting to deal with the diverse labour statuses that were emerging took time to develop. Conventions were adopted on part-time work in 1994 (No. 175), on home work in 1996 (No. 177) and on private employment agencies in 1997 (No. 181), but these have been poorly ratified, especially the first two which had only 11 and 5 ratifications respectively, as of 2008. Attempts to establish a Convention on contract labour were also unsuccessful – though they did ultimately give rise to a Recommendation, that is, a weaker instrument, on the employment relationship in 2006. The situation of domestic workers is now on the International Labour Conference agenda for 2010 and 2011, so progress continues, but it is slow.

Finally, in the past decade, as unemployment again declined in industrialized countries, at least until 2007, there have been signs of a resurgence of concern about conditions of work – for instance an increasing resistance by workers to the intensification of work,[36] a reversal of earlier attempts to reduce employment

---

[35] See, for instance, G. Standing: *Unemployment and labour market flexibility: The United Kingdom* (Geneva, ILO, 1986); W. Sengenberger and D. Campbell (eds): *Creating economic opportunities: The role of labour standards in industrial restructuring* (Geneva, International Institute for Labour Studies, 1994); P. Auer (ed.): *Changing labour markets in Europe: The role of institutions and policies* (Geneva, ILO, 2001); and more recently, D. Kucera and J. Berg (eds): *In defence of labour institutions: Cultivating justice in the developing world* (Basingstoke, Palgrave Macmillan and Geneva, ILO, 2008).

[36] F. Green: *Demanding work: The paradox of job quality in the affluent economy* (Princeton, NJ, Princeton University Press, 2005).

security, a revival of interest in minimum wage legislation and renewed efforts to extend various protections to part-time and other "atypical" workers. The European Commission has been an important actor in this process, publishing a series of communications and policy proposals on ways to respond to the growth of labour market fragmentation, and adopting Directives on part-time, fixed-term and now (probably) temporary agency work.[37]

In the ILO's work, the main thrust since 1999 has been to treat policies to improve the quality of work within the broader Decent Work Agenda (which we shall discuss further in Chapter 6), involving an integrated approach to rights at work, employment promotion and social dialogue, as well as the different aspects of social protection considered here. For instance, attempts have been made to include some aspects of conditions of work within integrated approaches to poverty reduction and development at the national level, as part of the ILO's contribution to the "PRSP process" – a World Bank-driven programme linking national poverty reduction strategies to debt reduction. This contribution included treatment of wage issues in Indonesia, Liberia, Pakistan and Peru, OSH issues in Ghana, Liberia and Mali, and better designed labour legislation in Tanzania and elsewhere.[38]

Another recent development within this framework is a new perspective on the informal economy, a concept which extends the idea of the informal sector to embrace ill-regulated and precarious wage work in or for formal enterprises. There is a certain convergence among ILO constituents on informal economy issues, but for different reasons. Workers' representatives broadly consider that the informal economy undermines efforts to raise standards, and should be formalized. Employers depict it as unfair competition for enterprises that respect labour regulation and tax codes, and reach the same conclusion as workers. Of course, neither fully represents the views of their constituencies, since many formal enterprises take advantage of lower production costs in the informal economy – while in many countries it offers the only realistic source of employment; but informal economy workers are poorly represented in trade union structures.

Nevertheless, this official convergence of views allowed the Office to present a strategy paper on decent work in the informal economy to the 2002 International Labour Conference, which included a variety of suggested means to

---

[37] One example among many is the EU's Green Paper on Labour Law: *Modernising labour law to meet the challenges of the 21st century* (COM/2007/0627), 24 Oct. 2007. See also the European Commission's Communication: *Towards common principles of flexicurity: More and better jobs through flexibility and security*, which was adopted on 27 June 2007.

[38] See D. Ghai: *ILO participation in PRSPs: An independent evaluation* (Geneva, ILO, 2005).

improve the quality of work in the informal economy, through schemes for realizing rights and extending social security (see Chapters 2 and 4 of this book), and local low-cost methods to improve safety and health (but not other conditions of work). The strategy can be summed up by the statement that "owners of micro- and small enterprises need to be convinced that job quality is good for business".[39] It was stressed that improving skills and establishing the appropriate environment for enterprise development would also enhance job quality. Employers argued for a light framework of regulation which would give enterprises as much freedom as possible, while workers continued to argue for progress towards the universal application of agreed labour standards. The Conference discussions broadly concluded that there was a need to "mainstream" (formalize) the informal economy, and to reinforce representation, implicitly within the existing tripartite framework.

The persistence and growth of the informal economy as a low-cost, ill-regulated environment with poor quality jobs suggests that there are powerful economic reasons for its existence. A positive relationship between job quality and productivity cannot therefore be taken for granted. Recent thinking has focused on the need for a step-by-step approach, establishing a basic floor and a modest framework of regulation.[40] But without adequate representation for the actors concerned – which so far has been beyond the capacities of the existing tripartite structure – and large-scale investment in raising economic capabilities, the informal economy seems likely to remain a large reservoir of poor quality jobs.

## The impact of the ILO's work – Some illustrations

Rather than attempt to cover all aspects of the quality of work, the remainder of this chapter examines three central aspects in more detail: hours of work; OSH; and minimum wages. Working time is where the ILO started, with Convention No. 1, and it has always been a core concern for both workers and employers, as well as often being a source of considerable conflict. Occupational safety and health is a highly technical subject, but it is an area of great importance for the quality of work. And minimum wages are a key link between the ILO's standards on the one hand, and living standards and poverty reduction on the other.

---

[39] ILO: *Decent work and the informal economy*, Report VI, International Labour Conference, 90th Session, Geneva, 2002, p. 68.

[40] For a statement of the approach, see V. Tokman (ed.): *De la informalidad a la modernidad* (Santiago de Chile, ILO, 2001).

As we shall see, these three topics illustrate different types of ILO work and influence. On hours of work, the ILO has contributed substantially to policy debates at different times, and the world has moved towards the 40-hour week first advocated by the ILO in the 1930s. But in recent decades, global frameworks appear to have lost influence on working-time policies in the face of widely varying national perspectives. Occupational safety and health, by contrast, is an area in which the Office has played a low profile but consistently valuable technical role, offering policy frameworks and information systems which have been widely used by specialists. And, on wages, the ILO was an important actor for many years, but its effort fell away sharply after the 1970s and as a result its presence in policy debates is now weak; an effort to remedy this situation has started recently.

ILO efforts to improve the quality of work can be broadly divided into four categories. First, there is the standard-setting process. Some 31 out of 76 "up-to-date" Conventions concern some aspect of the quality of work, in the sense we are using it in this chapter. While there are more international labour standards on the quality of work than in any other domain, the ratification record is uneven. Only three of the 25 Conventions adopted since 1965 in this field (excluding maritime Conventions) have been ratified by over 40 countries (the earlier Conventions have a better record). But, although the ratification record might be mixed, this amounts to a considerable attempt to establish an international framework for regulation. The influence on national legislative frameworks comes not only through ratification, but also because participants in Conference discussions are frequently involved directly in the design of national legislation, often with technical assistance by the Office.

Second, the Office has undertaken research into different aspects of wages and working conditions, and developed information systems, such as the *Encyclopaedia of Occupational Health and Safety*, discussed below. The intensity of these efforts, and the publications to which they have given rise, have varied over time. One interesting indicator of the ILO's attempt to analyse these three issues related to the quality of work can be found in the frequency of articles in the ILO's regular journal, the *International Labour Review*. This is by no means a perfect indicator because the journal itself has evolved over time and publication depends on editorial policy; what is more, not all issues make suitable subjects for articles in the *International Labour Review*. But it does offer a long time-series with a degree of continuity, covering all fields of ILO work, and so provides an indication of trends in interest and research efforts which are not readily available elsewhere.

Figure 1 shows the percentage of all published *International Labour Review* articles that have examined the three aspects of quality of work explored here. And it can be seen that they accounted for a substantial percentage of all articles

Figure 1 *International Labour Review* articles on aspects of the quality of work, 1919–2008 (percentage)

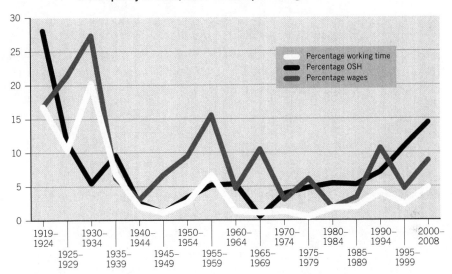

Note: Figure for OSH in 1919–24 was 46 per cent (reduced in the graph for scaling reasons).

until the mid-1930s. After this initial burst, the number of articles on working time declined and has not recovered; work on OSH also started high, declined to a fairly low level in the decades after the war, but picked up and maintained a fairly steady level from 1970 to 1990, increasing thereafter; work on wages has shown a very erratic trend, with notably little work published in the 1970s and 1980s. A recent recovery in the numbers of articles published on wages (and indeed also on hours of work and OSH) appears to reflect new priorities under the Decent Work Agenda.

Third, a substantial effort has been put into spreading the ILO's ideas on quality of work, through advocacy and awareness-building, working with networks of specialists, and a variety of technical cooperation projects and missions, notably under the PIACT. Much of this has involved creating capacity to develop and implement policy at the national level, in the shape of specialized institutions and labour administration systems, and the building up of labour inspection systems. Networks have been particularly important in the area of OSH.

Fourth, there has been a history of development of codes of conduct, such as safety codes, and their promotion by enterprises. This has included not only support to national policy development, but also increased attention to voluntary action such as corporate social responsibility. For instance, the ILO's Tripartite Declaration of Principles concerning Multinational Enterprises and Social Policy (MNE Declaration) (1977, revised 2000 and 2006) has a substantial section which declares that multinational enterprises should, inter alia, provide the best possible wages, conditions of work, and health and safety standards, within the framework of government policies. The ILO's employer constituents consider this declaration to be an important instrument to guide enterprise policies.

## Hours of work[41]

### Long-term trends

In Keynes's famous 1930 article on the economic possibilities for our grand-children,[42] he imagined the economic problem solved in 2030 by a century of economic growth, and work to a large extent replaced by leisure.

> Thus for the first time since his creation man will be faced with his real, his permanent problem – how to use his freedom from pressing economic cares, how to occupy the leisure, which science and compound interest will have won for him, to live wisely and agreeably and well.

He speculated about a three-hour shift and a 15-hour working week. In so doing, he was reflecting the general expectation of economists that rising incomes would be converted into both higher levels of consumption and shorter hours of work.

Broadly speaking, the historical record suggests that this is the direction of change, in the industrialized world at least, but working time is much less sensitive to income than is commonly believed. Even though we are not yet at 2030, Keynes's vision is clearly out of reach. In the consumer society, the constant emergence of new products and needs maintains the pressure for ever-higher incomes and consequently long working hours. Figure 2 shows a sharp decline in annual working hours from the nineteenth century up to the 1930s in industrialized countries, a flattening out or reversal of the trend through the Second World War and its aftermath, and a resumed downward trend up to 2000 – but the pace of decline is

---

[41] This section owes a great deal to two papers prepared for the ILO Century Project in 2008: J. Murray: *ILO and working conditions: An historical analysis*; and D. McCann: *Contemporary working time law: Evolving objectives, subjects and regulatory modes*, drafts available at: www.ilocentury.org; and to empirical research on working time by Sangheon Lee and Deirdre McCann.

[42] Reprinted in J.M. Keynes: *Essays in persuasion* (New York, W.W. Norton & Co., 1963), pp. 358–373.

**Figure 2** Long-term trends in annual working hours:
Selected countries, 1870–2000 (annual hours)

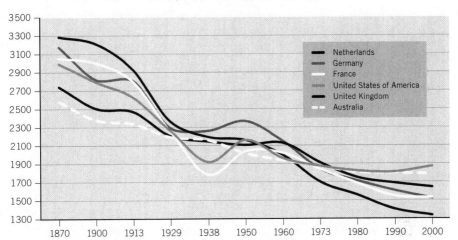

Source: Sangheon Lee et al., cited in footnote 43, figure 3.1, in turn based on M. Huberman and C. Minns: *Hours of work in old and new worlds: The long view, 1870–2000*, Discussion Paper 95 (Dublin, Institute for International Integration Studies, October 2005).

slow if set against the substantial rises in real incomes, especially during the post-war period, and particularly slow in the "Anglo-Saxon" countries in the figure.

What is more, surveys carried out for a recent ILO research project suggest that some 22 per cent of the world's workers were working more than 48 hours per week at the turn of the twenty-first century, more than 80 years after the adoption of the ILO standard (Convention No. 1) which set this as a maximum, for industrial workers at least.[43]

## Working-time standards and their impact

It was not an accident that the ILO's first Convention set a 48-hour limit on weekly hours of work in industry. Limits on working time, as we saw in Chapter 1, had been one of the principal demands of the international trade union movement for many years, and it was widely regarded as legitimate and a suitable subject for international legislation, not only to discourage competition through excessive work, but also as an important concession to workers' demands which could help to contain the influence of the Bolshevik Revolution. Moreover, hours of work

---

[43] S. Lee, D. McCann and J. Messenger: *Working time around the world: Trends in working hours, law and policies in a global comparative perspective* (Abingdon, Routledge and Geneva, ILO, 2007), p. 54.

remained on the ILO agenda throughout the 1920s and 1930s, with a series of Conventions covering specific aspects of working time, such as paid leave, and particular situations of groups of workers, including restrictions on night work for women. Much of the analytical work of the Office was devoted to this issue – no less than 84 articles published in the *International Labour Review* between 1921 and 1940 treated some aspects of hours of work.[44] By the end of the 1930s, a country which had ratified all the relevant ILO Conventions would be committed to a 40-hour week, with weekly rest and paid leave.

But very few countries had ratified all the relevant Conventions by that date; indeed, many industrialized countries had not ratified any. And the nature of the debate changed in the course of the period. From the early 1930s onwards, the issue was not prohibiting excessive working hours to avoid unfair competition, but rather work-sharing in order to maintain employment levels. That was the explicit aim of the Forty-Hour Week Convention (No. 47), adopted in 1935. There was considerable resistance from both employers and some influential governments to extending the scope of international instruments in this field; the Netherlands, the British Empire, Switzerland, and Canada were among those opposed to the 40-hour Convention, which they considered economically unrealistic. G.A. Johnston, an ILO official between 1920 and 1957, comments with respect to the 40-hour work Convention, that "even its warmest partisans had no illusions that it would be widely ratified". He describes the history of the treatment of the problem by the ILO "either as a melancholy chronicle of repeated failure or as an inspiring saga of sustained refusal to accept defeat".[45]

The ILO was the principal forum for international debate on working time in the 1930s, although the impact of its work was largely indirect. Political developments and social pressure at the national level were no doubt more influential than international action. For instance, it was the Front Populaire which introduced two weeks of paid holidays in France in 1936. Nevertheless, national actors, both trade unions and governments, used the ILO as a platform and a means to reinforce their national policy goals. Among other examples, the ILO was a point of reference in debate on working time in Germany in the 1920s.[46] Pressure for ratification from the Office, and in particular from its Director, shows how international and national debates intersected:

---

[44] But only 54 in the following 65 years up to 2006.

[45] G.A. Johnston: *The International Labour Organisation: Its work for social and economic progress* (London, Europa, 1970), pp. 165–166.

[46] There were several parliamentary discussions in the 1920s and it was a reference point for trade union demands. See S. Kott: *Albert Thomas, l'Allemagne et l'OIT (1919–1933): Dénationaliser les politiques sociales*, draft paper, Geneva, 2008.

... I went so far as to approach the dictatorships of Spain and Italy to drag ratifications out of them, as they needed to prove to the outside world that they were not reactionary. In France, I am trying as hard as possible at the moment to profit from the petty disputes between the radicals and socialists to obtain the necessary ratifications from the Senate.[47]

During the war, hours of work naturally increased again, but they started to decline once more in industrialized countries after 1950. The 1967 ILO General Survey on the subject concluded that considerable progress had been made as regards both national and international standards on hours of work, as well as in relation to the actual practices; the 1984 survey concluded that these trends had continued. The most recent such survey (2005) makes the case for continued standard-setting, in order to bring earlier standards into line with new working practices.[48]

The difficulty of demonstrating the ILO's contribution to this trend is illustrated by Sangheon Lee et al., who show that there is essentially no relationship across countries between ratification of the two main working time standards and the incidence of excessive work (defined as work in excess of 48 hours per week).[49] Countries having ratified Conventions Nos. 1 and 47 show as much excess work as countries that have not. But, of course, this proves nothing, since some countries with excessive working hours might ratify the Convention as part of an effort to deal with the problem, which would generate a positive relationship between ratification and hours of work – a point that is true of most standards.

In practice, national legislation has been gradually converging towards the aspirations of the Forty-Hour Week Convention, 1935 (No. 47), and the Reduction of Hours of Work Recommendation, 1962 (No. 116). Lee et al. argue that "the evidence from 2005 confirms that the 40-hour limit is now the dominant standard" across the world, in the sense that it is the standard to which the largest number of countries adhere. But there is a great deal of national variation, and international standards do not appear to be the main reference point. On the other hand, in many countries, the ILO's constituents have played an important role in national debate on working time policy, and they clearly draw on the work

---

[47] Albert Thomas, letter to M. Donau, Director of the Berlin Office, 9 December 1925, quoted in D. Guérin: *Albert Thomas au BIT, 1920–1932: De l'internationalisme à l'Europe* (Institut européen de l'Université de Genève, 1996), p. 31.

[48] ILO: *General Survey of the reports concerning the Hours of Work (Industry) Convention, 1919 (No. 1), and the Hours of Work (Commerce and Offices) Convention, 1930 (No. 30)*, Report III (Part 1B), International Labour Conference, 93rd Session, Geneva, 2005.

[49] Lee et al., op. cit., p. 53.

of the Office. As discussed in Chapter 1, international instruments have to be seen as one aspect of a wider social and political process, in which a good part of the influence of the Office comes from its work with its constituents and others at the national or local level.

### The "ILO approach"

Reduced working time is not an "ILO idea", but there is an ILO approach to the subject which is distinctive. First, it brings together a variety of different issues and attempts to put them in a common framework: the length of the working day; rules for overtime; rest days and holidays; maternity protection; the organization of part-time work; shift work and night work; and the relationship between work and family.

Second, as Murray points out,[50] the ILO approach provides explicitly for the state to play a role in preventing exploitation and providing for social reproduction. Some decisions may be devolved to the private sphere, through collective bargaining for instance, but within limits set by legally mandated norms and the obligation for all actors to be informed of their rights and entitlements.

Third, for many years, the ILO approach in this field – as in many others – was built around the figure of the male, full-time industrial worker. Limits on working time initially aimed to create space for what Murray describes as "masculine pursuits", including "gardening, running an allotment and keeping poultry, playing games and sports, and increasing knowledge through libraries, lectures and technical courses".[51] And various categories of what would today be described as "atypical" employment were excluded. Since women tended to be concentrated in these categories, there was a pronounced gender bias in the standards. A correction is currently under way, but it is not yet fully reflected in the ILO's instruments.

Fourth, there has always been at least lip service paid to the economic dimension of working time, in two main respects: at the micro-level, relating reduced or reorganized hours of work to improvements in productivity and efficiency; and at the macro-level, on the understanding that reduced working time was one instrument for employment creation. However, ILO research into the economic impact of working time policies has been limited, and there is little evidence to support the economic claims that are sometimes made. For instance, reduced working time seems to be a very blunt instrument for employment creation – the

---

[50] J. Murray, 2008, op. cit., p. 5.
[51] The Utilisation of Spare Time Recommendation, 1924 (No. 21), now withdrawn.

most recent experiment along these lines, the 35-hour week in France, is generally thought to have had only a limited impact on overall employment levels[52] – and, although this idea has returned occasionally to the ILO, it has had little influence on the ILO's agenda since the 1930s.[53]

The micro-level relationship is a double-edged sword. The increasing influence of neo-liberal economics in the 1980s, and in particular pressure for labour market flexibility, is one reason why there has been relatively little advance in working time regulation in recent years. The positions of the OECD and the World Bank were noted above. The World Bank's Doing Business surveys have taken the position that labour market regulation inhibits growth, including working hours regulation.[54] A similar perception underlies the long-running debate on the EU Working Time Directive, which limits the working week to 48 hours, with an opt-out provision allowing individual agreements between workers and employers to exceed this duration. The United Kingdom Government has succeeded in maintaining this opt-out, to the dismay of most other EU members.[55]

### The gender dimension

Policies for working time have an obvious important gender dimension, and one which has been understood differently at various points in time, as the ILO has moved from a "protective" approach to one of mainstreaming gender equality. Three issues in particular have been addressed:

- night work for women;
- maternity protection and;
- part-time work.

A Convention prohibiting night work for women in industry (No. 4) was adopted by the ILO at its first Conference.[56] Seen as a protective measure in a period when gender equality was a very distant goal, it met an important demand. But pro-

---

[52] See, among other sources, Pierre Boisard: *Working-time policy in France*, Document de Travail 34 (Paris, Centre d'Etudes de l'Emploi, 2004).

[53] One reason is that the ILO Workers' group does not have a common view on the issue. Unions from countries such as Brazil, France and Germany have promoted reduced working time as a source of employment creation, but unions in other parts of the world have given priority to different goals, including increased leisure, control of overtime or limiting excess work.

[54] See Chapter 1.

[55] On these issues, see McCann, op. cit.

[56] See also the discussion of this subject in Chapter 2.

tection also implied inequality (and by today's standards the Convention would be widely viewed as a means of protecting male jobs). Increasingly considered as a constraint on women's rights and opposed by the women's movement, it was denounced by a number of countries and eventually replaced in 1990 by a new Convention, which – unlike the earlier one – did not prohibit night work but rather demanded that alternatives be available for mothers during pregnancy and after childbirth. This is an interesting case, not only because of the change in the way the issue was understood over time, but also because of the pressure on the ILO to adapt its standards to social change. In this instance, the ILO was following national and regional thinking and action (in Europe at least), rather than leading it.

The pattern for maternity leave has been similar to that of night work, in the sense that the shift has been from directive to supportive. The protections provided in the Maternity Protection Convention, 1919 (No. 3), have not been greatly extended, even though the most recent revision was in 2000 – partly because of strong opposition to extending protection, led by the Employers' group, which voted en bloc against the new Convention, and some governments. But the provisions have been made more flexible, and there is greater attention to accompanying benefits and rights.

Part-time work is dominated by women, and is often poorly regulated. Much national labour legislation is subject to an hours-of-work threshold, and part-time work is one way of avoiding its application. Part-time workers are also much less easy to organize. There has always been considerable resistance to extending rights to part-time workers, and – as noted above – the Convention that was finally adopted in 1990 has not been widely ratified.

Murray[57] argues that the norm of the female worker derived from the early ILO Conventions differed from that of the standard worker. The female worker was not seen as a citizen as such, either of the workplace or within society as a whole. Her time away from work took her into the unregulated domestic realm. Furthermore, unlike men, women were not to have a say in the adaptation of their work to care needs, since the early Conventions were built on prohibitions (of work during the six weeks following confinement, of work during the night).

This approach started to change in the 1970s, as a rather belated response to growing female labour force participation, acknowledgement of the invisibility of much domestic and care work and increased attention to gender equality. The Workers with Family Responsibilities Convention, 1981 (No. 156), stated that it

---

[57] J. Murray, 2008, op. cit., p. 16.

was necessary to recognize and encourage the care work of men and women, and to integrate the demands of the domestic sphere with those of the paid workplace. Although this Convention calls only for the development of a national policy with rather broad provisions, it is an instrument that can and has been used effectively by the women's movement to promote gender equality goals.

As Murray puts it, "By the time of the new century, a much more sophisticated vision of the 'labour problem' of combining work and life was available. It was increasingly recognized that for [both male and female] workers with care responsibilities, time away from work was not time spent as the worker pleased, as posited in early ILO thinking. Rather, such workers needed to intersperse periods of work and non-work for various purposes, and for various lengths of time."[58] However, efforts to construct a better adapted policy framework in the ILO's work have to date been essentially restricted to research and advocacy.[59]

## Challenges

Working-time policy is not something that can really be analysed in isolation from the economic and social setting of work. Around the world, many people are working shorter hours than they would wish; this is notably true of much part-time work by women. And many of those who are working long hours, especially in self-employment or casual labour in the informal economy, do so at very low levels of productivity and wages in order to survive. For them, higher productivity or higher wages is a precondition for shorter working hours, which in principle many would prefer. The issue is not so much that in the informal economy work escapes regulation; it is rather that shorter working hours can only be achieved as part of a broader package of measures that also addresses output and income goals. In other words, policies for working time are not simply a question of regulation – they cannot be separated from problems of underemployment and productivity.

This is quite different from the over-simplified economic view that working time regulation is undesirable because it reduces flexibility and constrains employment creation. On the contrary, in all countries, such regulation provides important protections for many workers, and reducing the protection of workers in regular employment is most unlikely to have any beneficial impact on workers in the informal economy. This point is repeatedly made in ILO research. But it does suggest that more attention needs to be given to a policy framework for

---

[58] J. Murray, 2008, op. cit., pp. 17–18.
[59] See McCann, op. cit.

the working time of those who fall outside the scope of effective state regulation. So far, the ILO has had little to offer in this domain. It requires a better
understanding of the link between the legal, social, economic and developmental
dimensions of working time.

Overall, there is a sense that the ILO's legislative framework for working
time is fragmented and in some respects dated, and there are plausible arguments for a more integrated and coherent approach. This, at any rate, was the
view taken by the Committee of Experts in their 2005 General Survey. The concern is not only with the duration of work (hours, weekly rest, paid leave, among
others) in various sectors and for different groups of workers, but also with the
organization of working time, notably the ways to introduce flexibility for both
workers and enterprises. But the greatest challenge lies in the persistence of long
or inadequate working hours, despite the existence of extensive national and
international regulation. In many developing countries, more than 40 per cent
of workers work excessive hours.[60]

## Occupational safety and health

Protecting the life and health of working men and women was a natural priority
for action at the beginning of the twentieth century. There was widespread use
of dangerous chemicals. Prohibiting the use of white phosphorous in match-
making was one of the emblematic first causes of international labour legislation
in 1906, but there were many others. There were killer diseases such as anthrax
and silicosis. And accidents in the workplace were widespread, including a famous
fire in a garment shop in New York in 1911, which killed 146 people and led to
pressure for government regulation.

Over the last century, there has certainly been a considerable improvement
in safety and health in the workplace in industrialized countries. But two aspects
of this topic are surprising. First, the number of work-related deaths worldwide
remains enormous. An ILO estimate for 2002 suggests 2 million work-related
fatalities per year. What is more, the rate reported for India and China in these
estimates is, implausibly, slightly lower than that for industrialized market economies, so the real number of deaths is probably much higher.[61] Major accidents

---

[60] Lee and McCann, 2008, op. cit.; McCann, op. cit.
[61] ILO: *ILO standards-related activities in the area of occupational safety and health: An in-depth study
for discussion with a view to the elaboration of a plan of action for such activities*, Report VI, International
Labour Conference, 91st Session, Geneva, 2003, table 1, p. 9.

are unhappily common, some of them globally notorious (such as the Union Carbide disaster in Bhopal in 1984 which killed several thousand people, or the Kader toy factory fire in Thailand in 1993 which killed 188 people and injured 500 more).

Second, there is a huge margin of uncertainty around these figures. In many parts of the world existing information is insufficient to judge whether progress is really being made. Documenting OSH is plagued by difficulties of measurement and definition. Some occupational diseases take many years to develop, and formally establishing their link with the workplace may be problematic. Statistics are inconsistent. Is a road accident on the way to work to be counted the same way as an accident with a machine in the workplace? There is enormous under-reporting in many developing countries. Many industrialized countries do show statistical improvements at different points of time in accident rates and particular diseases,[62] but new processes and situations are always arising. And in developing countries, rapid economic change is as likely to exacerbate the problem as alleviate it.

The starting point for the ILO's work in 1919 was to provide an adequate knowledge base for policy purposes. At the first International Labour Conference, the Office was asked "to draw up a list of the principal processes to be considered as unhealthy". This, however, proved to be difficult, not only because of contradictory medical opinions, but because views of what was unhealthy were coloured by the economic implications. The problem is well illustrated in the work of the ILO in regulating white lead in paint. Although a Convention (No. 13) was adopted in 1921, which prohibited the use of white lead in some situations, debate on the issue was heated.[63] There were powerful economic interests at stake, notably among lead producers in Great Britain, and they fought a rearguard action against prohibition, arguing that lighter regulation would suffice – despite strong evidence of mortality through lead poisoning among painters. Albert Thomas was accused of allying himself with French and Belgian manufacturers of a zinc-based substitute. Where economic interests are at stake, precautionary measures are resisted.

The head of the ILO's Industrial Health Section was Luigi Carozzi, an activist from Milan who was a key figure in European networks for medical reform before the war. He was to lead the ILO's action throughout the entire interwar

---

[62] Ibid.

[63] J. Heitmann: "The ILO and the regulation of white lead in Britain during the interwar years: An examination of international and national campaigns in occupational health", in *Labour History Review*, Vol. 69, No. 3, Dec. 2004, pp. 267–284.

period.[64] The strategic issue for the ILO was to ensure that the field of occupational health was recognized as a concern in its own right, and to establish the ILO as a key player in international action. Carozzi pursued several lines. The first was to respond to the original demand for an adequate knowledge base through research. Some 57 articles on different aspects of occupational safety and health had appeared in the *International Labour Review* by 1926, and a series of studies on health risks and accident prevention appeared between 1924 and 1940. But it was clearly not possible for the ILO to be the premier research centre on such a wide-ranging and highly technical subject. Its comparative advantage lay rather in centralizing information and knowledge on some of the most serious occupational health risks.

This led, in Albert Thomas's words, to

a sort of encyclopaedia which would analyse from the triple point of view of the work to be done, the worker employed, and the environment in which he worked, the various tasks involved in human labour, the properties of the substances dealt with, the operations involved in handling and working up these substances, the possible sources and carriers of intoxication and diseases, the statistical data on the effects as far as known, the symptoms, the diagnosis, the therapeutic and prophylactic treatment, and the protective legislation already in existence.[65]

This was the *Encyclopaedia of Occupational Health and Safety*, an idea which has clearly proved its worth since, today, it is in its fourth edition and is widely circulated in three languages. The idea of a broad knowledge base on the subject has remained a central part of the ILO's strategy. It was reinforced in 1959 with the establishment of a permanent information centre (CIS) which still exists, today online, including both the *Encyclopaedia* and other sources. Some 140 institutions (both ILO constituents and independent institutions) are members. It is only one of a number of online databases, but in a Google search of "information on occupational safety and health" it comes up on the first page, along with several national information systems (but not when the search is for "information on preventing accidents at work"). It is, of course, hard to judge the true value of an information system of this type, since there is not much independent information

---

[64] The discussion on Carozzi's work and the ILO's work on silicosis is due to T. Cayet, P.-A. Rosental and M. Thébaud-Sorger: *Histoire du service d'hygiène industrielle du BIT*, paper prepared for the ILO Century Project, draft available at: http://www.ilocentury.org

[65] ILO: *Occupation and health: Encyclopaedia of hygiene, pathology and social welfare*, Preface to the first edition by Albert Thomas (Geneva, 1930).

on its use. At various times there has been some scepticism expressed in internal reports.[66] However, the programme does clearly have a base of users, since it is consulted regularly by specialists in the field.[67]

The second line pursued by Carozzi was to focus on one strategic cause. He chose silicosis. This was a killer disease, which was worsening with the mechanization of mining, but one which was not properly recognized, in part because of the economic interests involved. France, Belgium and the Netherlands all opposed recognition of the existence of the disease throughout the 1930s.[68] But the ILO had powerful arguments to show that silicosis was indeed a disease (along with all of the pulmonary and other infections which it induced), and one that was very much linked with the workplace – and Carozzi used them.

To do so, he relied on a third line of action: the mobilization of international networks, in which he was already a participant. This was brought to fruition at an important conference on silicosis held in Johannesburg in 1930, a location where there was a concentration of mining. This was the first meeting held by the ILO outside Europe. By mobilizing expert opinion, the ILO laid the ground for the general recognition of silicosis as an important domain for action. This in due course led to Convention No. 42, adopted in 1934, on workmen's compensation for occupational diseases, which specifically referred to silicosis, along with a number of other important diseases.

The importance of this example is to show how a number of complementary actions and approaches proved to be effective in ensuring impact. Networks, research, information, standards and advocacy all played a role, and established the credibility of the Organization's action.

A difficult period followed because of the war. After the war it took time to reconstitute the ILO's expertise in this field, and the division of areas of competence with the newly created WHO was conflictual. In the end, the ILO abandoned the strictly medical aspects of occupational health, in which the WHO had demonstrated a comparative advantage, and turned towards prevention, combining action on safety and health in one programme.[69] The research effort also

---

[66] See, for instance, ILO: *Report of the ad hoc Committee on the Occupational Safety and Health Programme*, Governing Body, 188th Session, Geneva, Nov. 1972, GB.188/9/5, para. 12. See also ILO: Evaluation of PIACT, op. cit., which commented that "there is a real need for feedback on how information provided by CIS is used", and considered that the information it provided was "of less immediate value to developing countries". The programme was redesigned in 1986 in the light of that evaluation.

[67] However, CIS staff do not have detailed information on this use. Some 2–3,000 queries per month are put to the database, but this is only one of several ways of accessing the information.

[68] Cayet et al., op. cit., p. 3.

[69] A Joint WHO–ILO Committee on Occupational Safety and Health was subsequently created and continues to meet, and there are some relatively modest joint activities.

declined. There were publications in the 1950s and 1960s on subjects as diverse as electrical accidents, and the particular problems and needs of developing countries, but other organizations, such as the newly created European Coal and Steel Community, could put much greater resources into research.

Throughout this period, ILO work focused on the development of codes of practice and some specific standards, as well as technical cooperation.

A number of Conventions which addressed particular safety and health risks were adopted from 1960 onwards, with the first, on radiation, the result of a long process of research and debate, including the development of model codes for safety regulations. In an extensive review of the ILO's achievements in OSH up to 1969, the two leading experts at the time – Marcel Robert and Luigi Parmeggiani – argued that the Organization's work had a considerable influence in the field of radiation, involving research, networks and promotion, in a process reminiscent of its action on silicosis 30 years earlier.[70]

The development and dissemination of model codes and codes of practice, which had started in the 1930s with a standard code of industrial hygiene, proved to be an important instrument for promoting ILO ideas. These codes were often based on the results of both expert and tripartite discussion, and some were developed in and promulgated by the sectoral (industrial) ILO committees, such as those on the Metal Trades or on Leather and Footware.[71] A particularly influential case, with visible impact, concerned the labelling of dangerous substances in the 1950s, in which the Chemical Industries Committee played a significant role. The danger symbols that were adopted have to a large extent acquired general use, having been incorporated in the recommendations of the International Organization for Standardization (ISO).

This approach has continued to the present day. Between 1972 and 2005, 41 such codes were adopted. It is not clear that all have had a major impact, but there is widespread evidence of their use in diverse situations. References to particular codes are fairly frequent on the websites of associations of manufacturers or occupational associations; they are used by ILO constituents and in ILO technical cooperation; they provide inspiration for national legislation; and they are used in international framework agreements. An example of the latter (among many others) is the model framework agreement of the International Federation of Building and Wood Workers (IFBWW), used in global agreements with

---

[70] M. Robert and L. Parmeggiani: *Fifty years of international collaboration in occupational safety and health* (Geneva, ILO, 1969), pp. 32–35.

[71] E. Weisband: *ILO industrial committees and sectoral activities: An institutional history* (Geneva, ILO, 1996), p. 125.

**Figure 3 Examples of danger symbols adopted by the ILO**

Note: Corrosion, explosion, fire, oxidizing agents and poison (left to right).
Source: Johnston, op. cit., p. 346.

a number of multinational companies, which cites the ILO codes of practice for health and safety in forest work, and on safety in the use of synthetic vitreous fibre insulation wools.[72]

The technical nature of much of this work did not, it should be noted, preclude diversity of approach. For instance, there were two very different visions of the promotion of safety at work: one, more "Latin" in origin, based on administrative regulation and organization; the other, more "Anglo-Saxon", based on individual responsibility and insurance. ILO safety codes have to accommodate these different perspectives.

The other important area of work during this period was technical advice and assistance to developing countries, which developed in the 1950s and 1960s, along with other aspects of the ILO's technical cooperation programme. Much of the effort at that time was devoted to developing national institutions with the technical capacity to research and oversee OSH policies, and a number of successes were claimed. Robert and Parmeggiani give the example of India, where a network of centres was put in place with ILO support.

Overall, it can be reasonably argued that the ILO played a significant role in the development of policies for occupational safety and health in industrialized countries, at least up to the 1960s. Robert and Parmeggiani claim a number of achievements: "one may count the control of anthrax, phosphorous poisoning, ankylostomiasis among miners, and lead poisoning among printers and painters".[73] They also point to the decline in silicosis. But they also identify what they regard as failures – increases in bronchitis, skin disease and allergic disorders, among others – and call for renewed and reinforced efforts.

---

[72] See: http://www.fitbb.org
[73] Robert and Parmeggiani, op. cit., p. 61.

In the 1970s, occupational safety and health was incorporated in the PIACT. In practice, however, the Office unit responsible for OSH pursued its own line, in particular developing a framework Convention for OSH policy, No. 155, in 1981, which is still receiving ratifications today. This Convention expresses the essentials of the ILO approach, involving tripartite cooperation, procedures for identifying and regulating dangerous and unhealthy situations, adequate systems of inspection and research and information-sharing among all parties concerned. There have been recent ratifications of Convention No. 155 by Algeria, Australia, China, New Zealand, the Republic of Korea and the Russian Federation, among others. The continuation of a modest but significant research programme can be seen in the flow of articles published by the *International Labour Review*.

Today's programme, called SAFEWORK since 1999, is carrying on in the same vein. The basic idea is that international knowledge systems and instruments can contribute effectively to improved occupational safety and health at national level. Within the ILO, this is a relatively uncontroversial area. Both employers and workers recognize its value, and together they form an effective lobby at both national and international levels. In a survey of member States undertaken for a 2003 review of the programme, 75 per cent of respondents indicated that they "have used the relevant OSH and labour inspection Conventions as guidance or as models in shaping their national legislation".[74] OSH figures in various codes for corporate social responsibility, notably including the ILO Multinationals Declaration. And, as a former Director of the programme, Jukka Takala, put it, "progress requires a safe and healthy labour force; no country can achieve a high level of competitiveness and productivity without taking care of the safety, health and well-being of its workers". He argues that the European Union's policies in this field have been influenced by the ILO, and that this can be seen in EU Directives and Resolutions of the European Parliament.[75] A new Convention, No. 187, pursues the framework-setting approach.

It is harder to argue that the ILO has been successful in making safety at work a high priority in development. Its technical cooperation work in this field has, in general, been poorly funded. Admittedly, the programme was reinforced at the end of the 1980s with pledges of long-term financial support, especially from Finland, in order to transfer knowledge and build institutions in Asia and Africa. The scale of the programme nevertheless remains limited. This is not to

---

[74] ILO: *ILO standards-related activities in the area of occupational safety and health: An in-depth study for discussion with a view to the elaboration of a plan of action for such activities*, Report VI, International Labour Conference, 91st Session, Geneva, 2005.

[75] Personal communication.

neglect the impact of a variety of local schemes and projects, regularly reported in ILO publications. But they tend to reach hundreds or thousands of workers rather than millions.

Beyond funding, there is also a question of the balance of the programme, which is, by its very nature, focused on formal institutions and regulatory frameworks. As the 2003 review recognized, much of the problem of occupational safety and health in developing countries lies in small and informal enterprises that are beyond the effective reach of such approaches. More flexible and better adapted policies are required. Yet, although the informal sector is a concern of the current SAFEWORK programme – and again there are examples of successful local impact, for example among homeworkers and workers in small construction sites in several countries in East Asia[76] – it does not appear to be high on the list of priorities.

One area of research that seems to have been relatively neglected is the economics of safety and health. Improvements in workplace health and safety should, in general, raise productivity. That is particularly true of accidents, which are costly. The ILO seems not to have taken advantage of this serendipity to research the economic benefits of accident prevention better. Much of its action has basically assumed that the value of improved occupational safety and health is self-evident – whereas, in reality, if the economics do not support the case, the policies will not be adopted. Slow progress in developing countries clearly reflects the costs of safety and health improvements, and more documentation of the economic benefits would help make the case for their adoption.

On the whole, the evidence supports the view that the ILO's work on OSH has been influential within its domain, and has been an important source of knowledge and support to national action. Its connections with global networks of specialists are illustrated by the regular World Congresses on Safety and Health at Work, which the ILO co-organizes, with several thousand participants. There are gaps in this work – notably, as commented above, with respect to economic analysis and the way to improve OSH in the informal economy – but it does illustrate how a consistent promotion of ILO ideas can help to drive forward a global policy agenda.

---

[76] ILO: *Decent work in Asia: Reporting on results 2001–2005*, Report of the Director-General, Fourteenth Asian Regional Meeting, Busan, Republic of Korea, Aug.–Sep. (Geneva, 2006), box 5.5, p. 71.

## Minimum wages

The ILO's work on wages can be divided into three main periods.

First, there was a period of broad concern and debate over wage policy in the early years of the Organization, starting with minimum wages in the 1920s and continuing with participation in debate on the role of wage policy in combating the effects of the Great Depression. Convention No. 26 on minimum wage-fixing machinery, dating from 1928, is one of only six Conventions, other than the fundamental Conventions on rights at work, with more than 100 ratifications. In the 1920s and 1930s, in the Director's Report to the annual International Labour Conference, he regularly included a review of wage developments, as one of the key dimensions of the world of work.

Second, after the war, progress on minimum wages was consolidated by addressing other dimensions of wage policy, such as the protection of wages and equal remuneration. At the same time, a debate emerged on the role of wage policy in economic development, to which the ILO contributed in the 1960s and early 1970s.

The third period, from the mid-1970s on, saw a decline in capacity and response on wage issues within the ILO. Figure 1 on page 109, showing *International Labour Review* articles concerning minimum wages, illustrates the deficit in ILO work. There is at present an effort under way to rebuild capacity in this area,[77] but the ILO was absent from debates on wage policies during a period when abrupt changes in real wages had a serious impact on workers around the world.

This section will focus mainly on minimum wages, as the pre-eminent ILO concern in this field.[78]

### The development of wage policy in the 1920s and 1930s

Among the goals identified in the ILO's Constitution, one is "the provision of an adequate living wage", and another the "recognition of the principle of equal remuneration for work of equal value". And labour should not be considered as a commodity – so its price could not be simply determined by demand and supply.

---

[77] Recent publications include F. Eyraud and C. Saget: *The fundamentals of minimum wage fixing* (Geneva, ILO, 2005); and J.Velasco and A. Marinakis (eds): *¿Para qué sirve el salario minimo? Elementos para su determinación en los países del Cono Sur* (Geneva, ILO, 2006). A database has also been established on minimum wage legislation (http://www.ilo.org/travdatabase/).

[78] This section is in large part a summary of a paper by Andrés Marinakis: *The role of the ILO in the development of minimum wages*, 2008, paper prepared for the ILO Century Project, draft available at: http://www.ilocentury.org

The most obvious point of departure was to set a floor to wages. When the ILO was created, minimum wages were applied in only a few countries. In Great Britain there were Trade Boards in certain industries ("sweated industries"), which aimed at preventing exploitation, especially of women and homeworkers. Australia and New Zealand fixed minimum wages by industry and regional districts. The United States had minimum wage laws in six states, and Canada in four Provinces. In France and Norway there were pockets of minimum-wage fixing in the textile industry, particularly concerning homeworkers.

At its very first Conference, the ILO was asked to explore this issue. A key question was whether there could be a single international minimum wage. In an internal note for the Director, a British official from the Statistical Section (and from 1929 to 1940 its Chief), James Nixon, pointed out that the determination of minimum wages was a very complex matter, very different from other labour standards.

> A minimum wage differs from other minimum standards in that the standard of living, expressed in terms of commodities or amount of money, differs so greatly from one country to another that it makes it almost – if not totally – impossible to fix an international standard.

He concluded that:

> Consequently, each State has to determine its own standard and all that an international Conference can do on this matter is to set certain principles which should be followed by each State.[79]

Nixon's conclusion was far-sighted, but it soon became apparent that existing information about the different national systems was fragmentary and the international community lacked the basic statistical data needed, whether on wages or on costs of living. Further consideration of a minimum wage required a stronger knowledge base.

A research programme was therefore launched, including country studies and new data collection. It concluded, against the conventional economic wisdom of the time, that:

> Evidence available from some ILO member countries indicated that minimum wage regulation promoted industrial peace, increased the level of output and

---

[79] ILO Archives, File N 104/0/0 (text in French), p. 5, paras 2–3.

sustained employment levels. In highly competitive labour markets, where employers were exceptionally powerful in reducing wages, minimum wage legislation could help provide a measure of countervailing power in support of disorganized workers.[80]

The idea of a common international minimum wage was still present during the technical discussions in the 1920s, which raised many concerns and doubts. However, this idea seems to have been definitively buried by the wording of the British proposal to include the wages item in the agenda of the 1927 Conference. In a memorandum sent by Humbert Wolfe, of the British Ministry of Labour, to the Deputy Director, Mr Butler, it is made clear that:

> ... there is no intention to suggest that wages should be fixed by the Convention itself, but merely that wage-fixing machinery in the various States should be examined. This means that at the most, the Convention might suggest some additional form of wage-fixing machinery to cover certain limited industries, but *could not in any circumstances suggest actual wage levels*.[81]

Humbert Wolfe played a very active role in this process as British Government delegate, and he was elected Chairman of the Committee on Minimum Wage-Fixing Machinery that prepared the questionnaire sent to the countries, so his views carried weight.

The Convention itself was adopted in 1928. The main aim was: "the elimination of the payment of unduly low wages to the workers and the elimination of unfair competition within employers with regard to wages".[82] In general, countries where collective bargaining was more developed were sceptical about the need to introduce minimum wage-fixing mechanisms, a position which remains common today (for instance, Denmark, Finland and Sweden, where collective bargaining remains strong, have not ratified the Convention). There was a belief that the growth of collective bargaining would render minimum wages redundant. And despite considerable debate on how the level of the minimum wage should be set, and the reference in the ILO Constitution to a living wage, the Convention says nothing about the principles which should guide the setting of

---

[80] Cited in A. Endres and G. Fleming: *International organizations and the analysis of economic policy, 1919–1950* (London, Cambridge University Press, 2002).

[81] H. Wolfe: *Memorandum with regard to the Minimum Wage item, proposed by the British Government for insertion at the 1927 agenda*, ILO Archives, File N 104/0/1, Geneva, 1925.

[82] ILO: *Minimum wage-fixing machinery*, Report draft and questionnaire, International Labour Conference, 10th Session, Geneva, 1927.

the minimum wage, save a reference to "exceptionally low wages". This is left to a Recommendation, but even the Recommendation is quite vague.

Nevertheless, Convention No. 26 and its accompanying Recommendation No. 30 must be seen as a real step forward. In the 1920s, very few countries had a minimum wage and there was very limited knowledge about the specificities of the application in each country. The ILO was given a concrete mandate to do research on this topic, spread the results of it through publications and conferences and develop the statistical definitions in order to make information comparable. In the following years this was the main course of ILO action. By the end of the 1930s, 22 countries had ratified Convention No. 26.

In the years after the adoption of the Convention, however, the idea of improving working conditions by setting a minimum wage in low-paying trades encountered a serious challenge with the crisis of the 1930s. The world economy entered a vicious circle of rising unemployment, reduced wages, lower demand and lower investment. On the wage issue, some economists were in favour of letting the economy find a new equilibrium point at a lower level (disregarding the social cost), while others believed that an increase in wages could help in reversing the cycle by stimulating demand (in the hope that inflation would lag behind, permitting real wage increases).

The ILO resisted the former view. Addressing the Conference in 1931, Albert Thomas formulated the wages dilemma:

> We are faced with two main tendencies. Some people are in favour of the workers' demands and say, with the Americans, "High wages are the foundation of industrial prosperity". Others maintain that there is only one way of alleviating the depression: to lower wages so as to reduce costs of production and consequently increase consumption.

He expressed his doubts on the wage cuts strategy:

> I also have the gravest doubts about the idea that wage reductions could provide a cure. The theory put forward on this subject might at most be valid for industries working for export. If, however, wages are reduced in any given country, they will be reduced in the neighbouring countries too. Besides, if it cannot be said with certainty that high wages are the cause of the depression, I believe very strongly that on the contrary, wage reductions will still further diminish consumption.[83]

[83] A. Thomas: *International social policy* (Geneva, ILO, 1948), pp. 92–93.

While the ILO was certainly not the most influential actor in this stand-off between neo-classical and Keynesian economics, its arguments were ultimately vindicated. Minimum wage policy could help to check a downward wage spiral, and a high wage policy could indeed assist in maintaining consumption levels. The ILO's research tried to provide empirical foundations for such policies. One notable example was its major study of wages, undertaken at the request of Henry Ford to establish the real level of wages in different locations where his company planned car production. His intention was to establish common wage levels and avoid accusations of social dumping. This study was in reality overtaken by the Depression, but it reflected the spirit of the times, which was that high wages and high productivity should go hand in hand with high employment and high output levels.[84] After the election of Roosevelt in 1932, this was reflected in United States policy proposals, for instance at the 1933 World Monetary and Economic Conference of the League of Nations. [85]

## Consolidation and expansion in the decades following the Second World War

The foothold in the wages field which the ILO had gained in the 1920s and 1930s was consolidated and expanded after the war. Conventions on protection of wages, on minimum wages in agriculture (excluded from Convention No. 26) and on equal remuneration for men and women workers were adopted and have since been widely ratified.

The key question, as far as work on minimum wages was concerned, was how to respond to the needs of low-income countries for a better link between wage policy and economic development. Minimum wages were on their agenda. In India, a Committee on Fair Wages had been set up soon after Independence, and its recommendations went very much in the direction of the original ILO idea of a living wage.[86] In Latin America, many countries had enacted minimum wage legislation – indeed, for populist governments, such as those of Peron in Argentina or Vargas in Brazil, this was a central policy plank.

At the beginning of the 1960s, the balance for the ILO with regard to the objective of disseminating the idea and application of minimum wages could be

---

[84] There is a lively account of this episode in V. de Grazia: *Irresistible empire: America's advance through twentieth century Europe* (Cambridge, MA, Belknap Press, 2005), pp. 78–93.

[85] ILO: *Report of the representatives of the International Labour Organization at the Monetary and Economic Conference*, Governing Body, 64th Session, Geneva, Oct. 1933, GB.64/13/914.

[86] Government of India, Ministry of Labour: *Committee on Fair Wages: Report* (Simla, 1949).

considered very positive. By 1969, Convention No. 26 had been ratified by 76 countries and was the third most ratified Convention.[87] This Convention, which applied only to manufacture and commerce, was complemented by Convention No. 99, concerning minimum wage-fixing machinery in agriculture, in 1951. Nevertheless, there was a feeling that the implementation of minimum wages had evolved beyond the framework of these Conventions, in particular for developing countries.

In November 1965, the Governing Body asked the Director-General to consider holding a meeting of experts on "minimum wage fixing and other problems of wage policy, with special reference to developing countries" in the agenda for 1967. The purpose of the meeting was to examine, first, the problems encountered in minimum wage fixing and, second, ways in which the ILO Conventions and Recommendations on this issue should be revised, if required.

The majority of the experts to be invited had to be from developing countries.[88] This constituted a major change when compared with the process that had led to Convention No. 26, which had been dominated by European countries. Dudley Seers, from the United Kingdom, was designated rapporteur for the first item on the agenda. He was Director of the recently created Institute of Development Studies of the University of Sussex and a leading development theorist. The developmentalist perspective cut across the whole report.

From the very beginning of the report, the minimum wages issue was put into a broader framework: "in developing countries, minimum wage fixing has to be seen as one of a battery of measures in the strategy of an attack on poverty, its major objective".[89] A key element of the development strategy was to change the existing structure of income distribution. The report clearly mentioned that minimum wage fixing has a limited impact on improving income distribution by itself, and that if wage increases were not absorbed by profits or increased productivity, they would result in higher prices – at the risk of worsening the situation. However, it also pointed out that: "Fixing of minimum wages can in any case be the most effective policy tool for one objective in any country. It can prevent the payment of particularly low wages to vulnerable groups of workers, and by doing so it can also make the distribution of income somehow better".[90] Criteria for setting the

---

[87] Only surpassed by the Right of Association (Agriculture) Convention, 1921 (No. 11) and the Forced Labour Convention, 1930 (No. 29).

[88] ILO: *Composition and agenda of committees and of various meetings*, Governing Body, 168th Session, Geneva, 1967, GB.168/15/10.

[89] ILO: *Report of the meeting of experts on minimum wage fixing and related problems, with special reference to developing countries*, Governing Body, 170th Session, Geneva, Nov. 1967, GB.170/6/10.

[90] Ibid.

minimum wage included the needs of the workers and their families,[91] the capacity to pay of employers and, significantly, the requirements of economic development.

In 1970, a new Convention on minimum wage fixing, No. 131, was adopted, but not without difficulty. The main two issues in contention were how to determine the needs of the worker, and how to take into account the capacity of employers to pay. In the Conference Committee, the treatment of the capacity to pay was a major area of disagreement between the Employer and Worker members of the Working Party. The Worker members argued that "in minimum wage fixing, as opposed to general wage determination, only social and not economic considerations should be taken into account" and also that it was very difficult to verify in practice if such capacity to pay existed or not.[92] The Employer members of the committee strongly supported the retention of the economic considerations, arguing that if they were ignored, this could result in inflation and unemployment, weakening the protective role of the instrument.

The Convention makes no reference to gender equality, apart from a preambular reference to Convention No. 100 on equal remuneration. In the debate on the Convention, the only point at which gender equality issues arose was in the context of a proposed amendment about taking the needs of the family into account in fixing minimum wages – implicitly the needs of (mainly male) breadwinners were greater than the needs of (mainly female) secondary workers. The amendment did not pass.

The final formulation of the Convention identified two broad and not necessarily consistent criteria for the setting of minimum wages:

a) the needs of workers and their families, taking into account the general level of wages in the country, the cost of living, social security benefits, and the relative living standards of other social groups;

b) economic factors, including the requirements of economic development, levels productivity and the desirability of attaining and maintaining a high level of employment.

At the end of this process, the ILO had a new instrument with a wider scope and content than Convention No. 26. This Convention promoted the idea of a minimum wage as one instrument among others for reducing poverty as part of

---

[91] "[A] wage is in no sense a living wage unless it adequately covers all who have to live with it" (ibid.).

[92] ILO: *Report of the Committee on Minimum Wages*, International Labour Conference, 53rd Session, Geneva, 1969.

a development strategy. This moment might be regarded as the high point in the long history of the minimum wage in the ILO agenda.

Convention No. 131 is an important instrument and one which has been fairly widely ratified by developing countries. But within a decade work on minimum wages had run into trouble on two fronts.

The first was an uneasy relationship with the ILO's work on development. The connection between minimum wage policy and development was emphasized by a Governing Body report on conditions of work in 1972: "The ILO ... must come to grips with the question far more than it has in the past of how initiatives in the fields of remuneration and conditions of work affect the potential for economic growth, employment expansion and the distribution of income" (para. 6). The report was concerned with rural–urban income differentials and the possibility that minimum wages would exacerbate inequalities between different social groups.[93]

The main ILO contribution to the development agenda at that time was the World Employment Programme (Chapter 5). This programme expanded rapidly in the 1970s but paid little attention to wages. The Comprehensive Employment Strategy Reports for a series of countries between 1970 and 1975 tended to damn minimum wages with faint praise. The Colombia report, for instance, recommended that "as long as unemployment and underemployment in Colombia have not been considerably reduced, minimum wage regulation should be used prudently ... it would seem undesirable to go much further than adjusting rates to increases in the cost of living".[94] The point was that minimum wages were in reality only respected in a part of the economy – the formal sector, where incomes were already relatively high. The development challenge consisted of raising incomes elsewhere, notably in the informal sector, which was highlighted by the 1972 Kenya mission report.[95] Minimum wages were unlikely to contribute much to poverty reduction, the main concern, because they could not reach the majority of workers. On the contrary, the goal was to put employment at the centre of development strategy, and wage policy should support that objective.

At the 1976 World Employment Conference, discussed in more detail in Chapter 5, the central theme was how to satisfy the basic needs of people in the shortest time possible. For the purpose of the discussion, "basic needs are defined as the minimum standard of living which a society should set for the poorest groups

---

[93] ILO: GB.188/FA/8/9, op. cit.

[94] ILO: *Towards full employment: A programme for Colombia* (Geneva, ILO, 1970).

[95] ILO: *Employment, incomes and equality: A strategy for increasing productive employment in Kenya* (Geneva, ILO, 1972).

of its people. The satisfaction of basic needs means meeting the minimum require-ments of a family for personal consumption: food, shelter, clothing; it implies access to essential services, such as safe drinking water, sanitation, transport, health and education".[96] The Conference adopted the principle of the basic needs strategy and favoured the consideration of labour-intensive methods of production.

Remarkably, there is little sign of a link between this development of poli-cies to satisfy the goal of basic needs and the discussion of needs which had long been a concern of minimum wage fixing. In essence, two agendas were developed in parallel. These issues were dealt with in two different ILO programmes, and there was little connection between them. The World Employment Programme had little time for standard-setting, and was developing a broader agenda con-cerned with growth and distribution. There was some reference to wage issues in the Declaration of Principles and Programme of Action adopted by the World Employment Conference, but it did not mention minimum wages. There was clearly an opportunity lost here to build a more coherent overall approach.

### Abdication

The second blow came with the emergence of the neo-liberal agenda in the 1980s, discussed above in connection with other aspects of conditions of work and in Chapter 5. Wage regulation was seen as contrary to market principles and a source of inefficiency. It would have been possible for ILO research to counter some of the more extreme views. After all, the economic literature on efficiency wages, which explored positive relationships between wages and productivity and pro-vided economic arguments in favour of minimum wages, started to develop in the mid-1970s. But ILO work on wages was merged with a Department concerned with industrial relations, and gradually atrophied.

The last major effort of that period was a 1981 review of minimum wage fixing practices and problems.[97] This comparative study of minimum wages and their evolution in a large number of countries provided a great deal of useful infor-mation. But it fell on stony ground. In much of the developing world, the 1980s was the era of structural adjustment. Stabilization policies aimed to squeeze out deficits through a reduction in domestic demand, involving a fall in real wages

---

[96] ILO: *Employment, growth and basic needs: A one-world problem*, Report of the Director-General to the Tripartite World Conference on Employment, Income Distribution and Social Progress and the International Division of Labour (Geneva, 1976).

[97] G. Starr: *Minimum wage fixing, an international review of practices and problems* (Geneva, ILO, 1981).

that would restore competitiveness. In an echo of the debates of the 1930s, it was argued that rules and institutions that restrict wage flexibility, such as a minimum wage, should be eliminated.

Despite the attack on the minimum wage during this period, the general practice was not to abolish the instrument, but rather to reduce the real level of the minimum wage through adjustments below the rate of inflation. For example, the United States did not adjust the nominal level of the minimum wage during the Reagan years. The same happened in Argentina during the "convertibility plan" (1992–2001), which fixed the exchange rate of the peso to the US dollar at parity. The minimum wage was maintained constant in nominal terms for almost ten years, as part of a strategy that assumed that wage flexibility could compensate for an overvalued local currency. In the case of Argentina, of course, the main result was to drive the economy into deep crisis.

One country that went against this general trend and decided to dismantle the minimum wage fixing system in the 1980s was the United Kingdom, in line with Margaret Thatcher's radical position in favour of liberalization of the economy. The United Kingdom had a very long practice with Trade Boards (later called Wage Councils) that fixed minimum wage levels in specific industries. In order to abolish them, the British Government decided that it should denounce Convention No. 26 which "as drafted lacks flexibility and therefore limits the Government's freedom of action in an area of vital public concern".[98] This was a long process, full of informal and formal exchanges, including a discussion between the Director-General of the ILO, Francis Blanchard, and Prime Minister Thatcher. The British Government considered, in particular, that minimum wages damaged job prospects for young workers. This view was highly debatable, and not supported by either British employers (the Confederation of British Industry) or workers (the Trades Union Congress). Nevertheless, the Thatcher Government went ahead and denounced the Convention, and subsequently also denounced Convention No. 99 (concerned with minimum wages in agriculture). The Government considered that the Convention's provisions were inappropriate for the United Kingdom and statutory control of pay was "inconsistent with its commitment to deregulation".[99]

In the late 1990s, under a Labour Party Government, the United Kingdom reintroduced a minimum wage. In July 1997, the Government appointed a Low Pay Commission, in order to analyse the introduction of a national minimum wage and its level. A year later this Commission presented its report, recommending

---

[98] *Financial Times* (London), 22 Mar. 1985.
[99] Letter to the ILO denouncing Conventions Nos. 99 and 101, 15 August 1994. ILO Archives, Standards Department.

the level at which the national minimum wage should be introduced, and how it should apply to young workers (which remained a concern).[100] The reintroduction of a minimum wage in the only country that had openly rejected it for the sake of flexibility is already a strong indication of the considerable value of this institution as an instrument for labour protection. After a long experience of labour market deregulation, there was a perceived need to reinstate some basic floors. This process also highlights the political nature of discussions on minimum wages.

What is striking in this case is that even after the reintroduction of the minimum wage, the Labour Government did not consider the possibility of ratifying any of the ILO minimum wage fixing Conventions, showing that there was a fundamental change of perspective. The report of the Low Pay Commission gives no indication that ILO Conventions were taken into account, and this was confirmed by a number of Commissioners who were consulted personally.[101] This could be taken as an indication that ILO standards were not perceived to be of much relevance to the United Kingdom towards the end of the twentieth century, or it might reflect the loss of importance of wage standards in comparison with others.

## Conclusions

The ILO played a significant role in building the framework for minimum wage policy and supporting its extension up to the early 1970s. Thereafter, the wage issue became marginalized, partly because of a decline in internal priority, and partly because of the shift in the dominant economic paradigm. Action by the ILO on wages did not cease, but it lost visibility. In the new debates in the 1990s on globalization and on fundamental principles and rights, wages did not return to the agenda.

The situation now seems to be starting to change. At the beginning of the twenty-first century, more than 90 per cent of countries have a minimum wage, making this one of the most extensively applied labour policies – and more countries are asking the Office for information and guidance.[102] There remains considerable scope for building a better understanding of the role of minimum wage

---

[100] *The National Minimum Wage: First report of the Low Wage Commission* (London, HMSO, June 1998).

[101] Personal communication between Andrés Marinakis (ILO) and John Cridland, William Brown and David Metcalf, all members of the Low Wage Commission at the time.

[102] For example, in East Asia alone, there have been recent requests for ILO expertise in this area from Cambodia, Hong Kong (China), Laos, Malaysia, Mongolia and Viet Nam (information from ILO Regional Office, Bangkok).

policy in the distributional goals of economic development strategy, and in poverty reduction. In recent years, there has an effort to rebuild the ILO's capacity on wage issues, but for the time being it is modest in scale.[103] With the turn of the tide back towards better regulation of market forces, the ILO has an opportunity to recover its earlier pre-eminence in this field.

## The challenges ahead

There is much evidence above of the impact of the ILO's work on the quality of employment, including some notable successes. Four general comments are worth making.

First, there has been a heavy reliance on standards and codes of practice. There are widespread indications that ILO standards have had a significant influence on national law and practice. As we have seen in the case of working time, there is substantial convergence around the basic ideas found in the ILO's international instruments. In other words, at least at the level of the legislative framework, there is increasing international agreement on the nature and extent of protection that should be provided to workers.

Nevertheless, the obvious risk of this strategy is to end up with well-designed instruments that are not applied in practice. Many of the codes and frameworks require a high-productivity, formal environment if they are to be fully implemented. These instruments can help to build such an environment, of course. But there is an urgent need to improve the quality of work in situations where formal standards are less effective or too costly, and that involves understanding the underlying economic mechanisms and incentives, and intervening in ways which make better jobs economically viable.

Second, in general, the research effort in this area has been uneven, both across subjects and over time, and this obviously weakens the impact of the ILO's ideas. It is clear that with so many subjects competing for resources within the ILO, major research programmes would be difficult to mount in all the areas discussed here. But more use could certainly be made of external networks. In recent years, there has been some revival in research on conditions and duration of work – and this needs to be sustained.

---

[103] However, a new regular publication on the topic has recently been launched. See ILO: *Global Wage Report 2008/09* (Geneva, 2008).

Third, the ILO's focus has always been on protection, risk and vulnerability. Yet there is also an appealing agenda to be developed on the positive dimensions of the quality of work – creativity, engagement, social inclusion, participation, fulfilment. And these are all issues which fit well into a broader concept of decent work, but which have received little attention in the ILO's work. The beginnings of an economic literature on "happiness" is a reminder that it is necessary to take into account a wider range of human goals.

Fourth, the fragmentation of the ILO's work into different, unconnected streams has been a source of weakness in the past. A better integration between the quality and quantity of work would be desirable. We shall return to that question in Chapter 6.

# Social protection[1] **4**

## Social protection for all?

It is estimated by the ILO that today only 20 per cent of the population world-wide enjoys adequate social protection. Paradoxically, the lack of coverage is especially concentrated where it is most needed. While in most of the industrialized world the rate of coverage is high, in sub-Saharan Africa and South Asia only a small fraction of the active population – in many countries in these regions only 5 to 10 per cent – has access to formal social security.[2] This is striking and inevitably raises questions about the effectiveness of both national and international social security policies.

The ILO is one of the few international organizations that has actively promoted social protection for all members of society since its creation in 1919. Social protection is now a much wider concept than it was in the early days. In current ILO terminology, it includes social security as well as conditions of work, occupational safety, migration and HIV/AIDS policies. In this chapter we shall mainly focus on social security (and social insurance in the early decades) as a means

---

[1] The principal author of this chapter is Jasmien Van Daele. Three articles provided key information for this chapter: S. Kott: *De l'assurance à la sécurité sociale (1919–1949): L'OIT comme acteur international*, paper prepared for the ILO Century Project, 2008, available at: http://www.ilocentury.org; E. Reynaud: "Social security for all: Global trends and challenges", in *Comparative Labor Law and Policy Journal* (2006), Vol. 27, pp. 123–150; J. Seekings: *The ILO and social protection in the Global South, 1919–2005*, paper prepared for the ILO Century Project, 2008, available at: http://www.ilocentury.org. With thanks to Véronique Plata for research assistance in the preparation of this chapter.

[2] W. van Ginneken: *Extending social security: Policies for developing countries*, Working paper No. 13 (Geneva, ILO, Social Security Policy and Development Branch, 2003), p. 7.

of ensuring income security in the face of various contingencies.[3] By creating a "social shield" against economic insecurity and hardship through the redistribution of income, social security has, from the beginning, been an essential part of the road to social justice for the ILO.

Over the years, both the objectives and the methods of the ILO to secure income security have changed in order to keep pace with transformations in both industrial(izing) societies and developing countries. We shall examine the changing role and influence of the ILO on the development of social security from a global perspective. Throughout its history, the ILO has been faced with the problem of the "global coverage", that is, coverage "for all", of income protection. The differences between the needs and capacities of the developed, industrialized world and the less developed countries have raised specific issues and problems in the field of social security. How has the ILO responded to these challenges? What type of social security models has it promoted (and why) and how effective have these been? This chapter does not try to give a full history. It reviews the role of the ILO in promoting income protection, from social insurance to social security, by tracing those key issues that reflect the ILO's long-standing values and principles and that have been at the centre of the debate throughout successive phases of its existence.

## The ILO social insurance model between the wars

In less than fifty years social insurance has conquered Europe
and is well on the way to conquering the world.[4]
(ILO, 1931)

The development of social protection is closely related to the history of industrial and capitalist societies, at least in its earliest decades. The modern welfare state has its origins in the nineteenth century "social question" (see Chapter 1), when the political elite became increasingly aware of the need for protective legislation to remedy the worst social evils of industrialization. This gave birth to a new concept of the state's social function: first, the incapacity to earn a living was recognized as a public responsibility; and second, it was no longer (solely) left to the workers

---

[3] For concepts of income security, see ILO: *World Labour Report 2000: Income security and social protection in a changing world* (Geneva, ILO, 2000), pp. 22–24.

[4] ILO: *The International Labour Organisation: The first decade* (London, George Allen and Unwin, 1931), p. 147.

to choose whether they would protect themselves against the most flagrant social risks. The state was now considered to be responsible for providing a minimum level of social protection for its community – although this was still very modest both in terms of benefits and categories of workers.

Germany, in particular, was a pioneer and leading exponent in this shift in thinking on social protection. Under Chancellor Bismarck, social Catholic state officials developed the first large-scale social insurance laws. In less than seven years, between 1883 and 1889, a national package of insurance against sickness, old age, invalidity and industrial accidents was put in place. The German Government tended to use social legislation as a means of "social imperialism". By providing economic security in the event of major risks and loss of income, the authorities hoped to integrate and bind the working class to the German nation-state, unified in 1871. Ultimately, social insurance was designed to guarantee the political stability of a young nation.

The first national legislation in Bismarck's Germany stimulated the creation of welfare policies in other European countries, notably the former Austro-Hungarian Empire, and later on also the Scandinavian countries. The diffusion process involved a complex reworking of external models to fit local and national circumstances rather than blind imitation. This was a process that took time. Before the First World War, relatively few states had social insurance schemes; these were limited in coverage and included only certain categories of workers (coalminers and railwaymen, for instance), especially those which were reasonably well organized.[5] In general, the economically weakest workers did not receive effective protection.

The First World War accelerated the development of social insurance because it brought about a considerable increase in pension, health, housing and rehabilitation demands. Politicians, bureaucrats and taxpayers were confronted with higher levels of public expenditure that necessitated new forms of government control and administration. At the international level, the ILO was one of the post-war institutional innovations concerned with promoting income protection.

In the first years of its existence the ILO's concrete output in the field of social insurance was "hesitating and uncertain", as stated by Albert Thomas in his report to the International Labour Conference in 1926.[6]

---

[5] For a general overview of the pre-war history of social insurance, see for example S. Kott, 2008, op. cit., pp. 4–6.

[6] ILO: *Report of the Director-General*, International Labour Conference, 8th Session, Geneva, 1926, p. 361.

Although the Preamble to the ILO Constitution in 1919 referred to "the protection of the worker against sickness, disease and injury, arising out of his employment" and "provision for old age and injury", as a means of establishing social justice, the nine General Principles which were to guide the ILO's work (see Chapter 1 and Appendix II) did not include income protection. After discussion in the Labour Commission at the Paris Peace Conference, the organization of voluntary insurance organizations was removed from the first draft of the General Principles. For reasons of political pragmatism and viability, the Commission agreed on a "minimum programme" of principles, on which there was already general agreement, in order to get it approved by the plenary Peace Conference.[7] The fact that Germany, Europe's most advanced country in terms of social insurance, was excluded from the 1919 peace talks, also explains why the issue was not incorporated in the General Principles.

In the international context of economic and monetary crises during the immediate post-war years, the ILO gave priority to working time regulation and other aspects of working conditions (see Chapter 3). Social protection was addressed at an early stage, but not very systematically or as part of a substantive long-term programme. Between 1919 and 1924, three partial problems of social insurance were treated in different Conventions and Recommendations: the extension of national social insurance to foreign workers; the extension to agricultural workers (which was initially strongly opposed by the French Government); and the provision of unemployment and maternity benefits. These instruments were mainly the product of immediate circumstances. The most obvious example was the Unemployment Convention No. 2 and Recommendation No. 1 of 1919 (see also Chapter 5), in the wake of post-war demobilization. In general, these early measures did not specify precise methods, the amount of the benefit or the distribution of costs; nor did they cover all risks or all categories of workers. No doubt this lack of detail had advantages, especially in questions that were hardly ripe for international codification immediately after the war.

By the mid-1920s, ILO policy on social insurance accelerated, reflecting a fast growing interest in the subject throughout much of the world. During and immediately after the war, social insurance in many countries had passed through serious crises. The rise in the cost of living, not always followed by a rise in wages, had reduced the efficiency of existing social insurance schemes. Pushed by a growing labour movement that was reinforced after the war, major reforms and legislative innovation were driven by national governments in various member States.

---

[7] For the debate in the Commission on International Labour Legislation, see J. Van Daele: "Engineering social peace: Networks, ideas, and the founding of the International Labour Organization", in *International Review of Social History* (Cambridge University Press, 2005), Vol. 50, No. 3, pp. 460–462.

After preparatory research by the Office, a systematic plan of social insurance was mapped out by the International Labour Conference in 1925. The standards developed between the wars had one common characteristic: they did not cover (yet) the whole population, but only specific sectors and categories of workers (industry, agriculture, migrant or maritime workers). Each standard covered a specific risk.

In a first phase, between 1925 and 1927, sickness insurance was identified as a first major priority – apart from industrial accidents. It was the branch involving the largest expenditure, and put the heaviest burden on production costs. In the first decade, the dominant ILO rationale for international action on social protection was the motive of economic competition. In 1925 the ILO's social insurance experts wrote in an *International Labour Review* article:

> Thus arises in the field of international competition a positively immoral inequality between states which have tried to protect their workers by insurance and those which, whether from parsimony or mere inertia, have done nothing of the kind. And there is no small danger that the inaction of some states may arrest the progress of those which are more advanced in ... systems of insurance.[8]

The ILO was slow to follow up its 1927 Sickness Insurance Conventions (Nos. 24 and 25, for industry and agriculture) with similar standards on other social risks. By the end of the 1920s, the ILO went through a period of introspection, reassessing its role in the face of the disappointingly slow rate of ratification of its Conventions (see also Chapter 3).

A new round of work on social insurance finally emerged during the 1930s, at a time when all national states were facing the consequences of the Great Depression. In a second phase, between 1932 and 1934, ILO standards dealt with old age, invalidity, unemployment and survivors' insurance (widows and orphans), both in industry and agriculture. This renewed enthusiasm for the expansion of social insurance in the early 1930s reflected three concerns. First, state and other elites became increasingly concerned about the growth of social expenditure. Broadly speaking, between 1920 and 1940, social insurance expenditure in Western Europe more than doubled.[9] Contributory schemes (see box 4 on page 145) were therefore seen as good strategy in order to raise revenues. Second, the politics of welfare shifted. In the cases of Germany and Denmark, social welfare reforms had been introduced

---

[8] ILO: "The ILO and social insurance", in *International Labour Review* (ILO, 1925), Vol. 11, No. 6, p. 764.

[9] P. Flora and A.J. Heidenheimer: *Development of welfare states in Europe and America* (New Brunswick, Transaction Books, 1981), p. 85.

by right-wing parties in the face of ambivalence or even opposition from the left. But in the 1920s, social-democratic parties made welfare a central component of their programmes. The left became the primary defender of a role of the state in welfare programmes. Third, and most importantly, a diverse scheme of social insurance was part of the governments' response to the worldwide economic crisis of the 1930s. The economic depression sharpened demands for income support during, and as a consequence of, periods of mass unemployment.

In promoting the compulsory contributory social insurance model in the interwar period, the ILO was not a trendsetter. It did not 'invent' this model, but reinforced and diffused basic principles that were already conceived and consolidated in national practices on an international scale. In fact, what the ILO promoted in its interwar standards mirrored exactly the structure of the German scheme.[10] This was no coincidence.

First of all, there were close contacts between Geneva and Germany that allowed for a direct exchange of knowledge and expertise. German delegates occupied crucial mandates in the work of the International Labour Conference. For instance, the German Government delegate, Andreas Grieser, chaired the Conference committee that prepared the draft Conventions on social insurance in the 1920s and early 1930s.[11] Grieser, Director of the Social Insurance Department of the German Ministry of Labour, also played an important role in the preparation of ILO social insurance standards as a member, from 1925 onwards, of the Correspondence Committee on Social Insurance. This ILO committee was established in 1922 as a 'reservoir' of technical experts, mostly high-level administrators and university professors (such as William Beveridge, Director of the London School of Economics and architect of the British post-1945 social security system[12]). These experts were recruited, on the basis of their competence, to advise ILO officials on technical issues and problems related to social insurance. Because of their pioneering expertise in social insurance, German specialists were very well represented on the ILO committee.[13]

---

[10] A remarkable detail illustrates the close connection between the German and ILO models. In 1981, the ILO's Social Security Department published a history of the ILO and social insurance, exactly one hundred years after the first German legislation on insurance. G. Tamburi: *The International Labour Organisation and the development of social insurance* (Geneva, ILO, 1981), p. 3.

[11] Andreas Grieser was President of the ILO Conference Committee on Social Insurance in 1925, 1927, 1929 and 1932.

[12] William Beveridge was a member of the ILO committee in 1925.

[13] In 1930, five of the 25 experts were German. See S. Kott: *Albert Thomas, l'Allemagne et l'OIT (1919–1933): Dénationaliser les politiques sociales?*, draft paper, Geneva, 2008; S. Kott: "Une 'communauté épistémique' du social? Experts de l'OIT et internationalisation des politiques sociales dans l'entre-deux-guerres", in *Génèses, sciences sociales et histoire* (Paris, Berlin, 2008), No. 71, pp. 26–46.

## Box 4 Social insurance versus social assistance

In the interwar period, the ILO promoted a particular model of social insurance. This was the compulsory contributory insurance scheme.

First, instead of the voluntary principle that had characterized the earliest forms of social insurance before the First World War, the ILO promoted a compulsory scheme from the beginning. The goal was to include as many wage-earners as possible. There was also a growing tendency to replace the voluntary principle with compulsory provisions within national insurance programmes.

Second, ILO standards prescribed that social insurance should be financed by contributions from employers and workers, sharing the social and financial responsibility for risks related to the loss of normal income. In its contributory model, the ILO thus concentrated primarily on private responsibility. The standards in the 1920s made no specific provisions for the public authorities; the ILO left it open to national laws or regulations to decide as to a financial contribution by the government. This changed during the 1930s, when the Depression triggered a more interventionist form of government participation. Then the ILO made more explicit reference to the role of public authorities in its social insurance standards.

Finally, in line with ILO standards, social insurance had – unlike private insurance companies – to be managed by self-governed institutions of the social partners under the administrative supervision of public authorities without any motive of profit. But, as no further conditions were prescribed in the early standards, the ILO stayed rather vague on the actual management of social insurance.

A minority group at the International Labour Conferences (and in its committees) defended a different type of income protection, namely social assistance. Social assistance was non-contributory and redistributive. General taxes, either local or national, were used to finance the various programmes providing fixed benefits to overcome social risks and to guarantee basic income security. Social assistance was based on the rights of all citizens, rather than of workers only. The right to benefits was linked to the membership of the community that was responsible for funding and managing the provision of benefits.

Scandinavian countries, Great Britain (and its colonies and dominions) and Switzerland favoured, each for different reasons, non-contributory schemes of social assistance rather than social insurance. Before 1919, some English-speaking countries had already introduced non-contributory schemes financed from public funds, going back to the long tradition of mutual aid or friendly societies. The Scandinavian countries, not yet widely industrialized, considered worker-based social insurance not applicable to a dispersed and mainly agricultural population. Agrarian workers were, after all, excluded in the social insurance standards developed by the ILO and Germany. And in Switzerland, compulsory contributory social insurance was blocked by the private insurance companies.

Over the course of time, the two models, contributory social insurance and non-contributory social assistance, would be combined in many countries.

The background, work and contacts of the permanent ILO officials in the Social Insurance Department also explain why the German model of social insurance was so prominent in the ILO. The Czech Oswald Stein, for example, joined the Department in 1922 and became its head in 1937. As a former, highly qualified government official in Prague and Vienna with a respected academic background in Central and Eastern Europe, he succeeded in developing close relations with social insurance departments and officials from the former Austro-Hungarian Empire and Germany. Stein was one of the driving forces behind the creation, in 1927, and the management of the International Conference of National Unions of Mutual Benefit Societies and Sickness Insurance Funds, an international association of insurance practitioners and experts promoting the development of social legislation. In 1947 this association became the International Social Security Association (ISSA).[14] All these international contacts and networks were important channels for the transmission of information and expertise on social insurance, modelled after the German scheme.

Second, the ILO favoured the German model because of its inherent focus on the concerns of workers and worker solidarity. Indeed, the reformist labour movement in Germany had supported compulsory contributory self-managed insurance since the end of the nineteenth century. Defended by the Germans, this type of insurance had become part, since the Amsterdam Congress in 1904, of the programme of the Second Socialist International. And the International Federation of Trade Unions prioritized this model in its first post-war conference in 1919. The political and trade union representatives backed this model of social insurance because the principle that the social partners should participate in the administration contributed substantially to the growth of the reformist labour movement. For the ILO, involving the three social partners closely corresponded to its tripartite structure and its institutional preference for collaboration between employers, workers and the state.

How effective was the ILO in the 'internationalization' of its preferred social insurance model? The real impact of the social insurance standards was relatively limited. They were not widely ratified, especially the survivors', invalidity and old-age insurance Conventions (1933–34). During the crisis years of the 1930s, ILO member States were generally not very keen on international commitments. This was especially true for member States outside Europe and Latin America. Within Europe, not surprisingly, Germany was the first country that ratified the

---

[14] On the history of the International Social Security Association (ISSA), see C. Guinand: "The creation of the ISSA and the ILO", in *International Social Security Review* (ISSA, 2008), Vol. 61, No. 1, pp. 81–98.

Convention on Sickness Insurance (Industry), 1927 (No. 24). In the case of Latin America, a small group of countries ratified most of the social insurance Conventions. Convention No. 24, for instance, was ratified prior to 1945 by Chile (1931), Colombia and Uruguay (1933), Nicaragua (1934) and Peru (1945). But Chile, Uruguay and Argentina, the pioneers in Latin American welfare state building, had already established embryonic social insurance systems early on, without much or any ILO involvement.

The social insurance Conventions were ratified by few ILO member States in the Anglo-Saxon world, Asia and Africa. The Indian Government, for example, decided against ratifying any of the 1927 Conventions and later also voted against the 1933 Conventions, a position which was not surprising since it coincided with that of the colonial power, Great Britain.[15] The opposition or indifference of the less industrialized countries to the international social insurance Conventions was an important cause of low overall ratification rates.[16] This may be attributed to special reasons that were rooted in the ILO identity of that time. During the interwar period, the ILO was a rather Eurocentric organization, mainly concerned with improving working conditions in industrialized countries.

In addition, changes in the international environment help to explain the limited impact of its social insurance standards. The dominant German model had seriously lost ground by the mid-1930s after Germany had left the ILO in 1933 (see Chapter 1). In the absence of German experts and delegates, there was more space for other social protection models that were on the rise at the time. In 1935, when Germany's membership officially ceased, the United States attended its first International Labour Conference as a new ILO member. Now that the strong influence of Germany had gone, the context of the ILO's work was entirely changed. A long-term state tradition in social insurance was totally absent in the United States. The isolationist position of the American Federation of Labor (AFL), which refused to join the International Federation of Trade Unions, implied that there was less support for the development of international regulation of social insurance schemes from within the United States. The entry of the United States into the ILO, however, was part of a broader national strategy to deal with the consequences of the worldwide Depression. In the context of Roosevelt's New Deal programme, a Social Security Act was elaborated in 1935. This Act was the first in the world to juxtapose these two words. But its legislative

---

[15] ILO: *Report of the Director-General*, International Labour Conference, 12th Session, Geneva, 1929, p. 170.
[16] Although Europe accounted for just less than half of the members of the ILO by 1931, it accounted for seven out of every eight ratifications of Conventions.

work was elaborated without taking into account any of the ILO standards. For instance, the Social Security Act did not foresee any sickness insurance, and the establishment of unemployment insurance was considered the responsibility of the different states of the United States.

We can reasonably conclude that the direct impact of ILO standards on national social insurance policies was limited, but standards were not the only means at the ILO's disposal. From its creation onwards, the Office made great efforts to become an international point of reference for research and expertise in this field, as in others. There were two main elements in the strategy.

First, information on very diverse social insurance schemes in many countries was collected and disseminated, and this work was reflected in numerous reports and international surveys – thereby facilitating the access of national labour administration officials and policy-makers to foreign experiences and data in an international comparative framework. For example, between 1924 and 1928, the ILO provided South African officials with extensive information on old-age pensions, unemployment and sickness insurance schemes across the world to help them in the preparation of South African legislation.[17]

The accumulation of all this information also served as a basis for the research activities of the Office itself. In the 1920s, a special research series on social insurance was launched as part of the *Studies and Reports* series.[18] In the *International Labour Review*, articles on very varied topics related to social insurance took off seriously around 1925, when a first set of social insurance Conventions was in the pipeline for the work of the International Labour Conference.[19] Generally speaking, the ILO's research work was to have a direct relationship with (and was consequently of direct use to) social insurance institutions and experts in the member States. Publications were therefore quite often country case studies.

---

[17] In one of its reports, a South African Government commission acknowledged that: "The International Labour Office at Geneva has been instrumental in collecting and collating much information and has published a large number of books and pamphlets on various aspects of the subject. These publications are a mine of valuable information. The issue of such books goes far to prove that the International Labour Office is amply fulfilling the first function for which it was created, viz., the collection and dissemination of information on industrial conditions and industrial legislation. At the 1927 Convention the delegates were furnished with a work in six volumes on Compulsory Sickness Insurance which deals in great detail with the schemes already in existence. This work and the other publications referred to have been of great assistance to us in our investigations." J. Seekings, op. cit., p. 18.

[18] ILO: *General problems of social insurance* (Geneva, ILO, 1925), Studies and Reports, Series M (Social Insurance), No. 1.

[19] For example, ILO: "The ILO and social insurance", in *International Labour Review* (Geneva, ILO, 1925), Vol. 11, No. 6, pp. 763–783; ILO: "The present tendencies of compulsory sickness insurance", in *International Labour Review* (Geneva, ILO, 1927), Vol. 15, No. 6, pp. 842–859; A. Tixier: "Sickness insurance at the International Labour Conference", in *International Labour Review* (Geneva, ILO, 1927), Vol. 16, pp. 773–803.

Second, ILO technical staff of the Social Insurance Department – well equipped with all this expertise – was put directly at the disposal of national governments. The organization of contact missions in the member States and the regions was part of this strategy. It was no coincidence that the ILO tried to broaden its mandate through operational activities in the 1930s, in the context of a declining impact of ILO standard-setting activities.

In 1930, the chief of the Social Insurance Department, Adrien Tixier, carried out the first technical cooperation mission in the history of the ILO. The Greek Prime Minister Venizelos wanted to introduce full-scale social insurance in Greece and had asked the ILO for assistance. However, due to basic problems – such as the lack of adequate statistics and trained officials and the fact that it was the beginning of the economic crisis – Tixier got no further than making recommendations for a general inquiry.

In 1935, when the United States was preparing its Social Security Act, the ILO's Social Insurance Department provided advice on how to set up the necessary administrative systems. John G. Winant, who had resigned as Assistant-Director from the ILO to become Chairman of the American Social Security Board (and who would return in 1938 to the ILO as the new Director), invited Adrien Tixier to the United States. Winant's view was that, for reasons of national prestige, a government should rather address itself to an international organization, of which it was a member, than a foreign government.[20] The ILO was for Winant, as a former high official of the Organization, a logical choice. And for Tixier it was obvious that it was in the ILO's main interest to strengthen its relations with the United States as a new member State by supplying technical expertise and advice. This was even more important, as mentioned earlier, because the American social security legislation did not take into account ILO standards.

From the 1930s onwards, the ILO played a growing role through its regional approach – more specifically by its support to regional conferences. The first conference of this kind was held in January 1936 in Santiago, and brought together the American member States in an attempt to pay greater attention to the special conditions in the region. The growing concern of the ILO for a regional approach was in part a strategy to counter its loss of influence, due to the crisis, in Europe. And for Chile, as the only country in all the Americas that already had compulsory insurance covering all risks and all workers (including agricultural), requesting the ILO's assistance was a strategy to defend this insurance, which was under attack from both the right and the extreme left on the Latin American continent.

---

[20] Mission report Adrien Tixier to the United States, 14 November 1935, ILO Archives, *SI 2/61/3*; Correspondence between John Winant and Adrien Tixier, ILO Archives, *XT 86/3/1*.

When discussing the applicability of the ILO social insurance model by adapting it to the regional specificities and acknowledging the problems caused by scattered, heterogeneous and non-industrial populations, the American member States were not always on the same page. For instance, while the Chilean Government delegation to the Committee on Social Insurance defended three types of capital accumulation (collective accumulation, individual accumulation and a mixture of the two), the Uruguay Worker delegate wanted to see the system of individual accumulation abolished; after all, "it is ironical to think of States talking about social protection when all the time it is really the worker who is contributing the capital for the insurance system".[21] The proposal of the Chilean Government was, however, accepted. As a follow-up to the Santiago Conference, a second International Labour Conference of American countries was held in Havana at the end of 1939. These conferences were important in the early days of the ILO's technical cooperation activities which would really take off after the Second World War.

## From social insurance to social security: The war as a transition period

The motive of our life should be social security[22]
(Ernest Bevin, British Minister of Labour, 1940)

The Second World War was a crucial period of transition for the global landscape of welfare reform. Just like the First World War, it triggered fundamental changes in social and economic life and its underlying paradigms, articulating a vision of a just and democratic post-war world. During the Second World War, the ILO shifted away from its traditional discourse on social insurance to a more integrated concept of universal social security. In 1941, Oswald Stein, chief of the ILO's Social Insurance Department, wrote: "A few years ago social security was little more than a slogan, a bare outline of an idea; today the slogan stands for a wide-visioned, constructive programme; and tomorrow the programme will have become an accomplished fact if humanity remains free and follows the road of progress."[23] Apart from Stein's article "Building social security", other key ILO

---

[21] ILO: *Record of Proceedings*, International Labour Conference of American States which are Members of the International Labour Organisation, Santiago (Chile), 2–14 January 1936, p. 149.

[22] O. Stein: "Building social security", in *International Labour Review* (Geneva, ILO, 1941), Vol. 44, No. 3, p. 248, citing *The Manchester Guardian*, 21 Nov. 1941.

[23] Ibid., p. 247.

publications in this field came out with titles such as "A new structure of social security" and "Approaches to social security".[24] This shift in ILO thinking was not only a consequence of an upsurge in new ideas in the quest for social justice during the war. It was also a reflection of a shift of power within the ILO.

The ILO's leaning towards the Anglo-Saxon world, initiated by the withdrawal of Germany in the mid-1930s, was intensified during the Second World War. With the evacuation of the Office from neutral Switzerland to Canada, the Organization openly chose the side of the Western Allies in their fight against authoritarian regimes. Based in Montreal, the ILO became especially dependent on the two leading nations that were organizing a new post-war world order, the United States and Great Britain – also the main funders of the Organization in war-time.[25] Due to the absence of a powerful international trade union movement that was seriously weakened in the war, the ILO had lost one of its strongest defenders. Consequently, the ILO was even more dependent on the governments of the major Allied powers. In this context, the ILO became gradually in tune with the thinking amongst the Western Allies, led by the United States and Great Britain.

On 5 November 1941, the International Labour Conference adopted a resolution committing the Organization to support the Atlantic Charter (see Chapter 2).[26] In the spirit of this agreement, the ILO Director Edward Phelan addressed the Conference: "We now recognise that social security is, like political security, indivisible and that the two are inseparable."[27] Phelan used the concept of social security in very broad terms as a guideline for future ILO policy, while referring to social insurance as the ILO's preferred model in the interwar period: "Social insurance has now become an integral part of the structure of society. It not only affords basic protection for the *citizen*, but it furnishes dividends in physical vigour, morale, and enjoyment to the *individual*, and in productive capacity and wealth to the community to which he belongs. Moreover, the reciprocal ties of responsibility which it involves contribute powerfully to social solidarity."[28]

---

[24] "'A new structure of social security': The work of the Inter-American Conference on Social Security at Santiago de Chile", in *International Labour Review* (Geneva, ILO, 1942), Vol. 46, No. 6, pp. 661–669; ILO: *Approaches to social security: An international survey* (Montreal, ILO, 1942), Studies and Reports, Series M (Social Insurance), No. 18.

[25] These two member States provided approximately one third of the total ILO budget.

[26] ILO: *Record of Proceedings*, International Labour Conference, Special Session, New York, 1941, pp. 142–143 and Appendix I (2), Resolution endorsing the Atlantic Charter, pp. 163–164.

[27] ILO: *The ILO and reconstruction*, Report of the Director-General, International Labour Conference, Special Session, New York, 1941, p. 98.

[28] Ibid., p. 48. Own emphasis.

The combined approach of social insurance and social security by Phelan in his address to the International Labour Conference characterized the ILO's policy position during the war. The compulsory contributory model promoted by the ILO in previous decades was still maintained, and the tripartite management principle of social insurance schemes reaffirmed, very much in line with the ILO's own identity of tripartism as a means to social democracy. In his *International Labour Review* article of 1941 Oswald Stein concluded: "Social insurance can and must remain an institution for civic education, the image and instrument of democracy in action."[29] But although the "old" strategy of social insurance was still defended, social assistance was no longer seen as being inherently inferior – in sharp contrast to the interwar period, when social insurance was clearly given priority over the principle of social assistance. The ILO tried to reconcile the two strategies: "Both approaches are needed in a complete programme of social security."[30] This attitude started to underpin not only the Organization's research work, but also its operational activities.

The Office became increasingly involved in technical assistance initiatives on social security on the American continent. This was nothing new, as the ILO had already made efforts to set up regional conferences and technical missions in this area in the 1930s. During the war, however, these efforts had been intensified. Housed in Canada, the Office was in much closer contact with the Americas than it had been in Europe. The ILO's social insurance experts travelled to Argentina, Bolivia, Brazil and Uruguay in an endeavour to improve labour statistics. In mid-1942, the Chilean Government asked for ILO assistance to reorganize its social insurance scheme. Requests from Latin American Governments to help strengthen their social insurance institutions provided ILO officials with great opportunities to transfer and diffuse their knowledge and experiences as widely as possible; but this work also constituted a crucial part of the ILO's broader strategy to reinforce its legitimacy during the war, as its standard-setting activities ground to a halt.

With the help of the ILO, the growing concern with social welfare issues in Latin America led to the formation of a specialist body. First, in 1940, the Peruvian Government and the ILO established the Inter-American Committee to Promote Social Security in Lima as a joint initiative. Then, in September 1942, the first Inter-American Conference on Social Security was held in Santiago at the invitation of Salvador Allende, Chilean minister of Public Health, Social Insurance and Assistance (1938–41); at the time of the Conference, he was Vice-Chairman

---

[29] O. Stein, 1941, op. cit., p. 274.
[30] ILO: *Approaches to social security*, 1942, op. cit.

of the Workers' Insurance Fund in Chile.[31] Together with his colleagues from Argentina, Peru and Mexico, Allende was one of the four Conference delegates who pushed through the Declaration of Santiago de Chile, which was in line with the ILO's main position on social security during the war. The declaration specified the connection between social and economic security, placed social insurance within the general framework of social security and confirmed the worldwide role of social security, conceived as an instrument of solidarity to all peoples in their pursuit of well-being.[32]

In practice, the primary mechanism to achieve this goal would still be social insurance. Rather than emphasizing individual rights and citizenship, the Santiago Conference stated that workers needed social insurance so as to maintain their productive contribution to national welfare. Indeed, as Allende had declared earlier to the ILO Governing Body, "social insurance was one of the best means of assuring the social stability of a country and protecting democracy against the dangers which menaced it. Social insurance ... guaranteed to the worker and his family the necessary stability and the necessary assurances as to the future, which were the only possible basis for the greatness of a nation and the only source of its prosperity in the long run".[33] It is hardly surprising that a model of social insurance, involving employers and workers in the management structure, was promoted. After all, this was the model on which Latin American social insurance schemes were built and which had been favoured by the ILO for many years.

As a follow-up to the Santiago Conference, a Permanent Inter-American Committee on Social Security was constituted in 1943. The ILO funded most of the secretariat's expenses, including the salary of the Secretary-General. As such, the ILO had a permanent counterpart in Latin America for the more Europe-centred International Social Insurance Conference, created in 1927 with the help of the ILO and based in Geneva.[34]

In 1943 the ILO made a more open and clear shift to social security when the ILO's Social Insurance Department started actively promoting the Beveridge

---

[31] On the role of Salvador Allende, see G. Fajardo Ortiz: "Importancia de Salvador Allende Gossens en la organización de la primera Conferencia Interamericana de Seguridad Social", in *Revista CIESS* (2004), No. 8, pp. 7–22. For Allende's letter of invitation, ILO: *Governing Body*, 89–90th Session, 1940–41, Annex B, p. 64.

[32] "'A new structure of social security'. The work of the First Inter-American Conference on Social Security at Santiago de Chile", in *International Labour Review* (Geneva, ILO, 1942), Vol. 46, No. 6, pp. 686–687.

[33] ILO: *Governing Body*, 89–90th Session, 1940–41, p. 15.

[34] The International Social Insurance Conference, renamed in 1936, was the former International Conference of National Unions of Mutual Benefit Societies and Sickness Insurance Funds and became in 1947 the International Social Security Association (ISSA) (see also footnote 14).

model. Its officials Oswald Stein (since 1942 also Assistant-Director of the ILO) and Maurice Stack had offered their services in the preparation of the Beveridge Report. In 1942, they travelled to London to give evidence before the British Interdepartmental Committee on Social Insurance and Allied Services, chaired by William Beveridge, and to put documentation on social insurance legislation and administration in different countries at the committee's disposal. The ILO's report *Approaches to social security: An international survey* served as crucial documentation for this consultation work by the ILO officials and it was partly incorporated in the appendices to the final Beveridge Report. In July 1943, William Beveridge and his advisers were invited in Montreal to discuss the technical details of the new British social security model with the ILO's social insurance experts, Director Edward Phelan, and the Chairman of the Governing Body, the American Carter Goodrich. The Beveridge model defined social security in terms of contributory benefit programmes financed out of public funds raised through progressive taxation. The central pillar was the principle of universal coverage, thereby extending social protection to all citizens in industrial societies.

The ILO's preference for this model of social security has to be seen in the light of the international political changes of the time. By 1943, it was becoming clear that the Central Powers would most probably lose the war. The Allied forces, led by Great Britain, the United States and the Soviet Union, were accelerating their post-war reconstruction plans. But, in the negotiations on the creation of a new, improved international body to succeed the League of Nations, which would later become the United Nations, there seemed to be no leading role for the ILO. The Workers' group in the Governing Body pushed the Office for more action.[35] By supporting and promoting a new model of social security that had been developed by one of the main leading Western Allies, the Office was clearly adopting a strategy to carve out a role for the ILO after the war.

The shift in ILO thinking to social security paved the way for the debates in the International Labour Conference of 1944 and the Declaration of Philadelphia. One of the objectives specified by the declaration was the extension of social security measures to provide a basic income to all in need of such protection and comprehensive medical care. This was sketched out in two Recommendations adopted by the Conference: the Income Security Recommendation (No. 67) and the Medical Care Recommendation (No. 69). Both instruments contained a direct

---

[35] In 1943, *The Manchester Guardian* published two articles by the Belgian trade unionist and spokesperson of the Workers' group in the ILO Governing Body, Jef Rens. In "A plea for more speed" (March 1943) and "The ILO: Why is it inactive?" (September 1943), Rens criticized the ILO's invisibility and lack of political weight on the international reconstruction plans.

reference to the fifth clause of the Atlantic Charter, and their guiding principles revealed the unmistakable influence of Beveridge – with an explicit emphasis on social security as a fundamental and universal right for all citizens. Technically, the Recommendations were based on an integrated approach of social insurance and assistance, and stated that income security should be organized as far as possible on the basis of compulsory social insurance. The range of risks against which working people should be insured was identified: sickness, maternity, invalidity, old age (or death of a breadwinner) and unemployment. Provision for needs not covered by compulsory social insurance were to be made by social assistance for "all persons who are in want", more specifically for certain categories of persons, particularly dependent children and needy invalids, aged persons and widows. This would later be represented by Guy Perrin, one of the ILO's social security experts, in terms of a "doctrine of social security", that sought to reconcile social insurance and social assistance "within a totally new framework"[36], looking forward to a new era and a new role for the ILO in the internationalization of social security in the second half of the twentieth century.

## The challenge of "universal" social security

Our tripartite delegation will go away as it came, filled with the desire to contribute to the advance of social security so that poverty and the threat of war may disappear, and a better world be achieved.[37]
(Chilean Workers' delegate to the International Labour Conference, 1952)

In 1945, the whole world changed – and with it the attitudes towards social welfare. The aftermath of the Second World War saw a rapid increase in the number of countries that introduced or extended social security measures. As part of their reconstruction efforts, they systematically made efforts to assure income protection for their citizens. The decades after the Second World War have been widely characterized as the "Golden Age". The emergence of the welfare state was possible in a context of unprecedented rapid economic growth that made a broad-based political consensus in favour of government intervention sustainable. The ILO's approach to social security in the context of the emerging welfare state is most

---

[36] G. Perrin: "Reflections on fifty years of social security", in *International Labour Review* (Geneva, ILO, 1969), Vol. 99, No. 3, p. 257.

[37] ILO: *Record of Proceedings*, International Labour Conference, 35th Session, Geneva, 1952, p. 308.

clearly demonstrated in the Convention on Minimum Standards of Social Security (No. 102), adopted in 1952. The concept of social security as developed in this Convention, and the problems related to its "universal" application, are emblematic of the ILO's role in the first decades after the Second World War.

Once the ILO's position in the new UN system had been established, work by the Office on social security started in earnest towards the end of the 1940s. In 1949, the seventh International Conference of Labour Statisticians noted that differences in the administration and financing of social security schemes made international comparisons of social charges extremely difficult, and requested ILO officials to resume and expand the studies on the cost of social security schemes. The Office responded by sending out a questionnaire to the member States, structured around the new concept of social security as laid down in the 1944 Declaration of Philadelphia. This was the start of preparatory research by the Office that would lead, very quickly, to a new Convention.

In 1952, the Convention on Minimum Standards of Social Security brought together the whole range of branches that had been dealt with in different standards of the interwar period. It identified a set of flexible, globally-applicable minimum standards for nine contingencies: medical care; sickness; unemployment; old-age; employment injury; maternity; invalidity; survivors; and family allowances (the latter was the only subject that had not yet been covered by an ILO Convention). For each of these, it fixed a minimum level of protection in terms of the population covered and the benefits guaranteed, together with common organizational and management principles. The Convention also laid down the principal methods of enlarging the scope of social security systems, on the basis of statistical criteria, by distinguishing three categories of protection: for employed persons; for the economically active population; and for all residents with means below a certain level.

The 1952 Convention – adopted ten years after the Beveridge Report had come out in the United Kingdom – was in tune with the view of social security that had emerged from the Second World War and the Declaration of Philadelphia: that everyone should be given income security through full employment and social security. By extending the coverage and scope of international protection to broader categories of persons, Convention No. 102 incorporated the idea that every human being had the right to social security. But this right to a minimum of social security became not only a cornerstone of ILO post-war policy. In 1948, the United Nations General Assembly included it among the rights proclaimed in the Universal Declaration of Human Rights, and in 1966 the International Covenant on Economic, Social and Cultural Rights recognized "the right of everyone to social security".

The general principles of the 1952 Convention set the tone for the ILO's social security policy in the following decades. In the 1960s, four new Conventions were adopted: equality of treatment in 1962;[38] employment injury benefits in 1964; invalidity, old-age and survivors' benefits in 1967; and medical care and sickness benefits in 1969.[39] The underlying concept of social security, however, was the same as that in the Convention of 1952. The purpose of the new Conventions was to bring the different pre-war social insurance Conventions into line with the one of 1952, whilst allowing sufficient flexibility to encourage countries to ratify them. The interwar social insurance standards were systematically revised with a view to raising substantially the minimum standards of the 1952 Convention, in order to reconfirm the right to social security.

The broad concept of social security in ILO standards was not only the outcome of the view expressed during the war. It was also due to the Organization's efforts to respond to the international developments of the time. The growing number of newly independent countries after decolonization brought with it the need to adapt programmes to the requirements of the new member States, almost all of which were poor developing countries, whilst still paying attention to the social problems of the industrialized world. The main dilemma of ILO Conventions on social security in this era was to define exact standards of basic protection likely to be internationally accepted, while taking into account the specific needs of developing countries. By stipulating in the 1952 Convention that countries had to cover at least three out of nine branches of social security,[40] the ILO tried to secure a minimum level of protection, setting "a standard which is not so low that it represents no advance at all and not so high that it is really impossible of attainment by a majority of countries".[41] The desire for a flexible instrument, compatible with a wide variety of concepts and levels of protection, also led to the abandonment of the model of administrative and financial organization laid down in pre-war Conventions.

The 1952 Convention was adopted by 123 votes for, 32 against and 22 abstentions. Nearly every Employer delegate voted against, after speaking against it in committee at almost every stage. They maintained that the standards stipulated were not minimal, and that if the Conference were to adopt anything, it should be

---

[38] For the equality of treatment of foreign and migrant workers regarding social security, see W.R. Böhning: *A brief account on the ILO and policies on international migration*, paper prepared for the ILO Century Project, 2008, draft available at: http://www.ilocentury.org

[39] See C. Guinand: *Die Internationale Arbeitsorganisation (ILO) und die soziale Sicherheit in Europa (1942–1969)* (Berne etc., Peter Lang, 2003).

[40] Including one of the following five: unemployment, old-age, employment injury, invalidity and survivors.

[41] ILO: *Record of Proceedings*, International Labour Conference, 35th Session, Geneva, 1952, p. 318.

another Recommendation and not a Convention. The Convention was largely supported by Workers' and Government delegates. The Workers felt that it did not go far enough. They had even pushed for a discussion of advanced standards of social security, complementing the minimum standards. But this issue had been rejected early on in the debates. For some Workers' delegates, mainly those of the South, the Convention's standards were set too high, and they abstained. This was the case for the workers of Argentina, Burma, Costa Rica, the Dominican Republic, Guatemala, Haïti, Indonesia, Peru, the Philippines, Venezuela and Viet Nam.[42]

It is thus hardly surprising that, although the Convention was designed with special provisions for developing countries, it was ratified by very few countries from the Global South.[43] There were, of course, few developing countries – in terms of independent States – when the 1952 Convention was adopted. But later on, after decolonization, there was no significant increase in the rate of ratifications.[44] Although Asia was fairly well represented at the 1952 Conference, particularly by the most populous countries, only Japan ratified Convention No. 102. But Japan was rather the prototype of an industrialized country. As of the end of 2008, the 1952 Convention was ratified by 29 European member States, including a new wave of ratifications in Eastern Europe after the collapse of communist regimes in 1990. Some countries made legal adjustments to bring national legislation in line with international provisions.[45]

The limited direct impact in the developing world had undeniably to do with the concept of social security involved. In the 1952 Convention, the ILO promoted a combined approach of social insurance and social assistance (including either targeted or universal schemes). But, in practice, it still favoured contributory social insurance. The underlying model of reference was the industrial worker in wage labour. It included partial exemptions for "underdeveloped countries", allowing

---

[42] Ibid., p. 409.

[43] G.M.J. Veldkamp: "A new dimension for international cooperation in social security", in *International Labour Review* (Geneva, ILO, 1969), Vol. 100, p. 135.

[44] Out of the newly independent countries in Africa, five ratified over the course of time (Democratic Republic of Congo, Libya, Mauritania, Niger and Senegal). In Latin America, six ratifications were registered after 1952 (Bolivia, Costa Rica, Ecuador, Mexico, Peru and Venezuela). However, a number of Latin American member States had already developed social insurance schemes decades ago.

[45] See, for instance, L. Riva-Sanseverino: "The influence of international labour Conventions on Italian labour legislation", in *International Labour Review* (Geneva, ILO, 1961), Vol. 83, No. 6, p. 596; G. Schnorr: "The influence of ILO standards on law and practice in the Federal Republic of Germany", in *International Labour Review* (Geneva, ILO, 1974), Vol. 110, No. 6, pp. 561–562; M. Cashell: "Influence on Irish law and practice of international labour standards", in *International Labour Review* (Geneva, ILO, 1972), Vol. 106, No. 1, p. 63; J. Albalate Lafita: "The influence of international labour Conventions on labour law and social change in Spain", in *International Labour Review* (Geneva, ILO, 1979), Vol. 118, No. 4, pp. 452–453; S. Lagergren: "The influence of ILO standards on Swedish law and practice", in *International Labour Review* (Geneva, ILO, 1986), Vol. 125, No. 5, p. 318.

for a period of transition, in which the proportion of the population covered was a minimum 50 per cent of the *industrial* workforce (rather than of the total workforce or population). This underpinned the idea that developing countries were expected to evolve through a progressive process of industrialization in which workers gradually became wage-earners and corresponding forms of protection were introduced – just as had occurred in the industrialized welfare states. As such, the 1952 Convention was a typical example of the ILO's belief in 'modernization' by industrialization and democratization (see Chapters 3 and 5): as peasants were transformed into workers, and productivity rose, poor countries would be able to afford more ambitious social policies, including social security programmes.

However, the hopes that the social security model established in the industrialized countries would gradually be extended to the developing countries did not materialize. In practice, the wage-earner model in ILO social security standards would not become as widespread as expected in the Global South – where, in most cases, the informal economy was becoming increasingly important. Unorganized workers outside formal employment (see Chapter 5) were excluded from the ILO's social security model which, based on a long-standing tradition of tripartite-managed social insurance with a prominent place for powerful trade unions, reached only a core group of workers with formal jobs (see Chapter 3). The lack of social security coverage in the informal sector has been a major challenge for the ILO ever since.

As earlier, the ILO's most direct and specific influence in the field of social protection did not revolve around the ratification of relevant Conventions. The post-war decades were a period of rapid expansion of ILO technical assistance, with respect to both social security – social insurance, in fact – and development. The ILO social security experts continued their efforts in Latin America. In 1956 and 1957, for instance, they carried out a series of survey missions to help improve the national pension systems of Argentina and Peru. Closer to its headquarters, the European Community relied on the ILO to carry out the basic technical work connected with the harmonization of social security systems as required by the Treaty of Rome (1957). By way of example, the preparatory technical work for the introduction of a European system of social security for migrant workers designed to facilitate the free movement of labour within the countries of the European Economic Community (EEC) was completed, in 1958, under a joint working arrangement between the EEC, the European Coal and Steel Community and the ILO.[46]

---

[46] ILO: *Report of the Director-General (Part II)*, International Labour Conference, 43rd Session, Geneva, 1959, p. 38; C. Guinand, 2003, op. cit., pp. 244–267.

Over the years, the scope of technical assistance programmes broadened and new regions became part of the ILO's world of work. In the Middle East, Iran asked for ILO assistance in training staff and the improvement of administrative techniques of social security schemes. In Asia, the ILO set up programmes in Burma, Pakistan, Thailand and Viet Nam, amongst others, to help governments draft comprehensive laws covering the first stage of social security benefits.[47] Most of these programmes aimed at providing assistance in social security planning, explicitly taking into account the country's economic and social characteristics – in contrast to the ILO Conventions on social security that proclaimed a more "universal" scope. For instance, the Ottawa Programme of Social Security Reform, adopted by the Eighth Conference of American States in 1966, stated that maximum priority should be given to the extension of social security in the rural sector. In this context of an increase in technical assistance programmes, it is surprising that the World Employment Programme, the ILO's flagship contribution to the United Nations International Development Decade, paid very little attention to social security issues (see Chapter 5).

## Crisis and controversy:
## The Chilean pension model as an example

It was obvious that social security, which had
been conceived as a wartime dream, was in
danger of becoming a peacetime nightmare.[48]

After the first oil shock in 1973, the uninterrupted period of post-war economic growth came to an end. As the economic crisis deepened, demands upon social expenditure grew. But the shift in the dominant economic model during the 1980s (see Chapters 1, 5 and 6) implied a reduced overall role for the state and the promotion of private arrangements not only in production but also in social policy. In this context of privatization and neo-liberal policies there were substantial implications for the ILO and its approach to social security.

Much of the debate about welfare reform during this period focused on pensions. This is hardly surprising, since pensions accounted for a large component

---

[47] ILO: *The ILO in a changing world*, Report of the Director-General, International Labour Conference, 42nd Session, Geneva, 1958, p. 96.

[48] A. Parrott: "Social security: Does the wartime dream have to become a peacetime nightmare?", in *International Labour Review* (Geneva, ILO, 1992), Vol. 131, No. 3, p. 382.

of social expenditure due to spectacular demographic changes and the rise of life expectancy in the decades after the Second World War. The development and international diffusion of the Chilean pension model exemplifies the challenges the ILO faced in the field of social security between the 1970s and 1990s.

At the beginning of the 1970s, the Chilean social security system was one of the most advanced in the region: it covered all contingencies, reached virtually all the population and offered generous benefits. This put high pressure on the state's social expenditure, suffering from mounting financial deficits. In this context, in May 1981, the Pinochet regime instituted a radical reform of the pension system. This drastic structural reform was possible as it was imposed by an authoritarian government, which dissolved the parliament, banned political parties and trade union confederations and ruled the communications media with an iron hand, so that opposition to the reforms was eliminated or extremely weak.

The new Chilean model, inspired by Chicago-trained liberal economists,[49] was characterized by an individualization and privatization of pension provision, based on a compulsory personal savings scheme. Only workers contributed to the private pension plans. There was no employer contribution. The pension received on retirement was determined by the contributions made and the returns on investments. New financial institutions were created, which competed with each other for these private accounts and were responsible for investing the funds. This model gave the state a minor role. Apart from overall regulation, the state had to provide "assistential" means-tested pensions to those unable to reach a minimum pension. This model had both an ideological and a public finance rationale. In ideological terms, it reduced the degree of social solidarity to a minimum, while it individualized responsibility and relied heavily on market mechanisms. In terms of public finance, it allegedly eliminated the problem of deficits in social security systems because obligations could not exceed assets. It was also argued that the system could achieve higher coverage in developing countries because it was not dependent on a formal employment relationship. And finally, a key point, it was maintained that this system provided a new supply of investible funds for development, unlike pay-as-you-go pension (PAYG) systems. Similar arguments would underpin the introduction of a savings-based unemployment "insurance" system in the 1990s.

The Chilean model was clearly inconsistent with the ILO's approach. In 1992, the Thirteenth ILO Conference of American Member States in Caracas (Venezuela) emphasized that the state should continue to carry out its functions

---

[49] J.G. Valdés: *Pinochet's economists: The Chicago School of Economics in Chile* (Cambridge, Cambridge University Press, 1995).

and responsibilities as regulator, co-financer and guarantor of the pension system. The private sector should provide supplementary programmes, but was not essential for financing the general system.[50] This was also the bottom line of a critical review of the Chilean model by Colin Gillion, the head of the ILO Social Security Department, and Alejandro Bonilla, a senior staff member. They considered that the burden on the state was greatly understated in the Chilean pension model; in particular, it had to shoulder high transition costs in the move from a PAYG to a capitalization system. Without the employer contribution, the level of the pension was unlikely to be adequate. Due to the lack of a "safety net", risks were borne by the individual, whose pension would depend on the vagaries of the market at the time he or she retired. Consequently, the new pension system placed greater pressure on other social expenditures. The ILO also criticized the lack of solidarity between generations and social groups with different needs and capacities.[51]

Gillion and Bonilla developed an alternative model that was taken further in the ILO Director-General's report to the International Labour Conference in 1993, and by ILO official Subramaniam Iyer in an *International Labour Review* article.[52] Together with a strong criticism of the defects of the Chilean pension system, the ILO defended a three-pillar pension model for developing countries: a basic state pension financed from taxes on the PAYG-principle (first compulsory pillar); defined benefits from contributions by workers and employers administered by social security institutions (second compulsory pillar); and supplementary pensions run by private institutions (third voluntary pillar).[53]

In the pension debate, the ILO was eclipsed by the international financial organizations (the World Bank and the International Monetary Fund (IMF)), which were imposing structural adjustment programmes on indebted countries turning to them for help in dealing with their debt crises (see Chapter 5). In 1994, the World Bank proposed a model that became the leading influence on pension reform.[54] This model, largely based on the Chilean system, involved a new view of social security, whereby public pensions were considered primarily as an

---

[50] C. Mesa-Lago: "Pension system reforms in Latin America: The position of the international organizations", in *CEPAL Review* (1996), No. 60, p. 85.

[51] C. Gillion and A. Bonilla: "Analysis of a national private pension scheme: The case of Chile", in *International Labour Review* (Geneva, ILO, 1992), Vol. 131, No. 2, pp. 171–195.

[52] ILO: *Social insurance and social protection*, Report of the Director-General (Part I), International Labour Conference, 80th Session, Geneva, 1993; S. Iyer: "Pension reform in developing countries", in *International Labour Review* (Geneva, ILO, 1993), Vol. 132, No. 2, pp. 187–207.

[53] C. Mesa-Lago, 1996, op. cit., pp. 86–88.

[54] World Bank: *Averting the old age crisis: Policies to protect the old and promote growth* (Washington, DC and Oxford, World Bank and Oxford University Press, 1994).

instrument of anti-poverty strategy. Whereas the ILO favoured the improvement of existing pension systems (for instance, by raising the retirement age, providing less generous benefits and reducing administrative expenses) in order to face rising costs, the World Bank demanded structural reforms. It pleaded for a two-pillar pension model in the form of a modest universal social assistance pension financed from taxation (first tier) and mandatory individual savings (second tier), as in the Chilean model. Other aims, regarded by the ILO as essential – such as protecting against life's uncertainties, implementing principles of justice in terms of redistribution and (gender) equality, strengthening social cohesion and promoting social inclusion and solidarity – were not given priority.

The World Bank's energetic promotion of pension reforms was a powerful factor in the spread of this particular model across the developing and post-Communist world. Schemes on the lines of the Chilean model were adopted in other parts of Latin America, such as Argentina, Colombia and Peru. They were also emulated in Central and Eastern European countries in transition after the fall of the Communist regimes, where the planned-economy social security system had collapsed; but the ILO had little influence in helping to build new schemes. Poland, for example, where the ILO had played an important role in supporting the development of an independent trade union movement (see Chapter 2), nevertheless followed the World Bank model when reforming its pension system, as did Hungary. In Central and Eastern Europe as well as in Latin America, existing pension schemes were clearly in need of reform – and the private model was attractive to employers since they were not obliged to contribute, and to financial institutions keen to manage the funds. ILO advisers in the newly created multidisciplinary teams in both regions provided counter-arguments based on the ILO's three-pillar model.[55] But, although some countries (such as Uruguay) did introduce such models, overall the influence was limited.

Interestingly, once democracy had returned to Chile and centrist and centre-left governments had been elected, there was an increasing recognition of some of the disadvantages inherent in the private pension system. It was apparent that the new financial institutions were generating large commissions to the detriment of the final pensions delivered, and successive governments attempted to tighten regulation. This led, in 1997, to the bizarre situation of pension fund commission agents occupying the ILO office in Santiago in an attempt to put pressure on the

---

[55] A. Conte-Grand: *Reparto o capitalización. Gestión pública o privada. Aporte para las discusiones en material de seguridad social* (Santiago, OIT Equipo Technico Multidisciplinario para Argentina, Brasil, Chile, Paraguay y Uruguay, 1995); M. Cichon et al.: *Social protection and pension systems in Central and Eastern Europe* (Budapest, ILO Central and Eastern Europe Multidisciplinary Advisory Team, 1997).

Chilean Government to relax these regulations. Obviously, there was a perception that the ILO was influential. Subsequent reforms in Chile have strengthened the redistributive elements of the system, aiming at a more universal coverage and allocating public funds to finance the system, with special attention for incentives for the poor, young people and women to enable them to join progressively the contributory pension scheme. And this has meant moving back towards the ILO model. Moreover, in 2003, Poland ratified the ILO Minimum Standards of Social Security Convention of 1952, as did some other Central and Eastern European countries during the 1990s and after 2000.

Overall, it is clear that the development and spread of private pension schemes has changed the overall policy landscape. Across the world today, pension schemes, especially in the private sector, are much less likely to be defined benefit than defined contribution. Among workers, there is strong resistance to making pensions too heavily dependent on market forces. This trend is due to wider international economic developments rather than to the ILO itself. In 2000, the ILO published its major response to the World Bank pension policy in a compendium *Social security pensions: Development and reform*, containing a full analysis of the complex issue of pension reform at the turn of the century.[56] In contrast to the World Bank, the ILO argued for a system which would provide income security in old-age by adequate benefits, the extension of coverage and 'good governance' of pension systems. The ILO's response took its time. In hindsight, it took probably too long, as stated by the ILO's Head of the Social Protection Sector in 2008. His critical analysis summarizes the ILO's position in the whole debate:

> Our role in the pension reform debate so far has been to promote the idea of pragmatic parametric reforms rather than major dramatic changes that can incur major social risks. We have not been as successful as we should have been. The most likely reason is that we underestimated the power of the political economy and the hidden economic agendas. But we continued to give advice. Developments during the past few years showed that we were probably right in many ways, but we could not change the direction of reforms radically.[57]

---

[56] C. Gillion et al.: *Social security pensions: Development and reform* (Geneva, ILO, 2000); Summarized in C. Gillion: "The development and reform of social security pensions: The approach of the International Labour Office", in *International Social Security Review* (Geneva, ILO, 2000), Vol. 53, No. 1, pp. 35–63.

[57] ILO: *Pension reforms in Central and Eastern Europe in a global perspective: Lessons learned*, address by Assane Diop at the Wissenschaftliches Kolloquium "Internationale Entwicklungen in der Rentenpolitik", Berlin, 2 April 2008, p. 10.

# Social protection as part of an integrated ILO approach

*Decent work marks the high road to economic and social development,
in which employment, income and social protection can be achieved
without compromising workers' rights and social standards.*[58]
(Juan Somavia, ILO Director-General, 1999)

The Asian financial crisis in 1997–98 showed the dramatic consequences of underdeveloped social protection systems and demonstrated that good economic performance in itself is not enough to assure social welfare (see Chapter 5). There was a growing awareness that the globalization process that had been accelerating since the 1990s needed a strong social dimension in order to be inclusive and sustainable. This has been the underlying principle of all ILO policy in the last decade (see Chapter 6). In this context, the ILO reiterated its approach to social security, focusing on a general extension to people who were not yet covered. The issue of "social security for all" took the debate away from pension reform.

In June 2001, the International Labour Conference examined the issue of social security in order to define a concept that would meet the challenges that had been mapped out in the *World Labour Report* of 2000.[59] One of the key global problems facing social security is the fact that more than half of the world's population is excluded from any type of social security protection, mostly in the developing world. Those outside the formal labour market are beyond the reach of social security legislation, except for basic social assistance schemes in the more advanced countries. In the industrialized countries (including the economies of Central and Eastern Europe), social security systems face new demographic challenges, such as ageing and changing family structures, with important implications for the financing of social protection. Some consider that the current social security systems are too expensive and that they harm the process of economic growth and development. In a number of countries, there is dissatisfaction with the administration of social security, and calls for reform involve a review of the role of the state and the responsibilities of the social partners.

The documents prepared for the 2001 Conference, as well as a record of the debates, were put together in an ILO volume optimistically entitled *Social security: A new consensus.* But the discussions in 2001 suggest that, initially, there had

---

[58] ILO: *Decent work*, Report of the Director-General, International Labour Conference, 87th Session, Geneva, 1999.

[59] ILO: *World Labour Report 2000: Income security and social protection in a changing world* (Geneva, ILO, 2000).

been little consensus. The Workers' group in the Committee on Social Security stated that the ILO had made "too little progress" since 1944.[60] They emphasized the importance of increased employment and insisted that the extension of social security to the previously excluded should be subsidized without any reduction of benefits in existing schemes. The Employers' group, unsurprisingly, stressed the need for economic growth and warned about imposing excessive costs. They were especially concerned about the fiscal implications of ageing and of HIV/AIDS, and insisted that discussions should be at the national rather than international level, so as to take fully into account the national conditions and constraints. Government members were divided: some favoured the ILO setting legally binding minimum standards, while others pointed out that the ILO's social security Conventions had been ratified by only a few Members and they were consequently opposed to further standards on social security. Generally speaking, the positions staked out by the various parties were broadly those held since the 1920s.

The "new consensus" that came out of the 2001 International Labour Conference consisted of the reaffirmation that social security was a basic human right. The Conference noted that certain groups had different needs and some had very low contributory capacity. The highest priority should therefore be given to policies and initiatives that brought social security to those not covered by existing schemes. However, the conclusions of the Conference did not entail any substantial commitment on the part of the ILO member States. It was left to each country to determine a national strategy for working towards social security for all. The 2001 Conference therefore called on the ILO to launch a major campaign ("Global Campaign on Social Security and Coverage for All") in order to promote the extension of social security coverage worldwide.

A universal concept of social security was not so new. It was after all very much in line with the overall approach of the Declaration of Philadelphia and with the Universal Declaration of Human Rights and the International Covenant on Economic, Social and Cultural Rights. In all these instruments the extension of social security is seen as part of the implementation of a combination of complementary or interdependent rights and measures. In 2001 it was agreed that the ILO's strategy for the extension of social security should be closely linked to its employment strategy and to other social policies. This is one of the essential features of the Decent Work Agenda, adopted by the ILO in 1999. An integrated approach linking social security with other labour market issues in order to provide income security for a wider fraction of population is today the official goal of

---

[60] ILO: *Social security: A new consensus* (Geneva, ILO, 2001), p. 8.

the ILO's Social Protection Sector ("Enhancing the coverage and effectiveness of social protection for all"). This integrated approach was totally absent in the two previous decades.

Seen within the broader international environment, there is still a sharp divide between the ILO's approach to social security, based on universality, solidarity and redistribution, and that promoted by the World Bank in recent years, of "social risk management".[61] The social risk management approach has the advantage that it is wider than social security. It is about preventing risks and not just reacting to them, and providing "risk management instruments" to individuals, notably among the poor, as part of a wider strategy for development and poverty reduction. But it also means that the treatment of social risks is based on the idea of individual management; individuals are considered as entrepreneurs managing their own life and selling their skills on the labour market, and the state consequently has a very limited role. This tendency to downplay solidarity reflects a problematic ideological position because the pattern of distribution itself clearly affects the ability of individuals to protect themselves against social risks.[62]

The closest analogy in the ILO's agenda was a programme on socio-economic security, established in 1999 as part of an institutional effort to prompt a rethinking on social protection policies within the framework of the concept of decent work. The programme developed a model of socio-economic security, in which different forms of security needed to be addressed: labour market security, employment security, job security, work security, skill security and representation security – all of which complemented income security, traditionally the main focus of social security.[63] Substantial research was undertaken that involved extensive data collection, leading in some cases to conclusions at variance with the mainstream ILO approach. For instance, the programme highlighted the possible contribution to security of a "basic income" approach, implying a minimum income for all guaranteed by the state. It argued that basic income security was essential for real freedom and that it was the best way to target the most insecure and poor, as it complemented the very limited coverage of work-based social security schemes in developing countries. The programme also researched new forms of universalistic social protection such as categorical (by age) cash benefits or

---

[61] R. Holzmann: *Social risk management: The World Bank's approach to social protection in a globalizing world* (Washington, DC, World Bank, 2003). Robert Holzmann, Head of Social Protection in the World Bank, is a leading advocate of this approach.

[62] B. Deacon: "From 'safety nets' back to 'universal social provision': Is the global tide turning?", in *Global Social Policy* (London and New Delhi, Sage Publications, 2005), Vol. 5, No. 1, pp. 19–28.

[63] For a brief overview, see G. Standing: "From people's security surveys to a decent work index", in *International Labour Review* (Geneva, ILO, 2002), Vol. 141, No. 4, pp. 441–454.

universal school attendance allowances, practices that could inform social policies in developing countries.[64]

In contrast to the World Bank model of social risk management, the ILO's approach to socio-economic security did not become mainstream. When the programme came to an end in 2007, despite having generated a series of books, papers and databases which were widely referred to in the academic community, its influence on ILO policy had been limited. The Social Protection Sector, of which it was a part, was at the time divided into different programmes, conducted by separate units, each with its own approach, which made it difficult to develop a unified approach. Elsewhere in the Office, there were efforts to explore the notion of "flexicurity", or how to combine the need for flexible adjustment to competitive pressures from the global economy with a decent level of social security, especially in the developed world (see Chapter 5).

Meanwhile there was increasing emphasis on the central role social security could play for the reduction of poverty in the developing world. New solidarity-based approaches were developed with a particular focus on the informal sector and the large number of female workers engaged in it. The Strategies and Tools against Social Exclusion and Poverty Programme (STEP), for instance, aims at the extension of social security (in particular in health insurance) and the fight against social exclusion at the local level by developing community-based schemes for poor populations excluded from formal systems in the least developed countries. Financed by donor governments (mainly Belgium and Portugal), in 2008 it was operational in over 40 countries.

Essentially these programmes aim to reconcile a universal approach of social security – the principle of "social protection for all" – with special attention for the diversity of socio-economic realities in many countries and different groups whose needs, ability to contribute and employment and integration situations are fundamentally different. They all make the case for a minimum "global social floor" in order to meet the basic needs of uncovered communities and groups and thus lift a greater number of people out of poverty. The resurgence of concern with inequality on the international agenda in recent years suggests that there is an important space for the ILO to occupy, aiming to promote a fair pattern of access to labour market opportunities with mechanisms for solidarity and redistribution through social security, within a coherent overall approach.

---

[64] ILO: *Economic security for a better world* (Geneva, ILO Socio-Economic Security Programme, 2004).

## Conclusion

The ILO's history of action in securing social protection throughout the twentieth century was one of variable success. Its main contribution came not through generating new ideas or models of social protection, but rather through acknowledging, reinforcing and spreading existing models that were already in place in key countries. This was most clearly the case during the interwar period. By mobilizing expertise – generated by ILO officials as well as relevant international networks – and consensus-building among political leaders, trade unions and employers, the ILO was a "propelling" force for the international diffusion of social protection programmes.

What the ILO promoted in its first decades of existence was a particular model of social insurance, based on compulsory contributory schemes as derived from the German experience. In relation to the industrialized world, the ILO was the springboard from which the Bismarckian concept of social insurance was able to reach other countries. Despite a visionary commitment – enshrined in the 1944 Philadelphia Declaration – to a more universal social security, social insurance was still the dominant frame of reference for ILO policy in the second half of the twentieth century.

The effects of concrete ILO action deserve further research. In assessing its different roles in general terms, it may reasonably be argued that the ILO was more effective in providing and mobilizing labour expertise, and dispensing technical cooperation, than in its standards work on social protection, especially in those developing countries that needed it most. Yet, as was well summarized in a conference of British social insurance experts (of which one was William Beveridge) in 1925, the ILO standards nevertheless had their role to play:

> The rules are general, the agreements are conditional, and the loopholes visible to the naked eye. Yet, after all, that is as it should be. In Geneva you get an atmosphere in which the backward nations – and every nation is backward – become really conscious of the pressure of public expectation, and anxious to come up to the level of the more progressive. Give them a mild convention, an easy convention, which the reactionaries at home will not be able to tear to pieces; give them a permissive convention, allowing them, at their own time, to make intolerable conditions tolerable, and shameful conditions decent.[65]

---

[65] *Social insurance in its national and international aspects and in relation to the work of the ILO and the League of Nations. Report of the conference organized by the League of Nations Union and the London School of Economics, November 1925* (London, Faber and Gwyer, 1926), p. vii.

Looking back at the past 90 years as a whole, the influence of the ILO seems to have been greater when viewed from the industrialized world than from the Global South. Its long-standing institutional preference for social insurance, tripartite-based and focusing on workers in formal employment, explains why the ILO was not always able to successfully promote "social protection for all", although it has been successful in promoting social protection for some. The recent shift in emphasis towards extending social security to the population as a whole recognizes the need for a new approach, and identifies priorities for the future. Yet in the context of a wide range of socio-economic situations and the scale of the differences between countries, the ILO has acknowledged the huge practical difficulties involved in promoting the implementation of universal social security in all its member States.

While progress towards guaranteeing adequate social protection for all is slow and difficult, the ILO remains an essential actor, if progress is to continue. More recently, with the call for an integrated approach in the Decent Work Agenda, the ILO has conceded that:

> there is no single right model of social security. It grows and evolves over time. There are schemes of social assistance, universal schemes, social insurance and public or private provisions. Each society must determine how best to ensure income security and access to health care. These choices will reflect their social and cultural values, their history, their institutions and their level of economic development.[66]

---

[66] ILO, 2001, op. cit., p. 2.

# Employment and poverty reduction[1]

5

From the standpoint of an individual's welfare, having or not having work with an adequate income is a crucial dividing line. Employment is the means through which most people gain an entitlement to income and achieve a sense of social participation. Conversely, as countless studies have documented over the past century and beyond, the opposite state of being unable to find employment is an unmitigated disaster in terms of personal and familial economic hardship, humiliation, social exclusion and the psychological damage it inflicts. As a result, the prevention or reduction of unemployment has been high on the agenda of trade unions since their creation. From a societal point of view, high unemployment represents an unnecessary waste of potential output and human resources, often breeding social and political unrest and pathologies. Hence, the ILO's mandate of improving the welfare of workers cannot be realized solely through international labour standards. The promotion of international labour standards and steady improvements in the quality of employment will be most effective in an economic context where there is sustained growth in output and employment. Advancing productive employment, therefore, has to be a key objective of the ILO.

Not surprisingly, the ILO has, since its inception, devoted a major part of its work to employment issues. The Preamble of its Constitution included a reference to "the prevention of unemployment" among the items in the ILO's remit, and the second Convention it adopted in 1919, its first year of existence, related to unemployment (Unemployment Convention, 1919 (No. 2)). This instrument

---

[1] The principal author of this chapter is Eddy Lee.

provided for the communication of statistics and information on measures taken by member States to alleviate unemployment; on the setting up of public employment agencies; and the establishment of systems of insurance against unemployment. Interestingly, the accompanying Recommendation to this Convention (Recommendation No. 1) went further than this provision for the communication of information and referred to the notion – clearly far-sighted for its time – to the use of public expenditure to stabilize the level of employment.

Since then the ILO has adopted a number of other key instruments relating to issues of unemployment and employment policy, to which reference will be made at the appropriate points in the chronology of this discussion of the ILO's work on employment. Similarly, we shall explain the inclusion of the term 'poverty reduction' in the title of this chapter when we discuss the development of ILO's work on employment issues in developing countries (or underdeveloped countries as they were then called) after the Second World War.

This chapter undertakes a broad review of the ILO's work on employment since 1919. It describes the types of issues dealt with in each decade and assesses to what extent this action was in line with the major economic and employment problems of the day. For each period it also comments on the quality of the work undertaken, compared to the prevailing state of academic and policy thinking at the time. The implicit criterion for evaluation is that, at the very least, the ILO's work on employment should have recognized and responded to contemporary key issues, met minimal standards of academic quality and stimulated thinking and debate in policy and academic circles on solutions to major employment problems. This is admittedly a very broad evaluative framework. Nevertheless, it might still yield some useful lessons for the future. Indeed, even a simple comparison of what was actually done – by the ILO with what needed to be done given the economic circumstances and state of knowledge at the time – can expose major failings and omissions.

## The interwar period

The ILO's work on employment in the 1920s, the initial decade of its existence, was impressive from several standpoints. First, the range of issues it dealt with was vast and clearly unfettered by today's narrower conception of the role and competence of the ILO in the field of economic policy. This work ranged from specific national policies to reduce unemployment, such as increased expenditures on municipal public works and for dealing with the consequences of unemployment through the introduction of unemployment insurance, to key issues of global economic governance. Among the latter issues, there were studies on the relationship between monetary policy, economic fluctuations and the level of employment and the problems posed for national macroeconomic policy by the then prevailing international monetary system. Second, the work was at the frontier of technical knowledge of the day. It was solidly grounded in the system of labour statistics that the ILO was developing and produced a regular stream of authoritative reports on employment issues,[2] as well as scholarly articles in the *International Labour Review*. In particular, there was a major review of the employment situation in the world in the mid-1920s and studies examining new areas of economic policy, such as macroeconomic demand management and the relative effectiveness of different instruments for achieving this.[3] Third and perhaps most important, the work was at the forefront of progressive thinking on economic and social policy in its time. All the work on the important issues of national and international economic policy mentioned above was explicitly motivated by the ILO's fundamental goal of achieving social justice. There was a clear understanding that the ultimate objective of economic policies was to advance social justice and that they should be formulated, implemented and evaluated in this light.

The context in which this work took place was one where, in the aftermath of the First World War, the world was tentatively searching for a new model of governance for the global economy. The old regime of economic globalization under the hegemony of Great Britain had ended with the outbreak of the First World War and could not be easily restored. The economic domination of Great Britain was declining, while new economic powers, such as the United States, were on the rise. The most glaring manifestation of this unsettled state of global economic governance was the international payments system. The serious structural imbalances between surplus and deficit countries generated frequent monetary disturbances that placed serious constraints on national policies to achieve stability in the level of output and employment. Fluctuations in the level of output and employment thus featured prominently among the concerns of economic

---

[2] ILO: *Employment and unemployment*, Studies and Reports, Series C, of which 13 were produced in the 1920s; in addition, several Reports of the Director-General of the ILO on employment topics were also produced during this period.

[3] ILO: *Unemployment, 1920–23*, Studies and Reports, Series C, No. 8 (Geneva, 1924); H. Fuss: "Unemployment in 1925", in *International Labour Review* (Geneva, ILO, 1926), Vol. 14. On economic policy studies, see in particular ILO: "Bank credit and unemployment", in *International Labour Review* (Geneva, 1924), Vol. 9; P.W. Martin: "Overproduction and underconsumption: A remedy", in *International Labour Review* (Geneva, ILO, 1926), Vol. 14; H. Fuss: "Money and unemployment", in *International Labour Review* (Geneva, ILO, 1927), Vol. 16; and P.W. Martin: "The technique of balance and its place in American prosperity", in *International Labour Review* (Geneva, ILO, 1929), Vol. 20.

policy-makers at the time and the ILO's work on employment in that period rightly responded to this situation.

The ILO also addressed issues of national monetary policy and pointed out instances of misguided policies by monetary authorities that aggravated the problem of economic instability. Among the solutions it recommended were the establishment of Central Banks, the use of an employment index as a tool for demand management and an examination of the potential role of wage policy as a means of raising aggregate demand in periods of recession.[4] Above all, there was a clear realization that the primary cause of the difficulties in economic management was the deficient international monetary system. The ILO also made it clear that this deficiency could only be overcome through cooperative international action, such as coordinated international responses to financial crises. International economic and financial policies thus loomed large in the policy consciousness of the time and the ILO's work again correctly reflected this.[5]

The nature of the Organization's work on employment remained essentially the same during the 1930s. A significant difference was, however, that it was linked more directly to the advocacy of solutions for the overriding problem of the early 1930s – the Great Depression. This global economic crisis began in 1929 and led swiftly to mass unemployment in many countries. The unprecedented rise in unemployment overwhelmed the capacity of the then known mechanisms of coping with unemployment, namely unemployment insurance and local level public works. There was clearly a dire need for additional instruments of policy to counteract the widespread social distress that had been generated by the economic collapse. The ILO responded well to this challenge.

Its earlier work on national and international monetary policies, as well as its work that was in the vanguard of thinking on counter-cyclical macroeconomic policies, now stood the Organization in good stead in the face of the Great Depression. The ILO was in the forefront of the advocacy of a coordinated international effort to bring about a reflation of the global economy. As early as 1930, a paper in the *International Labour Review* discussed issues of global macroeconomic management and the need to deploy reflationary policies.[6] This was followed by four papers in the *Review* in 1931 on the international policy coordination required to achieve global reflation; on the need for a structural reorganization of the global

---

[4] A.M. Endres and G. Fleming: "International economic policy in the interwar years: The special contribution of ILO economists", in *International Labour Review* (Geneva, ILO, 1996), Vol. 135.

[5] ILO: *Unemployment in its national and international aspects*, Studies and Reports, Series C, No. 9 (Geneva, 1924).

[6] J.R. Bellerby and K.S. Isles: "Wages policy and the Gold standard in Great Britain", in *International Labour Review* (Geneva, ILO, 1930), Vol. 22.

economy; and on the social effects of the economic depression.[7] That same year, an important report stating the case for a set of international actions to overcome the Great Depression was published. A key part of these actions was a coordinated international programme of public works to raise effective demand in the global economy. There was also a discussion of the harmful effects of the spread of 'beggar-my-neighbour' protectionist trade policies and the importance of preserving an open international trading system. All this work must have helped to pave the way for the resolution adopted at the International Labour Conference in 1932, which called for a comprehensive programme of concerted international action on monetary, trade and public works policies as the means of overcoming the Great Depression.[8] At the 1933 World Monetary and Economic Conference, the ILO advocated coordinated international action which addressed both economic and social goals, but this call was sadly not heeded.

This focus on public works in the 1930s was in tune with contemporary progressive thought on economic and social policy. In the United States, the disastrous "laissez-faire" economic thinking and the orthodox monetary and fiscal policies it inspired, had led to the Great Depression and was replaced by Roosevelt's New Deal. This was also the period when there was significant ferment in the discipline of economics – a noteworthy aspect of which was the development of the body of thought now described as Keynesian economics. To its credit, the ILO clearly chose the winning side in the battle of economic doctrines in the 1930s, as it had done during the previous decade. It should, of course, be noted that this was the side whose ideas were far closer to the core ILO values of tripartism and social justice than the alternative laissez-faire school of economics. Equally, however, there was also a sound intellectual basis for this choice that had been established by ILO economists.

The work that emerged in response to the Great Depression continued until the end of the 1930s. In 1933, a paper was published on the social impact of a return to the Gold Standard.[9] In 1937, the eminent economist Abba Lerner

---

[7] P.W. Martin: "Finance and industry. The international significance of the Macmillan report", in *International Labour Review* (Geneva, ILO, 1931), Vol. 24; and P.W. Martin: "Finance and industry: The Macmillan report as a basis for international action", in *International Labour Review* (Geneva, ILO, 1931), Vol. 24; G. de Michelis: "A world programme for organic economic reconstruction", in *International Labour Review* (Geneva, ILO, 1931), Vol. 24; and H.B. Butler: "The social effects of the economic depression in North America", in *International Labour Review* (Geneva, ILO, 1931), Vol. 23.

[8] P.W. Martin: "World economic reconstruction: An analysis of the Economic Resolution adopted by the International Labour Conference", in *International Labour Review* (Geneva, ILO, 1932), Vol. 26.

[9] P.W. Martin and E.J. Riches: "The social consequences of a return to Gold: An analysis of certain current proposals for an International Money Standard", in *International Labour Review* (Geneva, ILO, 1933), Vol. 27.

wrote an article in the *International Labour Review* in which he presented the key ideas contained in Keynes's book published the previous year, *The General Theory of Employment Interest and Money*.[10] In 1938, a study further explored the role of public works in bringing about economic stabilization.[11] In the same year, one of the ILO's leading economists published two articles on the role of economic planning, an idea that was commanding greater interest in the wake of the evident failures of laissez-faire economics revealed by the Great Depression and of enthusiastic reports of impressive economic progress in centrally-planned economies.[12]

The 1920s and 1930s thus appeared to have been a good period in the ILO's work on employment. It chose the right issues in each period and played a credible role of policy advocacy in line with its mandate to alleviate unemployment and advance social progress. The credibility of its advocacy owed a great deal to its solid and pioneering work on economic and financial policies and their effects on the level of economic activity and employment.[13] It also quite rightly seized the opportunity to play a major role in the discussion of international economic issues – despite the fact that its primary vocation was the formulation of international Conventions designed to improve the welfare of workers. It would, of course, only be fair to note that the landscape of global governance prevailing in that period made it relatively easy for the ILO to claim such a prominent role on issues of international economic and financial policy. The only other potential rival at the time was the League of Nations.[14] While it is true, as discussed elsewhere in this volume, that there was some rivalry with that organization

---

[10] A.P. Lerner: "Mr Keynes's 'General Theory of Employment, Interest and Money'", in *International Labour Review* (Geneva, ILO, 1936), Vol. 34.

[11] ILO: *Public works policy*, Studies and Reports, Series C, No. 19, (Geneva, 1935), which led to the adoption by the 1937 International Labour Conference of two Recommendations relating respectively to international cooperation in respect of public works and the national planning of public works.

[12] P.W. Martin: "The present status of economic planning: An international survey of governmental economic intervention", in *International Labour Review* (Geneva, ILO, 1936), Vol. 33.

[13] It is of interest to note that Keynes himself recognized this. The *General Theory* (op. cit.) contains (p. 349) the following key observation on employment policy: "It is the policy of an autonomous rate of interest, unimpeded by international preoccupations, and a national investment programme directed to an optimal level of domestic employment which is twice blessed in the sense that it helps ourselves and our neighbours at the same time. And it is the simultaneous pursuit of these policies by all countries together which is capable of restoring economic health and strength internationally, whether we measure it by the level of domestic employment or by the volume of international trade." In a footnote to this passage Keynes noted that "the consistent appreciation of this truth by the International Labour Office, first under Albert Thomas and subsequently under Mr. H. B. Butler, has stood out conspicuously amongst the pronouncements of the numerous post-war international bodies".

[14] A. Alcock: *History of the International Labour Organisation* (London and Basingstoke, Macmillan, 1971).

on international economic issues, for example, vis-à-vis the organization of the World Economic Conferences of 1927 and 1933, there was no doubt that the ILO was unchallenged in so far as the relationship between economic policies and employment was concerned.

Before moving on to the 1940s, it might be useful to note briefly the evolution that had occurred in the conceptualization of the unemployment problem and of policies for dealing with it. The concept of unemployment had emerged in the context of the Industrial Revolution and the changes it brought about in the structure and mode of employment. During this period, wage employment in urban factories and offices had replaced peasant agriculture and rural wage employment as the dominant mode of employment. While rural economies had experienced seasonal and weather-induced fluctuations in the level of economic activity and hence of employment, the impacts of these fluctuations had been broadly spread out across rural communities and there had been no distinct class of unemployed persons as a social category. In the new industrializing urban economy the situation was very different, with open unemployment emerging because of rural–urban migration in search of employment and fluctuations arising from the business cycle. The policy attitude to this new social phenomenon of unemployment – equated with pauperism – had initially been a harsh one. The Poor Laws that were introduced to deal with this problem had a clearly punitive and deterrent intent, the underlying view being that unemployment was the result of indolence and clearly the fault of the individuals concerned.

By 1919, largely as a result of the earlier work of the trade unions and progressive social thinkers, this attitude had given way to a more enlightened view of the problem. It was now recognized that unemployment was caused by factors other than the personal failings of the unemployed persons themselves. These included seasonal factors, trade or business cycles and frictions or inefficiencies in the labour market. Accordingly, perspectives on policies for dealing with the problem changed as well. As reflected in the ILO's 1919 Unemployment Convention (No. 2), it was now accepted that government had an obligation to relieve unemployment through the organization of public works, the provision of unemployment benefits and the bringing about of improvements in the functioning of labour markets (for example, by creating public employment agencies).

By the end of the 1930s, the view of the responsibilities of government had evolved even further. Until then, the attitude had been that this responsibility was limited to dealing with the effects of unemployment after it emerged. This arose from the then conventional wisdom that markets were self-regulating and were best left free from any state interference. The notion that there was a more activist and also benign role of the state in preventing and mitigating unemployment through macroeconomic policies was a hard-won trophy of the Keynesian revolution in economic thought. This led naturally to the concept of "full employment" and the responsibility of governments to ensure this.

It goes without saying that virtually all of this work on employment related to the situation in the developed countries. This was a reflection of the composition and governance of the ILO in a period when imperialism was still deeply entrenched. The serious problems of unemployment, underemployment and poverty that undoubtedly prevailed in the underdeveloped world had yet to enter the Organization's consciousness.

## The Second World War and its immediate aftermath

In contrast to the 1920s and 1930s there was less research and policy advocacy on employment issues in the 1940s. This was partly due to the fact that during the first half of the decade the Second World War was still in progress and much of the effort of the reduced staff of the ILO in this period was devoted to preparing the Organization for a changed role in the post-war world. In this connection, the International Labour Conference, held in New York in 1941, discussed the "social objective in the coming period of reconstruction". Major problems were anticipated in the transition of economies from a war footing to normal peacetime functioning, among them fears of a slump and a rise in unemployment. The total mobilization for war had in fact created full employment in the major economic powers. At the same time, the evolution of thinking on employment policy was leading to a commitment to the objective of full employment. Beveridge's study on full employment was in preparation during the war and culminated in influencing the White Paper on Employment Policy that was issued in the United Kingdom in 1944.[15] Keynesian ideas had also spread across the Atlantic and the United States Employment Act was adopted in 1946. Thus the bar of expectation in terms of employment policy had been raised in the two major economies of the post-war world. This made it all the more important to find a means of reducing the impact on unemployment of demobilization and the restructuring of the economy to meet normal peacetime demand. The ILO made

---

[15] W. Beveridge: *Full employment in a free society* (London, George Allen and Unwin, 1944); and United Kingdom, Ministry of Reconstruction: *Employment Policy* (London, HMSO, 1944).

a contribution through a study on the employment problems in the transition to peace and in the longer-term.[16]

A key development during the first half of the 1940s was, of course, the preparation of the ground for the adoption in 1944 of the Declaration of Philadelphia. As has been discussed earlier in this volume, this redefined the mandate of the ILO for the post-war world. From the standpoint of the ILO's work on employment, the most important development was the inclusion in the declaration of a reference to the goal of full employment. This new mandate was immediately followed-up at the International Labour Conference held in Paris in 1945, where there was a discussion on policies for realizing the goal of full employment. In this respect, the ILO was quick to confirm its commitment to this new goal – a concept which its own work in the 1930s had played a role in developing.

Apart from this, there was little noteworthy new research or contributions to discussions of international economic policy in the immediate aftermath of the Second World War. There was a revival of pre-war work on public works, and studies were published on the role of public investment and development works in achieving full employment.[17] In 1945 a paper on full employment policies by Michal Kalecki, an eminent economist who was then on the staff of the ILO, was published in the *International Labour Review*.[18]

What explains this relatively fallow period of ILO work on employment issues in the first five years after the end of the war, despite the enhanced mandate conferred upon it by the Declaration of Philadelphia? Part of the explanation must surely lie in the fact that the ILO had to find its way in the much more elaborate structure of global governance that had been adopted from 1945 onwards. There was now the United Nations – of which the ILO became just a specialized agency. The UN itself, through ECOSOC, was given a mandate to work on international economic and social policy, including on employment issues. This was due, in part, to pressure from the USSR in the Cold War era. It was wary of the strength of the influence of the West over the ILO and saw the UN as a potentially more promising arena. In addition, the Bretton Woods institutions were given primary responsibility for international economic and financial policies. Thus, in contrast

---

[16] ILO: *The maintenance of high levels of employment during the period of industrial rehabilitation and reconstruction*, Report II, 27th Session of the International Labour Conference, Paris, 1945 (published in Montreal, 1945).

[17] The main study was ILO: *Public investment and full employment* (Montreal, 1946). See also D.C. Tait: "Development works and full employment", in *International Labour Review* (Montreal, ILO, 1946), Vol. 54, and other studies on the topic discussed therein.

[18] M. Kalecki: "The maintenance of full employment after the transition period", in *International Labour Review* (Montreal, ILO, 1945), Vol. 52.

to the pre-war period, the ILO now had to operate in a crowded and competitive structure of global governance. Although the Declaration of Philadelphia had given it a mandate to deal with international economic and financial policies from the standpoint of their social impact, this role was not, in the context of the new architecture of global governance, a very strong or clear-cut one. Although it could justify a place for itself in examining and scrutinising international economic policies from a social perspective, whatever it did unilaterally along these lines risked being operationally irrelevant, given the stronger and more direct mandates – as well as the vast financial resources – of the World Bank and the IMF.

## The 1950s and 1960s

The 1950s marked the beginnings of the extension of the ILO's work on employment issues to the developing world. This was the period of decolonization and the emergence of new states that expanded the membership as well as the preoccupations of the ILO. Until then, most of the work on employment policies had focused on the industrialized countries. Similarly, its work on international economic and financial policies had been conducted from the vantage point of their impact on these same countries.

The 1950s have been described as the beginning of the 'Golden Age' of high growth and full employment in the industrialized countries. The post-war recovery was faster than expected, and the Japanese and German economies began their take-off into higher growth. Full employment at levels of unemployment as low as 2 to 3 per cent – barely imaginable from today's standpoint – prevailed in most industrialized countries. The growing acceptance of the goal of full employment in the industrialized countries thus accorded with this empirical demonstration that it was indeed feasible. However, it was the United Nation's ECOSOC, and not the ILO, that assumed the lead role on this issue.

In 1950, ECOSOC adopted a resolution on national and international policies for the attainment of the objective of full employment.[19] This called on States Members to consider national action to maintain full employment and for the creation of an international environment that supported the attainment of full employment globally. The international environment was to include an increase in world trade, the stabilization of international investments and the

---

[19] United Nations: *ECOSOC resolution (No. 290(XI)) on full employment*, Document E/1849 (Geneva, 1950).

need for all countries to consider the international consequences of national policies. ECOSOC was aware of the fact that most of this discussion was from the standpoint of the industrialized countries and commissioned a report devoted specially to the employment problems in developing countries.[20] This report was prepared by an eminent group of experts that included two subsequent Nobel Laureates in Economics, Theodore Schultz and Arthur Lewis, and was discussed in ECOSOC in 1951.

The report drew on the then emerging discipline of "development economics" to highlight the very different nature of the unemployment problem in developing countries compared to that in the industrialized countries. A key difference was that in developing countries the main problem was not unemployment but underemployment, which was due to deficiencies of land and capital in relation to the labour supply. The main remedy, therefore, lay in accelerating the process of economic development as a means of generating the increased capital stock necessary for creating new employment opportunities. A basic requirement was to create the preconditions for economic development which included: an institutional framework to remove the obstacles to – and to provide the incentives for – an increase in entrepreneurship and investment; the provision of a basic level of education for the population; the development of skills and the administrative capacity to plan and implement development programmes; and institutions and policies for increasing saving and domestic capital formation. At the same time the report emphasized that the support of the developed countries was essential for the success of these national efforts by the underdeveloped countries. The developed countries were called upon to reform trade policies that hindered market access for developing countries, encourage increased flows of private investment to these countries and provide increased aid and technical assistance. Apropos the latter, the report recommended that the United Nations should establish an International Development Authority to manage the process. The key recommendations of the report were adopted by ECOSOC in a resolution of 1951, thus paving the way for the growth of United Nations action in promoting economic and social development.

There was some evidence that this work by the UN began to influence a shift in the ILO's work on employment to the developing countries. In 1951, the ILO's Asian Advisory Committee considered the subject of "Underemployment in Asia: its causes and remedies, with special reference to social aspects of capital formation for economic development". The committee recommended further investigation of the problem, particularly by means of field enquiries. Work on this issue

---

[20] United Nations Department of Economic and Social Affairs: *Measures for the economic development of underdeveloped countries*, Document E/1986 (New York, 1951).

continued in subsequent years, and in 1956 two studies reviewed government policies towards employment and underemployment in developed and underdeveloped countries respectively.[21] The study on the latter group of countries surveyed development plans in a number of countries with special reference to their expected effect on employment. It noted that most of these plans did not contain any estimates of the extent to which their implementation would increase employment and overcome unemployment and underemployment. It also highlighted the paradoxical situation in some countries of underutilization of industrial capacity, while there was severe underemployment in agriculture, and advocated increasing output in agriculture alongside that of industry in order to provide a market for increased industrial output. The ILO also addressed key issues in development economics, such as the problem of investment policy – especially the matter of the best use of capital resources to raise the rate of economic growth. This involved a comparison of the relative merits of a capital-intensive versus a labour-intensive growth strategy. The related issue of production techniques and employment creation was also discussed by the Asian Advisory Committee in 1957.[22]

However, basic issues as to the relationship between development strategy and employment did not appear to occupy centre stage in the ILO's work on employment in the underdeveloped countries in the 1950s. The second half of the 1950s marked the beginning of the ILO's work in fielding advisory missions and implementing technical cooperation projects in developing countries. These did not deal with matters of development strategy and employment but rather with those of vocational training and productivity enhancement.

To situate the motivation for the work on vocational training, it is necessary to recall the main preoccupations of employment policy in the industrialized countries at the beginning of the 1950s. As noted earlier, this was a period of full employment. Instead of a fear of unemployment, the main policy concern was over shortages of both skilled and unskilled labour. The problem of skill shortages sparked off an interest in education and skill development policies and in the issues and techniques of educational and manpower planning, while the problem of shortages of unskilled labour was dealt with through increased immigration from developing countries. And interest in skill shortages in the industrialized

---

[21] ILO: "Employment and unemployment: Government policies since 1950 I", in *International Labour Review* (Geneva, ILO, 1956), Vol. 74; and "Employment and unemployment: Government policies since 1950 II", in *International Labour Review* (Geneva, ILO, 1956), Vol. 74.

[22] ILO: "Some aspects of investment policy in underdeveloped countries", in *International Labour Review* (Geneva, ILO, 1958), Vol. 77; and ILO: *The comparative employment potentials of different methods of production and their respective roles in industrial development*, Document AAC/VIII/D.6, Eighth Session of the Asian Advisory Committee, New Delhi, November 1957.

countries directed attention to an aspect of the employment problem in developing countries that became prominent in the 1950s and 1960s – the relative lack of educated and skilled labour needed for economic development in these countries. Manpower planning was seen as an important means of overcoming this problem, as it set out to identify skill shortages and project future skill requirements in order to guide investments in expanding educational and training facilities to meet these requirements. Within this framework, the ILO began its technical assistance in developing vocational training systems in developing countries under the then United Nations Programme of Technical Assistance. This was the largest component of ILO technical assistance – and by 1956 some 40 countries had received ILO assistance in this field.[23]

At the same time, there were also ILO productivity missions to several countries. The focus of these missions was "to demonstrate how, by the application of modern management and industrial engineering methods, better use could be made of the resources available to industry ... without the need for additional large-scale investment or the expenditure of foreign exchange, which is generally scarce".[24] The rationale also included the notion that while vocational training to raise the productivity of workers was important, it should "not obscure the often greater importance of the productivity of capital".[25] The focus was thus on the modern industrial sector and on introducing modern management and production planning techniques to "backward" countries. This, together with the fact that the work on vocational training was also mostly directed at modern industry, meant that there was a very marked urban and modern sector bias in the ILO's work in the developing countries during this period. All this work was very much in keeping with the 'modernization' school of thought that held sway at the time. Marxist literature dismissed such thinking as a manifestation of neo-colonialism, since it ignored the importance of class struggle and structural change for achieving development.

The main impression that emerges from the ILO's work on employment throughout these years is that its role had diminished in comparison to the key position it had held in the pre-war period. It was the UN rather than the ILO that played the lead role on policies for full employment in the industrialized countries – and that initiated work on employment problems and policies in the underdeveloped countries. Although there was some work on development strategies

---

[23] ILO: "International technical assistance in vocational training", in *International Labour Review* (Geneva, ILO, 1957), Vol. 75, pp. 514–529.

[24] ILO: "ILO productivity missions to underdeveloped countries", in *International Labour Review* (Geneva, ILO, 1957), Vol. 76, p. 2.

[25] Ibid., p. 6.

and employment, these were by no means innovative or major contributions to academic or policy thinking at the time. And, as just noted, the bulk of its advisory and technical assistance work did not focus on central issues of development and employment policy, but on the narrower ones of raising labour and capital productivity in the small modern sectors of underdeveloped economies.

But the situation began to change in the 1960s. The ILO's work on employment in this period paved the way for the launching of the World Employment Programme (WEP) in 1969 and the major influence on development and employment policies that that Programme was to have in the 1970s. A major factor behind this change was decolonization and the accession to ILO membership of most newly independent developing countries. This pushed the Organization to begin to address the economic and social problems of developing countries, prominent among which were issues of employment and poverty.

A highly significant development occurred at the outset of the decade. In 1961, a major report prepared by a group of eminent development economists that included Benjamin Higgins and K.N. Raj was published.[26] A key message was that successful economic development might not be sufficient to increase employment and that special efforts were required to achieve the latter. Employment should thus be a separate objective of development policies. The report raised vital problems that were subsequently analysed in depth by the WEP in the 1970s. Among these were the scope for raising employment at a given level of investment through changing the composition of output and the techniques of production; the imperative need to raise the level of saving and investment; and the importance of raising the productivity of existing scarce resources as a means of increasing the volume of capital and consumption goods that would be available to support a higher level of employment.

This report served as background documentation for a general discussion of employment problems and policies at the International Labour Conference in 1961. And this, in turn, led to a Preparatory Technical Conference to discuss employment policy with particular reference to employment problems in developing countries, with a view to formulating a standard to be adopted by the Conference. In 1964, the Conference duly adopted the Employment Policy Convention (No. 122) and an accompanying Recommendation. The Convention requires ratifying governments to declare and pursue policies to promote full, productive and freely chosen employment, and to consult the social partners in the process.

---

[26] ILO: *Employment objectives in economic development*, Studies and Reports, New Series, No. 62 (Geneva, 1961).

The adoption of this Convention was a significant development from several standpoints. First, it clarified and formalized the ILO's commitment to the goal of full employment in all member States, regardless of their level of development. While such a goal had been widely accepted in industrialized countries, doubts had still lingered over the applicability and feasibility of full employment in developing countries. Second, there was now a legal framework for the coordinated promotion of policies for achieving full employment through both the supervisory machinery for ILO standards and the advisory services and technical assistance provided by technical departments. Third, the Convention highlighted the importance of embedding employment policies within core ILO values; employment had not only to be "full" but also "freely chosen", and the policies for achieving this should be designed with tripartite involvement.

There was, of course, other work on employment in the 1960s. The advisory and technical cooperation work on manpower planning, vocational training and productivity enhancement continued to expand. A major report on employment and economic growth was published in 1964, which addressed the industrialized countries' emerging concern in employment policy over such matters as the impact of automation and structural change on employment and the countervailing policies required to preserve full employment.[27] With reference to developing countries, studies were published on the concept of unemployment and underemployment, on techniques for manpower planning and on the problem of the choice of technique.[28] Such work no doubt contributed to the body of knowledge that underpinned the launching of the WEP.

Pursuant to the adoption of Convention No. 122, follow-up action was taken at ILO regional conferences in the 1960s. The Ottawa Plan for Human Resources Development for the Americas region, the Asian Manpower Plan and the Jobs and Skills Programmes for Africa, were adopted in 1966, 1968 and 1969, respectively. These titles are quite revealing of the fact that most of the ILO work at the time was still focused on problems of manpower planning and vocational training and not on the large issues of development strategy that were soon to take centre stage. Indeed, these actions at the regional level were integrated into the WEP that came into operation in 1969.

---

[27] ILO: *Employment and economic growth*, Studies and Reports, New Series, No. 67 (Geneva, 1964).

[28] N. Islam: "Concepts and measurements of unemployment and underemployment in developing countries", in *International Labour Review* (Geneva, ILO, 1964), Vol. 89; M. Debeauvais: "Manpower planning in developing countries", in *International Labour Review* (Geneva, ILO, 1964), Vol. 89; and W. Galenson: "Economic development and the sectoral expansion of employment", in *International Labour Review* (Geneva, ILO, 1963), Vol. 87.

## The World Employment Programme

David Morse, who was then at the helm of the ILO, described the aim of the WEP as follows: "to halt and indeed reverse the trend towards ever-growing masses of peasants and slum dwellers who have no part in development".[29] He believed that this goal would be achieved by providing the masses with the skills needed for productive work, by accelerating rural development and industrialization and by promoting the growth of international trade. He also emphasized that the focus on employment was necessary because productive work was the only path to a better life for people in poor countries, that the programme had to be global in scope because it could not succeed without help from the industrialized nations, and that the WEP was part of the United Nations Second Development Decade.

The launching of the WEP was significant for a number of reasons. First, it marked the formal beginning of an ILO concern with problems of poverty reduction in developing countries. The "masses" who had no part in development then are the poor of today's international efforts to achieve the Millennium Development Goals. As Morse himself recognized, this marked a major departure for the ILO. He stressed that the adoption of the WEP would "entail some changes in habits of thought and work. The main concern will be with those who do not have work (clearly meaning productive employment) rather that with those already in employment".[30] Second, adopting this broadened objective clearly implied that there had to be a parallel broadening of the scope of the ILO's work to key issues of overall development strategy. Third, the description of the WEP constituted an important and specific restatement of the core ILO value that the ultimate goal of all economic policies was the attainment of social objectives. In stating that employment was the only path to a better life, Morse elaborated on the point by saying that "there is no clearer and more concrete form of social participation than fruitful employment" and that, therefore, "even if it means slower economic growth, employment-oriented development is to be preferred on social grounds – so long as it does not result in actual economic stagnation".[31]

From the standpoint of its work on employment, the launching of the WEP was clearly a turning point for the ILO. It marked the end of the hesitant search for a role in the post-Second World War period, when it was confronted with the emergence of the United Nations and the Bretton Woods institutions – a search

---

[29] D. Morse: "The World Employment Programme", in *International Labour Review* (Geneva, ILO, 1968), Vol. 97, p. 518.

[30] Ibid., p. 520.

[31] Ibid.

that had led it, inter alia, to find safe niches in fields such as vocational training and manpower planning. Despite being of practical importance in their own right, these areas were not exactly at the cutting edge of the academic and policy thinking on employment and development issues at the time. Against this background, the launching of the WEP was a bold and welcome initiative to reclaim the high ground that the ILO had occupied in the pre-war period.

The WEP began with a bang, producing the first of several comprehensive employment policy reports in 1970. That report was on Colombia.[32] Produced by a team led by a leading development economist, Dudley Seers, it had a major impact on the academic and policy debate on development at the time. Lest there be any confusion among readers unfamiliar with these reports, it is important to point out that most of them were far more than just routine country reports by international organizations. They represented the outcome of considerable preparatory research work and the combined talents of a sizeable team of high-quality international development experts specially recruited for each country mission. Not surprisingly, these reports were highly respectable products in terms of their academic quality, as well as being both bold and innovative in their analyses and policy recommendations.

The Colombia report set the ambitious tone that was to characterize the work under the WEP in its first few years. Asked to produce a consistent set of policies for eliminating unemployment in Colombia, it proposed what amounted to a radical change in development strategy. In the words of the head of the mission: "The unemployment crisis requires, in fact, analysis not just of growth of unemployment itself but of the whole development process. To cure it requires a fundamental rethinking of development – not just 'providing jobs' to mop up open unemployment".[33] There were several key elements to the proposed strategy. One that was to dominate WEP thinking was the notion of the need to increase the employment intensity of the growth process. It was argued that a strategy of achieving high growth through a reliance on capital-intensive sectors and techniques of production would not only fail to generate many jobs but would also, through its indirect effects on the exchange rate and wage levels, reduce the amount of employment created in agriculture and other labour-intensive sectors.

According to the report, the route to an employment-intensive strategy required both conventional and radical measures. The conventional measures,

---

[32] ILO: *Towards full employment: A programme for Colombia*, prepared by an inter-agency team organized by the International Labour Office (Geneva, 1970).

[33] D. Seers: "New approaches suggested by the Colombia Employment Programme", in *International Labour Review* (Geneva, ILO, 1970), Vol. 102, p. 380.

in line with a neo-classical framework of analysis, would involve the removal of incentive biases which favoured the capital-intensive sectors and the adoption of capital-intensive techniques of production. Tax and other incentives for capital-intensive sectors, interest rate subsidies and an overvaluation of the exchange rate would need to be removed. At the same time, the costs of labour (especially those arising from the provision of fringe benefits) should not be raised unduly. But this was not considered to be sufficient. Radical structural change was also required. The distribution of income needed to be made much less unequal because "it is hardly conceivable that a high level of employment will be achieved in Colombia so long as the distribution of income is such as to generate a heavy demand for goods and service with big import requirements (allowing for both capital goods and intermediate products) and heavy skill needs, but little demand for goods and services incorporating a high content of unskilled labour".[34] A call was thus made for strong redistributive measures such as increased taxes on the rich, land reform, the control of monopoly and a widening of educational opportunities. A strategy of this kind would require a tight coordination of policies and hence "any government that adopted a full employment strategy would have to develop an appropriate system of planning".[35]

The second WEP mission, also led by Dudley Seers, was to Ceylon (now Sri Lanka) in 1971.[36] This raised the same core issue of the labour-intensity of growth but also drew attention to the problem of educated unemployment that was concentrated among young people. Ceylon was different from Colombia in that it had a socialist government, a significantly lower level of inequality in the distribution of income and progressive government expenditures on health, education and social welfare. Yet this lower inequality, held to be an important requirement for ensuring a better employment outcome in the Colombia report, was not sufficient to avoid a serious employment problem. A basic reason for this was that the same policy bias towards capital-intensive sectors and techniques that was found in Colombia also prevailed in Ceylon. In addition there was a "lack of controls on the introduction of foreign technologies that involve heavy foreign exchange costs".[37] Another reason was that, in spite of the lower income inequality, land was scarce in relation to labour in Ceylon and, unlike Colombia, there was no land frontier that still remained to be exploited. This scarce land

---

[34] Ibid., p. 387.

[35] Ibid.

[36] ILO: *Matching employment opportunities and expectations: A programme of action for Ceylon* (Geneva, 1970).

[37] D. Seers: "New light on structural unemployment: Lessons of a mission to Ceylon", in *International Labour Review* (Geneva, ILO, 1972), Vol. 105, p. 100.

had therefore to be redistributed in order to increase labour absorption in the rural areas.

Yet another reason was the dysfunctional education system that generated a serious problem of educated unemployment. The rapid expansion of education had "outrun the capacity of the economy to provide the sort of jobs that those with secondary school qualifications felt they are entitled to expect – broadly speaking, office jobs".[38] The report recommended that the problem be tackled by urgently reforming the education system to make it more oriented to practical skills rather than paper qualifications; overhauling the wage and salary structure in the economy to reduce the wide differential in favour of white-collar jobs; greatly expanding "para-professional labour forces in education and health"; and creating a "national youth service".[39]

At the same time, the report did not overlook the basic requirement for policy reforms to allow Ceylon to break out of the trap of a chronic balance of payment deficit and low growth. It advocated reforming the capital-intensive import-substitution strategy and the mobilizing of resources to fund employment creation through a reduction in unsustainable welfare expenditures, as well as increased taxation of the rich and general wage restraint. The mission held that these measures would raise both growth and employment while also increasing equity.

The third WEP mission was to Kenya in 1972, and this time it was led by another two well-known development economists, Hans Singer and Richard Jolly – who, like Dudley Seers, were also from the Institute of Development Studies of the University of Sussex in the United Kingdom. The report is significant in that it made two major contributions to development thinking in the period.[40] The first was the presentation of a development strategy based on "redistribution with growth", while the second was to draw attention to the significance of the "informal sector" for employment and development in developing countries.

The first contribution was essentially a more sophisticated presentation of the case for redistribution that had been made in the first two reports. The latter, as pointed out by a critic, had recognized high growth as a prerequisite of the strategy it recommended but had treated it largely as a *deus ex machina*. The Kenya report confronted the problem of the potential conflict between growth

---

[38] Ibid., p. 102.

[39] Ibid., p. 106.

[40] ILO: *Employment, incomes and equality: A strategy for increasing productive employment in Kenya* (Geneva, 1972).

and redistribution by stating that the two could be reconciled. "The emphasis is on growth as well as redistribution because of the low level of income per head in Kenya and the high proportion of the population living in the rural areas at near subsistence level. In view of these two facts, neither growth nor income distribution alone would be adequate. Both are needed and must be linked in a comprehensive strategy."[41] In arguing for a complete restructuring of the economy, the report was also mindful of the fact that resources had to be found to finance this. It took the view that "the resources for this restructuring would be found from a redistribution of the fruits of growth".[42] A more moderate slant was therefore given to the advocacy of redistribution, with the emphasis being shifted away from expropriation towards redistribution at the margin of the increments to GDP. This probably accounted for the World Bank's adoption of the concept in a major study on development strategy published in 1974.[43]

The second major contribution of the report was to argue the case for a revision of policy attitudes to the informal sector in developing countries. Although the concept was not invented by the mission, its report was responsible for transforming it into an important development policy issue. The framework for analysing the informal sector was the broader definition of the employment problem in developing countries that was set out in the report. This included not merely open unemployment but also the problems of underemployment and of low wages and low returns to work. The report noted that "mention of this sector often conjures up a picture of fictitious, marginal, parasitical or illegal activities" which "for a newly independent country" appears to represent a "reversion to primitive conditions, a denial of modernization and progress". Contrary to this stereotype, the report argued that "the informal sector, both urban and rural, represents a vital part of the Kenyan economy and that its existence reflects a necessary and, on the whole, beneficial adjustment to the constraints imposed by the prevailing economic situation". Accordingly, the report recommended "a major shift in government policies concerning the informal sector – a shift towards active encouragement and support" and stated that "what is needed are positive new policies for promoting the informal sector and linking it with the formal sector".[44] It is of interest to note that this concept has come to be an important issue for ILO work ever since, although it was initially rejected by

---

[41] H. Singer and R. Jolly: "Unemployment in an African setting: Lessons of the employment strategy mission to Kenya", in *International Labour Review* (Geneva, ILO, 1973), Vol. 107, p. 104.

[42] Ibid., p. 104.

[43] H.B. Chenery et al.: *Redistribution with growth* (London, Oxford University Press, 1974).

[44] Singer and Jolly, op. cit., p. 107.

the ILO constituency and the staff outside the WEP on the grounds of being beyond the mandate of the Organization.

These three reports defined the main issues that were addressed in the WEP's research and advisory work, undertaken both by the Office in Geneva and the regional employment teams that were established in Africa, Latin America and the Caribbean, and Asia during the 1970s. Other comprehensive employment policy missions were to follow during this period (the Philippines in 1974, the Dominican Republic in 1975, and Sudan in 1976), but none of them raised fundamental issues in the same way that the first three had done.[45] If anything, these later reports represented an adjustment of the WEP line towards less radical approaches to solving the employment problem in developing countries. For example, the report of the Philippines mission, headed by an economist from Yale University, Gus Ranis, highlighted the need to liberalize the economy and to move away from failed policies of capital-intensive import substitution towards a strategy of export-led industrialization. It argued that such a strategy, by promoting the growth of labour-intensive exports in line with the underlying comparative advantage of labour-abundant developing countries, would be the most effective means of rapidly raising the demand for unskilled labour. At the same time, economic liberalization, by reducing market failures, discrimination in the allocation of credit, monopoly power and the protection of inefficient industries, would also be the most effective way of improving the distribution of income. Similarly, the Sudan mission, led by the Norwegian economist Just Faaland, also adopted a more moderate and conventional policy stance.

The research work of the WEP covered a wide range of topics on key issues of employment policy in developing countries, as well as on international economic issues affecting employment and development. Major programmes, involving both in-house staff and external research collaborators, covered such areas as technology and employment; income distribution and employment; manpower planning and labour market information systems; rural employment; the urban informal sector; emergency employment schemes involving measures to increase capacity utilization and rural public works; and population and development. In addition, work was carried out on international issues which included the impact of the trade liberalization of employment – both in the North and the South; multinationals and employment; international sub-contracting and

---

[45] ILO: *Sharing in development: A programme of employment, equity and growth for the Philippines* (Geneva, 1974); ILO: *Inter-agency employment mission to the Dominican Republic* (Geneva, 1975); ILO: *Growth, employment and equity: A comprehensive strategy for the Sudan* (Geneva, 1976).

employment; international migration; and the transfer of technology.[46] Along-side these activities, there was an extensive programme of advisory services and technical assistance to diagnose employment problems, as well as to formulate and implement employment policies. This work was carried out by Geneva-based staff, the regional employment teams and resident teams of experts serving under country-based technical cooperation projects.

All this work generated a vast body of knowledge on employment issues in developing countries. This consisted, inter alia, of new survey data generated from field research; analyses of empirical relationships on the determinants of employ-ment, income distribution and poverty; studies on the functioning of rural and urban informal sector labour markets; and analyses of key issues of employment policy. In addition, the ILO came up with more practical products, such as actual drafts of chapters on employment and manpower policy in national five-year plans. It also published manuals on topics including the techniques of employ-ment and manpower planning and the design of labour-intensive public works.[47]

There can be little doubt that the WEP was the leading source of ideas and new thinking and expertise on employment issues in developing countries throughout the 1970s. And this may be attributed to the sheer volume and gener-ally high technical quality of its work. It was able to operate on such a large scale because it was able to convince donors of the strategic importance of the issues it addressed for achieving growth with equity in developing countries. Indeed, the programme offered a promising alternative to the failures of the develop-ment strategies of the 1950s and 1960s. But the size of this effort alone would not have been enough if the resources available had not been used to secure the involvement of economists from leading academic institutions throughout the world – and to recruit a cadre of young economists with doctorates from some of these same institutions. This provided a guarantee that the work undertaken would be of high technical quality and at the forefront of knowledge in its day. Furthermore, the involvement of leading outside economists in its activities lent prestige to the programme in the eyes of member States and the academic com-munity, while also providing a valuable conduit for the dissemination of WEP ideas. Last, but not least, the achievements of the WEP in this period owed much to the dynamic leadership of Louis Emmerij.

The work of the WEP in its first six years reached a defining moment with the organization of the World Employment Conference in 1976. The Conference

---

[46] ILO: *Bibliography of published research of the World Employment Programme* (Geneva, 1978), first edition. Eight other editions were subsequently published in the series until 1991.

[47] Ibid.

marked the ILO's entry into the series of World Conferences that had been organized by the UN and its agencies in the preceding few years on global issues, such as the environment, the food crisis, trade and development and population. The report prepared for the Conference, stressed that "the focus should be shifted towards meeting the basic needs of the masses".[48] It also spelt out in broad terms the major redirections of development policy required under a basic needs approach. Emphasis was placed on the "redistribution with growth" strategy that had been developed in the Kenya mission, highlighting both the acceleration of growth and the redistribution of income as key means for achieving equitable development. In addition to this core issue of a basic needs strategy, the Conference had agenda items on international manpower movements; the role of multinational enterprises in employment creation in developing countries; technologies for productive employment creation in developing countries; and labour market policies in developed countries. Apart from the last item, there were clear North–South differences on these issues in the context of the then acrimonious debate on the establishment of a New International Economic Order. Not surprisingly, the Conference outcome reflected compromises reached between the G-77 and developed country positions on these issues. Similarly, on the core issue of a basic needs strategy, there was no clear endorsement of the strong redistributive thrust of the strategy that the Office report had originally proposed. "Representatives of a few industrialized countries and some Employers' delegates felt that the report overemphasised structural change and redistribution ... [and] did not adequately emphasise rapid economic growth."[49] On the whole, however, the Declaration of Principles and Programme of Action adopted by the Conference did give a progressive thrust to development strategy by highlighting the need to focus on the alleviation of absolute poverty. It set the goal of the satisfaction of the basic needs of the poor within a generation. It also stressed the importance of international economic reforms and cooperation in order to reinforce action taken at the national level. In these two respects it anticipated the similar consensus reached by the international community around the Millennium Development Goals that were adopted in 2000.

The WEP was therefore given a major international mandate. But it was also set a very lofty target – no less than the universal abolition of absolute poverty

---

[48] ILO: *Employment, growth and basic needs: A one-world problem*, Report of the Director-General of the ILO to the Tripartite World Conference on Employment, Income Distribution and Social Progress and the International Division of Labour (Geneva, 1976).

[49] L. Emmerij and D. Ghai: "The World Employment Conference: A preliminary assessment", in *International Labour Review* (Geneva, ILO, 1976), Vol. 114, No. 3, p. 304.

within a decade – that was to prove impossible to achieve. The "basic needs strategy", although based on key elements of WEP work up to that point, had not, in fact, been specifically thought through and developed. The term had emerged in the throes of writing the report for the World Employment Conference, and was intended to encapsulate the key common elements of the development strategy being developed in the WEP's work. This had some unfortunate unintended consequences. The term "basic needs" begged a host of questions of both a technical and political nature. What were these needs? How were they to be measured and their progress monitored? Who was to define them, and through what process? Did the term not give a paternalistic slant and a mechanical supply-side focus to the complex process of poverty reduction? Did it not give the impression that it would condemn poor countries to aspiring to no more than drab, bare essentials for a long time to come?[50]

Given these difficulties, it is not surprising that the basic needs approach failed to blossom. Some technical work was undertaken to flesh out the strategy, and basic needs missions were fielded to a few countries. But on the whole, the ILO did not follow-up fully on the mandate it had been given by the World Employment Conference to prepare statistics, studies and strategies on basic needs in all countries. This was a reflection of the fact that the consensus reached on the concept at the World Employment Conference had only been superficial. There was support for the strategy from the Carter Administration, and the World Bank flirted briefly with the concept[51] – but by the early 1980s it had ended up in the cemetery of overblown United Nations ideas.

Despite this setback, the key components of WEP work continued throughout the rest of the 1970s. There were no more comprehensive employment policy missions, but scaled-down versions of such missions were fielded – principally by the regional employment teams. Research on the core issues of employment policy followed on, especially in the regional employment teams in Latin America and Asia, as did advisory and technical assistance programmes. Much of this work was of solid technical quality, but it failed to generate new ideas for solving the employment problem in developing countries. The high-water mark of new thinking had clearly been passed.

---

[50] D. Ghai et al.: *The basic-needs approach to development: Some issues regarding concepts and methodology* (Geneva, ILO, 1977).

[51] P. Streeten: *The distinctive features of the basic needs approach to development* (World Bank, Washington, DC, 1977).

# The 1980s

The decade of the 1980s was a difficult and turbulent one for the global economy. It started with the second oil shock that triggered stagflation and rising unemployment in the industrialized countries, as well as acute economic distress in many developing countries. For the industrialized countries, the 1980s marked the definite end of the era of full employment that had prevailed throughout the "Golden Age". The social and political consensus centred on the welfare state also began to crumble with the electoral victories of Margaret Thatcher and Ronald Reagan in the United Kingdom and the United States, respectively. The free-market doctrine they espoused began its ascent, challenging some of the key assumptions that had guided the ILO's work in the first six decades of its existence. In spite of the fact that most continental Western European countries remained unaffected by this "Anglo-Saxon" ideological shift, its influence began to spread quickly elsewhere. From a free-market perspective, the economic and social benefits of international labour standards and the labour market regulation they promoted were not the self-evident truths that they were to the ILO. On the contrary, the default position was that they represented potential distortions of the market that could reduce economic efficiency and growth. The same position extended to all other areas of prevailing economic and social policy and led to programmes of privatization, market deregulation and the erosion of welfare states funded by progressive taxation. In this context, the role and status of trade unions and of collective bargaining and social dialogue were invariably diminished.

It is important to note that the regime change in the United Kingdom and the United States was not a purely political phenomena but was linked to and fuelled by a parallel shift to the right in the discipline of economics. The postwar Keynesian consensus began to crumble in the face of the rise to prominence of neo-classical economics. In the realm of macroeconomic policy, the failure of traditional Keynesian policies to solve the problem of stagflation lent credence to monetarist arguments and to the notions of "rational expectations" and a "natural rate of unemployment". Within this neo-classical framework, the objective of maintaining a pre-determined level of full employment through manipulating monetary and fiscal policies was a serious delusion. The optimal policy, it was argued, was to allow the level of unemployment to find its natural rate unhindered by macroeconomic policy interventions that could only lead to rising inflation. And the only way to lower the rate of unemployment was through supply-side policies centred on restoring flexibility to labour markets that had become seriously distorted by the combined effects of protective labour legislation, excessive trade union power and generous welfare benefits that destroyed the incentive to work.

This neo-classical view of the employment problem thus struck against the core assumptions of all the main areas of the ILO's work, that is, the work on labour standards, employment, social protection and social dialogue.

This shift in economic doctrine soon began to impact on the developing countries. The second oil shock triggered off severe balance of payments and debt crises in many Latin American and sub-Saharan African, as well as a few Asian, countries. These countries had to turn to the IMF and the World Bank for help and were met by the full blast of the icy wind of neo-classical thinking on development. In line with current thinking, it was held that the optimal path to development was an adherence to laissez-faire policies, and that it was deviation from this strait and narrow path that had led to developmental failures, including the current crises in these countries. The only path to salvation was for these countries to adopt structural adjustment programmes that would purge their economies of the toxic effects of dirigiste and redistributive policies. And they should be subjected to the same prescriptions applied to the industrialized countries, consisting of privatization and public sector retrenchment, market deregulation, trade and investment liberalization and restrictive monetary and fiscal policies. Many indebted countries underwent this therapy but there were few cases where the expectations that they would be quickly restored to economic health were fulfilled. What was clear, however, was that the application of these programmes entailed high social costs in terms of rising unemployment and underemployment, falling real wages and incomes, and increased poverty. All in all, the 1980s was a period of stagnant per-capita income in Latin America and decline in sub-Saharan Africa, and has been referred to by some economists as the "lost decade" for development.

It might have been expected that these events would trigger a strong response from the ILO, especially given its recent leading role on issues of employment and development and its basic mandate to ensure social justice in the global economy. There was, in fact, a response – but a strikingly muted one in comparison to the high profile of the WEP's work in the preceding decade. In Latin America, the region hardest hit by the crisis of the early 1980s, the regional employment team (PREALC) did confront the issue in its advisory and research work. It documented the employment impact and highlighted the social costs of the crisis, and by the end of the decade it advocated policies for repairing the social damage that had occurred. It depicted this as a necessary repayment of the "social debt" that had been incurred during the period of crisis and adjustment.[52] But the impact of this work was largely confined to Latin America. The employment teams in the

---

[52] PREALC: *Meeting the social debt* (Santiago de Chile, 1988).

other regions did not undertake similar work. Neither was there any significant mobilization of effort in Geneva to address the social costs of structural adjustment. Only a small unit consisting of a handful of professional staff was deployed to address this issue alongside other international economic issues, such as trade liberalization and employment. The WEP was thus largely absent from the scene and the major response of the UN system came instead from UNICEF, which published an influential report entitled *Adjustment with a human face*.[53] This contained a critique of the policies of the Bretton Woods institutions as well as proposals for more socially-sensitive adjustment policies. Ironically, two of the main report's authors – Richard Jolly and Frances Stewart – had been major contributors to the WEP's work in the 1970s.

What explains this strange episode of the dog having failed to bark? A basic reason was that there was no political consensus to allow the ILO to advocate alternative policies to those of the IMF and the World Bank. The major economic powers that pushed for neo-liberal policies in the Bretton Woods institutions were hardly likely to encourage dissent from the ILO. At the same time, the workers' and employers' groups within the ILO held strongly divergent views on the issue. While the workers were strongly in favour of more socially-oriented policies, the employers sympathized with the neo-liberal rationale for structural adjustment policies. Another factor was that the WEP did not have a strong in-house technical capacity on the macroeconomic policy issues that were at the heart of the structural adjustment debate. And given the WEP's orientation towards fundamental structural issues of development strategy rather than shorter-run issues of actually managing monetary and fiscal policies, this capacity had never been strong. Now it was further weakened because the WEP was scaling down in terms of funding and staff numbers. The ILO was thus in no position to formulate academically respectable alternatives to conventional structural adjustment programmes that could have served to increase political support for a more socially-oriented approach.

This is not to say that the ILO was totally absent from the scene. Trade unions across the developing world protested about the negative effects of structural adjustment programmes on employment (especially public sector retrenchment), real wages and the cost of living in general. These resentments were aired in various ILO forums. However, the employers were determined to prevent the ILO from engaging in the issue, their argument being that structural adjustment was a macroeconomic issue and hence outside the mandate of the ILO. They were also strongly opposed to any suggestion that the ILO should strengthen its in-house capacity to deal with

---

[53] G.A. Cornia, R. Jolly and F. Stewart (eds): *Adjustment with a human face, Vol. I: Protecting the vulnerable and promoting growth* (Oxford, Clarendon Press, 1987).

macroeconomic issues. In the event, the only substantive ILO response was the organization, rather late in the day, of a high-level tripartite meeting on structural adjustment in 1987. The political impact of this meeting was limited, given the lack of consensus on the need to put forward an alternative ILO position.

Despite this central failing, other work was, of course, undertaken by the WEP during this period. Much of this reflected the continuing momentum of work programmes that had started in the 1970s. A major study, by Amartya Sen, *Poverty and famines*, was published in 1981, for example.[54] This work proved to be highly influential and Sen went on to win the Nobel Prize in Economics in 1998. The regional employment teams continued to produce country studies on employment and development and to provide advisory services and implement technical cooperation projects. In fact, much of the influence enjoyed by the ILO in the developing countries during this period was due to the substantive research and advisory work carried out by these regional teams. This was especially true of the Regional Employment Programme for Latin America and the Caribbean (PREALC) and the Asian Regional Team for Employment Promotion (ARTEP). In the early 1980s, the technology and employment programme examined the effects of higher energy costs on developing countries and conducted studies on new and renewable sources on energy. The rural employment programme undertook a series of studies on the food crisis in Africa in the second half of the 1980s and on rural labour markets and employment.[55] The International Institute for Labour Studies conducted studies on industrial districts and the development of small- and medium-sized enterprises, as well as on labour market institutions and employment.[56] A *World Labour Report* was launched in the early 1980s and employment was one of the core areas covered by this report, alongside issues such as social protection and industrial relations.[57] From the perspective of employment and poverty reduction issues, these reports failed to give new life to an intellectually flagging WEP. In the late 1980s, there was a single-handed attempt to confront the advocacy of labour market flexibility through a series of case studies of industrialized countries – but their impact on changing the policy debate was limited.[58]

---

[54] A.K. Sen: *Poverty and famines: An essay on deprivation and entitlement* (Oxford, Clarendon Press, 1981).

[55] ILO: *International Labour Review* (Geneva, ILO), Vol. 127, 1988; and Vol. 128, 1989. These were special issues, devoted to both these topics, respectively.

[56] W. Sengenberger and G. Loveman: *Smaller units of employment: A synthesis report on industrial reorganization in industrialized countries* (Geneva, ILO, International Institute for Labour Studies, 1988).

[57] ILO: *World Labour Report* (Geneva, 1984).

[58] G. Standing: *Unemployment and labour market flexibility: The United Kingdom* (Geneva, ILO, 1986). This was the first in a series of country studies which covered Austria, Finland, Germany, Italy, the Netherlands, Spain and Sweden.

## The 1990s

The 1990s saw the formal demise of the WEP and the beginning of a long and haphazard search for a new paradigm and political thrust for organizing the ILO's work on employment and poverty reduction.

In terms of the broad context of employment and development, the 1990s was a period of profound change. The fall of the Berlin Wall in 1989 triggered off a major economic and social crisis in the countries of the former Soviet bloc, and these countries embarked on the hitherto unprecedented challenge of making the transition from a centrally-planned to a market economy. The early years of this process witnessed a massive drop in output and the emergence of mass unemployment and poverty in countries that had never before experienced such trauma during the communist era. The collapse of communism also gave a boost to the process of economic globalization that had begun to take off with the ascent of neo-liberal economics in the previous decade. From that perspective, globalization was a logical extension of the market economy from a national to a global scale – a process that promised immense gains in terms of increased economic efficiency and higher growth. Now that communism no longer held sway, there was no credible alternative to the globalization project; on the contrary, there were now many more willing recruits for the expanding global market economy. These included not only the countries in the former Soviet bloc but also China and many other developing countries, including giants such as India and Brazil.

A significant development at the beginning of the 1990s was that the lead role in managing the process of transition to a market economy in the former Soviet bloc was assigned to the IMF and the World Bank. The financial and technical assistance provided to these countries thus came with the same strong neo-liberal policy conditionality that had been applied to developing countries under structural adjustment programmes. The added twist was that a "big bang" approach was favoured, which advocated that the key elements of the transition process – such as privatization; price, trade, exchange rate and capital account liberalization; the creation of a free labour market – should be implemented in one fell swoop. The IMF and the World Bank clearly showed little awareness of, or regard for, the fact that well-functioning market economies required a supporting structure of institutions, such as a legal system to ensure property rights and the enforcement of contracts; regulatory and policy regimes to prevent market failures and the abuse of market power; and, last but by no means least, systems of social protection, particularly in situations of major economic and social upheaval.

The ILO therefore faced a difficult external environment when it tried to respond to the drama of transition. Internally, the ILO was also undergoing a difficult major reorganization of its field structure. From 1992 onwards, Multidisciplinary Teams (MDTs) were established which comprised technical specialists in the ILO's main spheres of competence – such as employment, labour standards, social protection, industrial relations and enterprise development – as well as an advisor each for relations with worker and employer constituents of the ILO. Fourteen such teams were set up. They replaced the regional employment teams of the WEP and the other regional centres on training and labour administration. A basic rationale for this change was the need to capitalize on the inherent synergies that existed across the different disciplines of ILO work, and thus ensure a more coherent and greater impact from ILO assistance to its member States.

From the standpoint of ILO's work on employment, this change resulted in a fragmentation and consequent weakening of its capacity in the field. Instead of regional employment teams comprising each of eight to 12 economists who undertook research and provided advisory services on development policies and employment, these specialists were now dispersed across three or more MDTs in each region. A critical core of economic expertise in each region was thus lost. As the process developed, the problem was exacerbated by the adoption of a looser definition of what constituted work on employment issues. No longer confined to issues of economic policy relating to employment, the definition of an 'employment specialist' now included more practical areas of work, such as the promotion of small enterprises, the organization of income-generating activities and vocational training. Most of the MDTs did little research because they were fully taken up with day-to-day technical advice on relatively narrow topics.

In the mid-1990s, the World Summit for Social Development, discussed in Chapter 6, became an important focus of attention for the ILO's work on employment, both in the preparation of the Summit, and in its follow-up. The first *World Employment Report*[59] was prepared for the Social Summit. It attracted the attention of the media and other international agencies, including the Bretton Woods institutions. The second report, published in the following year, had even more of an impact and re-established the ILO, albeit briefly, as a significant player on employment issues.[60] The reports highlighted the gravity of the employment problem in developed, transition and developing countries, and urged concerted international action to deal with it. They reaffirmed that, contrary to the neoliberal view, the goal of full employment was still a desirable and feasible policy objective. In so doing, they refuted claims that the "end-of-work" was imminent and that full employment was thus an obsolete goal. They also argued that

---

[59] ILO: *World Employment 1995: An ILO report* (Geneva, 1995).

[60] ILO: *World Employment Report 1996/97: National policies in a global context* (Geneva, 1996).

the employment problem could not be solved through increased labour market flexibility alone, but instead required a combination of complementary macroeconomics, incomes, labour market and product market policies. The reports also called for cooperative international action to ensure that the potential for globalization to benefit all countries and increase employment creation was realized – rejecting the view that trade with developing countries was a major cause of the high unemployment in many industrialized countries. An agreement was reached between the ILO, the IMF and the World Bank to exchange drafts of their flagship reports for comment prior to publication. The ILO was also given observer status in the Interim Committee of the IMF. And, in 1997, it was invited, alongside the OECD, to be a regular participant in the annual Labour and Employment Ministries of Meetings of the G7 (later G8) countries.

In 1997, the Asian financial crisis began and sparked off a severe economic contraction with very high social costs in terms of increased unemployment and poverty. As was the case with the structural adjustment programmes of the 1980s, the policy conditions imposed on the debtor countries were highly controversial. Critics blamed these policies for worsening the economic contraction and increasing the social suffering associated with the crisis. While again absent from the macroeconomic policy debate, the ILO did respond fairly credibly to the crisis by highlighting its social costs and the need for swift ameliorative action.[61] It used the occasion to stress the importance of developing sound institutions for social protection and social dialogue during good times, pointing out that such institutions might have greatly reduced the social cost of the crisis and facilitated the process of economic adjustment and recovery. In practice, the ILO also managed to obtain, with the support of the then Managing Director of the IMF, Michel Camdessus, progress on the ratification of core labour standards and on social dialogue in two crisis countries – the Republic of Korea and Indonesia.

The crisis also drove home the point of how important an influence the accelerating process of globalization was becoming for the work of the ILO. Trade, investment and financial liberalization were being implemented in a growing number of countries, and this was obviously having an impact on employment and earnings. The process put a premium on sound economic management and strong social and labour policies as the means for maximizing the benefits from globalization. The ILO had begun to recognize and address these issues. As mentioned above, the first two *World Employment Reports* discussed the relationship

---

[61] ILO: *The social impact of the Asian financial crisis*, report for the ILO Tripartite Meeting on the Asian financial crisis, Bangkok, Apr., 1998; and E. Lee: *The Asian financial crisis: The challenge for social policy* (Geneva, ILO, 1998).

between globalization and employment. In 1996, the International Labour Conference had a general discussion on employment on the basis of a report entitled *Employment policies in a global context* [62] which was in fact based on the second *World Employment Report* – then in an advanced stage of preparation.

The ILO then produced a series of in-depth country studies on the social impact of globalization, the results of which were to be presented for discussion in the Governing Body.[63] The individual country studies, together with a synthesis volume, were well received by the Governing Body, and beyond. They made a strong case for enhancing the social impact of globalization through improved economic and social policies, including the strengthening of core labour standards and social dialogue.

As may therefore be seen, the ILO did make some significant contributions to the issues of employment in the 1990s. But the technical capacity of the Office on matters of economic and employment policy continued to decline. The replacement of the regional employment teams by MDTs weakened that capacity in the regions, with a strong knock-on effect on the effectiveness of work in headquarters. Indeed, Geneva had now lost a large part of its access to first-hand knowledge on regional and national perspectives and priorities on employment issues, as well as to valuable contacts in academic and policy circles. There was little extra-budgetary support for research and no systematic effort to maintain economic expertise through the process of recruitment. Not surprisingly, much of the work appeared to be ad hoc and merely a belated reaction to events and issues. The WEP had put the ILO "ahead of the curve", whereas now it was lagging seriously behind. The decade was thus largely a missed opportunity for the ILO to prepare for the employment and labour market challenges that were to come with the deepening and widening of globalization at the beginning of the twenty-first century.

---

[62] ILO: *Employment policies in a global context*, Report V, International Labour Conference, 83rd Session, Geneva, 1996.

[63] R. Torres: *Towards a socially sustainable world economy: An analysis of the social pillars of globalization* (Geneva, ILO, 2001). This is a synthesis volume of the series entitled: "Studies on the social dimension of globalization", which comprises country studies on Bangladesh, Chile, Republic of Korea, Mauritius, Poland, South Africa and Switzerland.

## The 2000s

The introduction of the decent work concept in 1999 changed the frame of reference for work on employment and poverty reduction. Although one of the four newly created sectors of the Office was devoted to different aspects of employment policy, its subsequent work is best considered within the context of this dominant and holistic new paradigm, which called for stronger interaction between work on employment and other aspects of the ILO's agenda. We examine this further in the next chapter.

This observation notwithstanding, some elements of work on employment in the earlier mould can still be identified. In 2000, a study was published on successful employment policies in four small European countries, arguing that the source of success lay in supportive labour market institutions and social dialogue, rather than in labour market flexibility.[64] Since then, work on the industrialized countries has centred on issue of "flexicurity" – or how to combine the need for flexible adjustment of labour markets to competitive pressures from the global economy with a decent level of social protection.[65] Work on employment problems and policies in developing countries has mainly taken the form of country studies and reports, with their problems being addressed in the context of global studies. Studies on the impact of globalization on employment and poverty were published in 2003 and 2004, and the fourth edition of the *World Employment Reports* published in 2001 addressed the issue of the employment and development implications of the digital divide and of the information economy in general.[66] There has been little further work on this issue. The fifth and only other issue in this series consisted of three essays on productivity and employment.[67] A Global Employment Forum was organized in 2001, and similar events have since been held in several other countries – including China. Following the Global Employment Forum, a ten-point Global Employment Agenda was launched and, since that time, has been extensively discussed in the Employment and Social Policy Committee of the Governing Body. Compared with earlier work on employment, there is a greater focus on entrepreneurship and enterprise development, which reflects the merging of units undertaking work on employment and

---

[64] P. Auer: *Employment revival in Europe: Labour market success in Austria, Denmark, Ireland and the Netherlands* (Geneva, ILO, 2000).

[65] P. Auer: *Protected mobility for employment and decent work: Labour market security in a globalized world* (Geneva, ILO, Employment Strategy Department, 2005).

[66] ILO: *World Employment Report 2001: Life at work in the information economy* (Geneva, 2001).

[67] ILO: *World Employment Report 2004–05: Employment, productivity and poverty reduction* (Geneva, 2005).

labour market policy and on skill development with a previously independent programme on enterprises.

The issues covered within the Global Employment Agenda extend beyond employment to include such matters as occupational safety and health, social protection and rights at work. As noted above, it is better to consider its role – in the quest for a coherent and substantive contribution to thinking on issues of employment and poverty reduction in an era of increasingly pervasive globalization – within the Decent Work Agenda as a whole. For, as we shall see in Chapter 6, the ILO has in fact responded to the challenges of globalization, including those of employment, mainly within the context of its decent work strategy.

# Decent work and a fair globalization     **6**

Decent work is based on the efforts of personal dignity, on democracies
that deliver for people, and economic growth that expands opportunities for
productive jobs and enterprise development ... Decent work is about the right
not only to survive but to prosper and to have a dignified and fulfilling quality
of life. This right must be available to all human beings. We rely on the ILO
to continue its struggle to make decent work a global reality.
(Nelson Mandela, message to the 2007 International Labour Conference)

This chapter considers two interrelated themes. The first is how far the ILO
has pursued an integrated agenda, in the sense of an agenda which brings
together its action in different fields in a coherent way. The second is the strategy
it has adopted to introduce social goals in the international policy agenda. These
themes are interrelated because the key global policy issue is achieving a better
balance between economic and social progress. At the same time, the ability to
build a coherent national policy agenda depends on international factors and
forces – most obviously when competitive pressures from the international market
restrict the scope for national social policy.

The first section of this chapter discusses the development of an integrated
approach in the early days of the ILO, and the second considers this aspect of its
work in the decades after the Second World War, when it received less priority.
The third section describes the renewed efforts of the 1980s and 1990s, through
proposals for a social clause and through global summits which promoted a broad
social agenda. The fourth section discusses the current Decent Work Agenda,
explicitly designed as an integrated goal to which both economic and social policies should contribute, and the central element of a strategy to reassert the ILO's
central role in building a social dimension to the global economy. And a final section draws some threads together and looks ahead to the medium term.

## A social foundation for the international economy:
## The early years

There are some parallels between the issues the ILO faces today and those it addressed in the 1920s. Both periods were times of globalization. The 1920s saw the tail end of the process of international economic integration which started in the nineteenth century, while the last two decades have ushered in a new phase of globalization of production and finance as well as trade, on the back of the neo-liberal wave of the 1980s. In both cases, a central issue was how to embed social progress in the workings of the international economy. And in each period the ILO was an important actor.

As we saw in Chapter 1, the ILO set out in 1919 to establish international labour standards, not just to prevent a race to the bottom, but more positively to provide an international mechanism for a race to the top, a way of ensuring that labour conditions improved alongside economic growth in all countries.

But it was quickly acknowledged that progress in labour standards could not be achieved without at the same time considering both the economic conditions which were needed for such progress, and the impact of social advance on economic growth. It was therefore not surprising that the agenda of the ILO rapidly expanded to embrace economic issues. Albert Thomas strongly believed that "the Organisation has the right, it may even be said the duty, of considering the effects that the realisation of its programme of social reform may have in the economic sphere".[1] Thomas attempted to consolidate this affirmation of the ILO's territory with a major "enquiry into industrial production throughout the world, considered in relation to conditions of work and cost of living". This monumental exercise was contested by the employers, who were opposed to this expansion of the work of the Office: "... the ILO's role is to bring about international cooperation with a view to establishing lasting social laws, and not to propose solutions of a general nature to transient economic situations".[2] But it was ultimately completed and published in several volumes, despite financial difficulties, and its value was acknowledged, for instance by participants at the 1927 World Economic Conference.[3]

---

[1] B.W. Schaper: *Albert Thomas: Trente ans de réformisme social* (Paris-Assen, Presses Universitaires de France-van-Gorcum, 1956), forthcoming in English under the ILO Century Project.

[2] P. Waline: *Un patron au Bureau International du Travail* (Paris, Editions France-Empire, 1976), p. 43, quoting his "patron", the French Employer delegate Alfred Lambert-Ribot.

[3] ILO: *The International Labour Organisation: The first decade* (Geneva, 1931), p. 258; T. Cayet: "The International Labour Organization and the International Management Institute: A fruitful strategy of influence", paper presented to the Conference "The ILO: Past and present", Brussels, 5–6 Oct. 2007, organized by the International Institute of Social History, Amsterdam, Ghent University and others.

As Chapter 5 shows, a fruitful line of economic analysis subsequently developed in the ILO's work.

This idea that economic and social policies need to be considered together is a constant theme in the ILO's history. It is a core ILO belief that social justice cannot be subordinate to economic considerations. When times get hard, however, social aims take a back seat in the struggle between social and economic interests. Albert Thomas constantly argued for the primacy of social goals: "Economic and social questions are indissolubly linked and economic reconstruction can only be sound and enduring if it is based on social justice."[4] He often spoke about the integration of economic and social policy, and his reports to the Conference tried to address the totality of the world of work.[5]

One difficulty, of course, was the range of issues which the ILO was trying to tackle. Very quickly there were a number of distinct areas of work within the ILO, each with its own agenda – social insurance (Chapter 4); occupational safety and health (OSH) (Chapter 3); international migration covered by a Permanent Migration Committee of the Governing Body[6] (Chapter 2); work on agricultural labour; on working time; and so on. Problems of internal fragmentation appeared very early on. In a 1923 report prepared by Adrien Tixier, Head of the Disablement Service, he found the different divisions of the Office compartmentalized, and duplicating each other's work on many subjects.[7] This is perhaps inevitable in an organization such as the ILO, which aims to be present in policy debates on a wide variety of issues; it was certainly still true in 1999, when the Director-General's Report to the International Labour Conference spoke of "an institutional tendency to generate a widening range of programmes without a clear set of operational priorities to organize and integrate their activities".[8] It is difficult and often unwise to neglect subjects which are specific in nature but important – policies for disabled workers, for example, or maternity protection. But the Office then has to rely heavily on external networks of expertise if it is to have a critical mass in each subject, making it that much harder to develop an integrated approach.

---

[4] ILO: *Report of the Director-General to the International Labour Conference*, 10th Session, Geneva, 1927, para. 52.

[5] Schaper, op. cit.

[6] See W. R. Böhning: *A brief account of the ILO and policies on international migration*, paper prepared for the ILO Century Project, 2008, available at: http://www.ilocentury.org

[7] D. Guérin: *Albert Thomas au BIT, 1920–1932: De l'internationalisme à l'Europe* (Geneva, Institut européen de l'Université de Genève, 2006), p. 25.

[8] ILO: *Decent Work*, Report of the Director-General, International Labour Conference, 87th Session, Geneva, 1999.

The other difficulty in developing an integrated approach is one of discipline. Various disciplines have been represented among the staff – law and economics are the two main ones – and they tend to be applied in different ways in different parts of the Office. Work on standards requires legal expertise, work on employment economic analysis, and the approaches differ considerably. Much economics is about trade-offs, so that economists will tend to consider possible adverse economic effects of higher standards, as well as the social impacts of economic policies, and develop a flexible policy response. On the other hand, a legal approach generally involves a framework of fixed principles and rights, to which economic relationships are seen as subordinate. This divide is not easy to bridge, and it tends to lead to different disciplines dominating in different parts of the Office's work. This separation is a practical one, but it affects the coherence of the ILO message. A segmentation by discipline and subject specialization also limits the extent to which ILO staff can move from department to department during their careers, so that even long-serving officials may have only a partial view of the work of the Office.

In the 1930s the ILO continued to work on a broad front, addressing both social and economic issues. The economic crisis reinforced a belief in the need for coherence between international economic and social policy. The League of Nations proved incapable of occupying this space,[9] so the ILO was effectively the main player at the international level. After Albert Thomas's death in 1932, his successor, Harold Butler, pursued the same line. He believed that "it was as essential to examine the social implications of financial and economic policy as it was to consider the financial and economic implications of social policy".[10] But as the economic crisis unfolded, the political environment became increasingly unfriendly to coordinated international action, and the ILO's work tended to concentrate on its distinct fields of specialization.

The underlying integrated, internationalist vision re-emerged during the Second World War, along with a broad commitment to both social and economic advance. The report of Edward Phelan, then Acting Director, to the 1941 New York Conference stated that "the general social objective of economic security based on social justice is to be the mainspring of concerted political effort".[11] He

---

[9] Clavin and Wessel argue that this was more due to resistance by member States than to lack of capacity of its secretariat. P. Clavin and J.-W. Wessel: "Transnationalism and the League of Nations: Understanding the work of its economic and financial organisation", in *Contemporary European History* (Cambridge University Press, 2005), Vol. 14, No. 4, pp. 465–492.

[10] S. Hughes and N. Haworth: *The ILO involvement in economic and social policies in the 1930s*, paper prepared for the ILO Century Project, 2008, pp. 19–20, available at: http://www.ilocentury.org

[11] ILO: *The I.L.O. and Reconstruction*, Report by the Acting Director of the International Labour Office to the Conference of the International Labour Organisation, New York, October 1941 (Montreal, 1941), p. 97.

reiterated the need to address economic and social goals together, and mapped out a programme with a substantial focus on employment, wages and social security, drawing inspiration from the Atlantic Charter (see Chapters 2 and 4). The Charter expressed the "desire to bring about the fullest collaboration between all nations in the economic field with the object of securing, for all, improved labor standards, economic advancement and social security".[12]

Three years later this led to the 1944 Declaration of Philadelphia, which we have discussed in other chapters. It contains the following statement of an integrated goal for the ILO: "All human beings, irrespective of race, creed or sex, have the right to pursue both their material well-being and their spiritual development in conditions of freedom and dignity, of economic security and equal opportunity" and declares that it is a responsibility of the International Labour Organization to examine and consider all international economic and financial policies and measures in the light of this fundamental objective.

## From planning to deregulation: The post-war decades

The Declaration of Philadelphia pledged ILO cooperation with other international bodies in "measures to expand production and consumption, to avoid severe economic fluctuations to promote the economic and social advancement of the less developed regions of the world, to assure greater stability in world prices of primary products, and to promote a high and steady volume of international trade". All of these were seen as means to the achievement of the ILO's fundamental goal. Nevertheless, immediately after the war, the design of the new multilateral system denied the ILO's claim for a broad economic mandate. As noted in Chapter 5, responsibility for economic and financial issues was entrusted to the Bretton Woods institutions, and co-ordination of economic and social policy issues to the United Nations Economic and Social Council. While ECOSOC ultimately proved to be a rather ineffective body, it was some time before the division of labour within the UN system was settled, for the fields of work of the ILO overlapped with those of a number of other specialized agencies and programmes of the United Nations itself.[13]

---

[12] *Atlantic Charter*, signed 14 August 1941 (Washington, Department of State Executive Agreement Series No. 236).

[13] Discussed in some detail by A. Alcock: *History of the International Labour Organisation* (London and Basingstoke, Macmillan, 1971), pp. 188 ff.

Within this new framework, political considerations, especially the tensions of the Cold War, made it difficult to maintain a broader, global vision during the early post-war decades (Chapter 1). ILO standard-setting continued, especially on human rights (Chapter 2), but the strong connections between standard-setting and the growth of the international economy were much less in evidence than between the wars. The prevailing economic model was concerned with the national economy. Indeed, the main justification for the expansion of international trade was to provide resources for domestic growth, and import substitution models dominated thinking in developing countries. The social agenda was also essentially defined by national priorities. As noted in Chapter 3, the 1955 "Ohlin report"[14] claimed only a rather modest role for labour standards in the process of expanding trade and regional integration within Europe.

Another illustration of the relatively limited scope for a global approach in this period is provided by the ILO's Industrial Committees. Mainly created in the early post-war period, these committees were originally conceived as forums for international tripartite discussion on policy issues in specific sectors (mining, textiles, steel, transport, among others) where there were important international concerns, leading to international collective agreements.[15] The sectoral committees could consider the whole range of ILO concerns, and therefore might be seen as constituting a first step towards global collective bargaining. The outcome was, however, much more limited. Their scope, as ultimately defined by the ILO Governing Body, was confined to broad issues of international cooperation, and they were given little power beyond the adoption of resolutions and the definition of codes of conduct. Their influence came mainly from the diffusion to the national and local level of desirable workplace practices. According to Haas, "the entire approach to international collective bargaining gave way to more modest efforts at advice to specific industries".[16] In reality there was very little space for the development of global policy.

The ILO's engagement with development expanded rapidly during this period, as discussed in other chapters. The newly independent developing countries gave higher priority to concrete national action to promote productivity

---

[14] ILO: *Social aspects of European economic co-operation*: Report by a group of experts (Geneva, 1956). See Chapter 3.

[15] This was the original idea of Ernest Bevin, the influential British labour leader and Minister of Labour during the war. See E. Haas: *Beyond the nation state: Functionalism and the international organization* (Stanford University Press, 1964), p. 293. The history of the committees is described in E. Weisband: *ILO industrial committees and sectoral activities: An institutional history*, ILO Sectoral Activities Programme, Working Paper 100 (Geneva, ILO, 1996).

[16] Haas, op. cit.

growth, employment creation and poverty reduction, than to international labour standards.[17] While there was a surge in ratifications of ILO standards by many of the newly independent countries, there were clearly also conflicts and inconsistencies between the priorities of developing countries and some of these standards. Maul cites the cases of forced labour and freedom of association, where ratification of the standards was seen as marking a break with the colonial past, but was often not followed by implementation, because governments were wary of politicized trade union movements or industrial conflict, or considered that compulsory labour in the interests of development could not be compared with colonial forced labour. This divergence of views was also found within the Office. Maul cites conflicting internal memoranda prepared by the economics section and the standards department, in which the former "postulated the primacy of economic development, which it viewed as an essential prerequisite to the realisation of social rights", whereas the latter "accused the economic camp of being too quick to concede the necessity of using coercion and limiting rights, without exploring how the same goals might be achieved in compliance with ILO standards".[18]

The ILO's action was basically concerned with national development – to which, of course, there was necessarily an international dimension. The United Nations Conference on Trade and Development (UNCTAD) was created in 1964, and called for changes to the world trading system which would make it more conducive to development.[19] This, however, had little immediate impact on the ILO's agenda. The ILO's African and Asian regional conferences in the 1960s did call on the Organization to intervene on international commodity markets, but this was opposed by Western governments.[20] The World Employment Programme, the principal ILO contribution to the United Nations International Development Strategy, mainly addressed national strategies for employment and (later) basic needs. It did eventually develop proposals for international action, which formed part of the Director-General's report to the 1976 World Employment Conference.[21] These

---

[17] D. Maul: *The ILO involvement in decolonization and development*, paper prepared for the ILO Century Project, 2008, available at: http://www.ilocentury.org. See also the oral history interview with S.K. Jain, former ILO Deputy Director-General, on the same website.

[18] D. Maul: *Menschenrechte, Sozialpolitik und Dekolonisation: Die Internationale Arbeitsorganisation (IAO), 1940–1970* (Essen, Klartext, 2007), publication in English forthcoming in 2009 under the ILO Century Project.

[19] R. Jolly, L. Emmerij, D. Ghai and F. Lapeyre: *UN contributions to development thinking and practice* (Bloomington, Indiana University Press, 2004), pp. 104–106.

[20] Maul, 2007, op. cit.

[21] ILO: *Employment, growth and basic needs: A one-world problem*, Report of the Director-General to the Tripartite World Conference on Employment, Income Distribution and Social Progress and the International Division of Labour (Geneva, 1976). See Chapter 5 for more details.

included assistance for trade adjustment, policies to increase the gains from international migration for sending countries, greater transfers of technology and a code of conduct for multinational enterprises. But there was little follow-up.

Perhaps this is not surprising. As noted in Chapter 1, this was a time of political tensions and economic difficulties. Neither workers nor employers supported the developing countries' call for a New International Economic Order (NIEO), which was strongly opposed by many industrialized countries, and delivered only meagre results for the countries in the South.[22] The ILO did not provide a promising forum for pursuing these issues further. A Multinationals Declaration was adopted in 1977,[23] following on from a similar OECD initiative, but although it made reference to development goals, notably employment creation, it provided no means to ensure that they were addressed. The second oil shock and subsequent global recession, which could have provided a platform for the ILO to promote coherence between economic and social policies, as it did in the 1930s, instead provided the point of departure for a narrower economic model based on supply-side responses and neo-classical economics.

The growing influence of this new economic and political framework from the early 1980s onwards constituted a challenge to the ILO's view of the world, as discussed in Chapter 5. Whether or not the ILO could have successfully maintained a broader international social agenda in the face of powerful economic interests at that time is far from certain. But it can readily be argued that the ILO would have been much better placed to respond if it had previously invested in a more integrated approach. In the 1970s, activities concerning employment, labour standards, conditions of work and industrial relations were, in large measure, carried out independently of each other. The World Employment Programme, in particular, was a world of its own. "I built a fortress", said its director at the time, Louis Emmerij.[24] Within the fortress it was possible to do many things which could not be done within the regular bureaucratic framework, much to the fury of some of the ILO's constituents. At the same time, it meant that the basic needs strategy, dedicated to making the satisfaction of a range of basic human needs the central goal of development, did not draw on other relevant ILO work, on minimum wages, rights at work or social security. The labour institutions that the ILO was promoting through its standards and

---

[22] Jolly et al., op. cit., pp. 121–123.

[23] ILO: *Tripartite Declaration of Principles concerning Multinational Enterprises and Social Policy* (MNE Declaration) (Geneva, 2006). The World Employment Conference had considered this issue but had failed to reach agreement.

[24] Louis Emmerij: Oral history interview. See http://www.ilocentury.org

industrial relations work were in reality the essential foundation for the market economy, and were needed for a successful and socially responsible structural adjustment. But, in part because of the fragmentation of its work, the ILO was unable to convincingly demonstrate this.

## The re-emergence of international social policy

In the 1980s and early 1990s, there were two developments of particular importance for the ILO. The first was the resurgence of the debate on the introduction of a social clause in international trade. And the second was a broader effort, mainly in the UN system, to refocus international policy on social development. In neither case was the ILO initially the main actor; but, in both cases, ultimately the ILO found ways to react.

### The social clause

The idea of a social clause, that is, the obligation to meet specific social standards as a precondition for participation in international trade or access to trade preferences, has regularly returned to the policy arena, often as a result of pressure from trade unions. But, although it has been incorporated in some bilateral agreements, it has never been accepted as a global rule. Indeed, member States have always been unwilling to accept externally-imposed binding social constraints, and this was reflected in the original design of the ILO, based on the voluntary ratification of Conventions. After the Second World War, the 1948 Havana Charter, which was intended as the frame for an International Trade Organization (ITO), made explicit reference both to the goal of employment creation and to respect for fair labour standards as basic principles for the global trading system. However, the Charter was not ratified by the United States and the ITO never came into existence.

In the Uruguay Round of trade negotiations of the General Agreement on Tariffs and Trade (GATT), which was launched in Punta del Este in 1986, a small group of industrialized countries, led by the United States, pressed for the issue of trade and labour standards to be included in the negotiations. The international trade union movement, led by the ICFTU, also lobbied strongly for the issue to be addressed in the Round. Although these efforts failed, debate on the social aspects of trade negotiations intensified, and they were, for instance, addressed at the Trade Committee of the OECD. Three of the prominent actors on this committee – Abraham Katz, Kari Tapiola and Stephen Pursey – would later play important roles in the ILO as members of the Governing Body and staff.[25]

The point was that while the dominant ideology favoured the liberalization of trade, national politics demanded protection of existing jobs and incomes and recognition of the adverse side effects for some workers and enterprises. There were widespread calls for a level playing field. But the slope of the playing field depended on who was measuring it. A number of OECD countries, facing increasing competition from a small number of rapidly growing developing countries with authoritarian regimes and scant respect for labour standards, called for respect for basic rights at work. The idea of defining a set of minimum international labour standards to be respected by all in the context of their economic and commercial relations was not new. It had, for instance, already been raised by the United States Secretary of Labor, Ray Marshall, at the International Labour Conference in 1980,[26] and in a resolution at the Conference in 1977. But developing countries continued to see the international trading system as biased against them, and in need of the sorts of structural reform promoted by the NIEO, rather than incorporating labour standards in the trading regime, which might increase their disadvantages further. The international trade union movement as a whole was strongly in favour of a social dimension to trade, although trade union organizations from some developing countries – notably India – were more ambivalent.

A basic question was what standards might be included within a social clause. For trade unions, the core standard was, naturally, freedom of association, but there were voices calling for a much wider set of standards. Debate within the ICFTU led eventually to an agreement to promote a core set of rights, a package which connected freedom of association and collective bargaining to the politically more attractive rights to freedom from forced labour and discrimination (child labour was added later on).[27] Within the United States, tripartite discussion initiated by the employers followed a similar track.[28]

---

[25] Katz was United States Employer delegate to the ILO Governing Body from 1984 to 1999; Tapiola was Worker delegate to the Governing Body from 1991 to 1996 and was subsequently appointed to the Office as Executive Director; Pursey joined the Office from the ICFTU in 1999 and currently directs the Policy Integration Department.

[26] Noted in F. Blanchard: *L'Organisation internationale du travail: De la guerre froide à un nouvel ordre mondial* (Paris, Editions du Seuil, 2004), p. 224. See also: ILO: *Record of Proceedings*, Provisional Record No. 14, International Labour Conference, 66th Session, Geneva, 1980, p. 7.

[27] Source: Stephen Pursey, who was Chief Economist at the ICFTU at the time and one of the principal participants in this internal debate.

[28] Abe Katz: Oral history interview. See http://www.ilocentury.org

There was also reflection on these issues within the ILO during the same period, including exchanges between the Director-General, Francis Blanchard, and Arthur Dunkel, Director-General of GATT at the time. In 1989, a group within the Office suggested various possible mechanisms for promoting minimum labour standards, including the idea of a new Convention.[29] A tripartite meeting was held early in Michel Hansenne's term as Director-General that considered the linkage between trade and labour, including the possibility of a social clause, but the outcome was inconclusive.[30]

The issue came to a head in the reform of the governance of the global economy that led to the creation of the World Trade Organization (WTO), which was designed to consolidate the development of a comprehensive multilateral trading regime. The ILO had not been a significant actor in the GATT negotiations, but the Office was represented in the final GATT ministerial meeting in Marrakesh held in April 1994, which completed the Uruguay Round and confirmed the creation of the WTO. Once again, an important point of contention was whether the WTO should address the issue of labour standards, with the trade unions and a number of industrialized countries determined that it should, and most developing countries opposed. An ambiguous form of words was found at Marrakesh which permitted the issue to be considered again at the WTO itself.

At the 1994 International Labour Conference, the Report of the Director-General considered procedures that might strengthen action on fundamental rights in the context of globalization, expressed as enabling rights which would underpin progress in other fields, and included a section on the possibility of a social clause. The debate was lively. The Chairperson of the Workers' Group stated in no uncertain terms how the workers saw a social clause:

> Our social clause is opposed to child labour. Our social clause is opposed to forced labour. Our social clause is opposed to discrimination. On the positive side our social clause supports freedom of association. Our social clause sees free collective bargaining as the means of setting the wages and conditions of employment a country can afford in the light of its domestic circumstances. There you have it. The Workers' social clause – no more, no less.[31]

---

[29] Blanchard, op. cit., p. 231.

[30] This inconclusive outcome in the ILO was subsequently used as an argument by workers and some industrialized countries in favour of a social clause in the World Trade Organization. Source: Francis Maupain, ILO Legal Adviser during this period, personal communication.

[31] ILO: *Record of Proceedings*, International Labour Conference, 81st Session, Geneva, 1994.

But developing countries were opposed to the discussion of a social clause in the ILO. The June 1994 meeting of the Governing Body discussed an Office proposal to create a working party on the social dimensions of the liberalization of international trade. Despite a rearguard action by the Governments of India and Egypt to try and delay a decision, the proposal was eventually adopted. The Working Party first met in November 1994, and started a series of discussions on ways to reinforce the ILO's action; we shall return to this below.

In the end, the issue of a social clause was successfully kept off the WTO agenda by the G-77, who were deeply suspicious of protectionist motives among the industrialized countries who were promoting it. Instead, at the first WTO Ministerial Meeting in Singapore 1996, where the ILO Director-General was first invited and then "uninvited",[32] the international community reaffirmed that the promotion of labour standards was the responsibility of the ILO:

> We renew our commitment to the observance of internationally recognized core labour standards. The International Labour Organization (ILO) is the competent body to set and deal with these standards, and we affirm our support for its work in promoting them. We believe that economic growth and development fostered by increased trade and further trade liberalization contribute to the promotion of these standards. We reject the use of labour standards for protectionist purposes, and agree that the comparative advantage of countries, particularly low-wage developing countries, must in no way be put into question.[33]

The ICFTU put a positive spin on this text, since it acknowledged that trade and labour standards were indeed linked. Yet, in reality, it took the social clause off the agenda as far as the world trading system was concerned, and made it essential for the ILO to act.

---

[32] M. Hansenne: *Un garde-fou pour la mondialisation: Le BIT dans l'après-guerre froide* (Geneva, Editions Zoe, 1999), pp. 122–123.

[33] WTO: *Singapore Ministerial Declaration*, 1996, see: http://www.wto.org/english/theWTO_e/minist_e/min96_e/wtodec_e.htm

## The Social Summit

Meanwhile, another strand of thinking about international social policy had been developing in the international community, inspired to a great extent by the disastrous social consequences of the economic policies pursued in the 1980s, and by concern about the gung-ho imposition of naïve market models in the wake of the collapse of the Soviet Union and its social and economic model.[34] In the course of the 1990s, a series of United Nations Global Conferences addressed social issues. Starting with the Children's Summit in New York in 1990, it continued with the Earth Summit in Rio de Janeiro in 1992, the World Conference on Human Rights (June 1993, Vienna), the World Summit for Social Development (March 1995, Copenhagen), the Fourth World Conference on Women (September 1995, Beijing) and the Second United Nations Conference on Human Settlements (June 1996, Istanbul). These provided a platform for the many voices concerned to ensure that economic policies served social ends. While they could not, by their nature, create the countervailing power needed to force political change (unlike the social clause), they helped change the terms of the debate.

The ILO was not the initiator of any of these conferences, and was not a major active participant in the early stages. The Declaration of the World Conference on Human Rights, for instance, made little reference to the human rights dimensions of work and employment, with the exception of measures for the protection of migrant workers.

The World Summit for Social Development – known as the Social Summit – could not, however, be ignored. Convened by the United Nations General Assembly in December 1992, it was to address the critical problems of poverty, unemployment and social integration – issues at the heart of the ILO's mandate. The Summit was proposed by Juan Somavia, then Chilean Ambassador to the United Nations, in 1991, with the support of Chilean President Patricio Aylwin, and he was backed by the Secretary-General, Javier Perez de Cuellar, who appointed him as Special Representative to consult on the idea of the Summit. Somavia developed widespread support among governments, which reflected their concern with the social consequences of structural adjustment, including economic stagnation and growing poverty in Africa and Latin America, and the social costs of the transition process in the former Soviet bloc. He was subsequently appointed Chairman of the preparatory committee for the Summit.

---

[34] As Juan Somavia put it, "The Cold War was waged in the name of democracy and won in the name of the market". In T. Weiss et al.: *UN voices: The struggle for development and social justice* (Bloomington, Indiana University Press, 2005), p. 275.

Although the agenda of the Summit overlapped considerably with the ILO's spheres of interest, and Somavia met Director-General Hansenne in 1991 to inform him of the process and seek his collaboration, the ILO did not come substantially into the picture until the Governing Body discussed preparations for the Summit in November 1992. Employers', Workers' and Government delegates all expressed concern that the arrangements were going ahead without adequate ILO participation. The German Government spokesman commented that: "The Summit would deal with crucial problems and it seemed that the ILO would influence them only from the sidelines instead of playing a central role."[35] The Governing Body instructed the Director-General to approach the Secretary-General of the United Nations with a view to ensuring that there was adequate and tripartite ILO participation "in the preparation, the holding and the follow-up" of the Summit.

From then on, the ILO participated actively in the preparatory process for the Summit. The ILO's worker and employer constituents worked with Somavia, who was by then fully engaged in the organization of the Summit, and he addressed the High-Level Meeting on Full Employment at the 1994 International Labour Conference, where he called on the ILO's constituents to "look beyond" their immediate preoccupations.[36] The Office played a lead role on employment issues, providing substantive papers that set out the extent and nature of the global employment problem and analysed some national and international policies that could improve the situation.[37] The first *World Employment Report*, discussed in Chapter 5, was circulated at the Summit, where it provided a point of reference for the debate.[38] During the period leading up to the Summit, research was carried out by the International Institute for Labour Studies on an integrated approach to poverty reduction, and on policies to overcome social exclusion. To the satisfaction of the ILO, the Summit, a high-profile event with an unprecedented attendance of some 120 Heads of state and of government, adopted in its outcome document an endorsement of the goal of full, productive, and freely-chosen employment that was based on the language of the ILO

---

[35] ILO: *Report of the International Organizations Committee*, Governing Body, 254th Session, Geneva, Nov. 1992, GB.254/PV (Rev).

[36] "In government we need to look beyond the next election. In business we need to look beyond the next balance sheet. In labour we need to look beyond the next collective bargaining"; J. Somavia: *Employment: The first step out of poverty*, address to the ILO Informal Tripartite Meeting at Ministerial Level on Employment, Geneva, 10 June 1994, Record of Proceedings.

[37] See, for instance, ILO: *Contribution of the International Labour Organization to the first substantive session of the Preparatory Committee for the World Summit for Social Development* (Geneva, 1994).

[38] Hansenne, op. cit., p. 102.

Convention (No. 122) on employment policy. It also recognized the central role of employment in reducing poverty and social exclusion.

Worker members of the ILO played a prominent role in insisting on the importance of core labour standards in the governance of the global economy. The social clause issue was a key point of contention in the preparatory discussions. However, agreement was reached on language which affirmed a commitment to safeguard the interests of workers, including respect for the fundamental rights which had been asserted at the International Labour Conference the previous year. This was a breakthrough, the first formal international recognition of the special status of these rights, which became accepted as the core labour standards.

The Social Summit was able to reach this agreement because it set the promotion of core labour standards within a broad, coherent approach to social and economic development, embracing a range of key ILO concerns. The ten commitments adopted by the Summit overlapped in large part with the ILO's agenda. They included: poverty eradication; full employment; social integration based on the enhancement and protection of all human rights; equality between men and women; universal access to education; the development of Africa; structural adjustment programmes which incorporate social development goals; increased resources for social development; an enabling environment for social development; and stronger international cooperation. They offered a comprehensive approach which bridged the divide between rights and standards on the one hand, and development and poverty reduction on the other.

## The follow-up to the Summit

The ILO's follow-up to the Summit did not initially take full advantage of the space that had been opened up. However, action was taken in two fields: employment, and rights at work.

First, on employment, the ILO was given a mandate by the Social Summit to organize an inter-agency follow-up on the programme of action on employment. Some inter-agency meetings were organized and a series of country employment policy reviews were carried out. Some of these, such as the review in Chile,[39] were in fact organized on an inter-agency basis and took a broad integrated view, covering macro-economic policy, employment quality, industrial relations, labour legislation and gender equality. But the quality of these reviews

---

[39] OIT: *Chile: Crecimiento, empleo y el desafío de la justicia social* (Santiago de Chile, ILO, 1998).

varied, and little was done at the global level to take advantage of them. They do not appear to have had much impact on ILO thinking or actual policies on employment. There were also both political and technical exchanges with the heads and staff of the IMF and the World Bank, and participation in meetings on employment under the auspices of the G7 (later G8).[40] But although the importance of employment policy was acknowledged in these exchanges, there was little concrete evidence of change in policy at this level – indeed, shortly afterwards, the IMF demonstrated its lack of concern with employment goals in its erroneous response to the Asian Financial Crisis (Chapter 5).

Second, and more productively, the Social Summit helped to provide a partial exit from the impasse over the social clause. Taking advantage of the international affirmation of core labour standards beyond the ILO at the Summit, the Office launched a campaign for their ratification. Meanwhile, the Governing Body initiated the development of a new instrument based on these standards, the Declaration on Fundamental Principles and Rights at Work and its Follow-up. The key feature of this instrument was its universality – that is, it laid down principles and rights that all countries were to respect by virtue of their membership of the ILO, irrespective of whether they had ratified the standards concerned. It thus could be treated as a first step towards the building of a universal social floor to the global economy. It also included a follow-up to assist countries in realising these principles, and regular reporting on progress towards them.

The Declaration emerged from a rich and complex process, involving both political and institutional questions, to which this account cannot do justice. In addition to the outcomes of the Social Summit and the WTO Singapore meeting, it drew on work at the OECD[41] and in the International Financial Institutions, as well as the process within the ILO referred to above. Another source of this idea lies in the United States employer community. According to Abe Katz, their representative on the Governing Body at the time, the US Council for International Business was, in the late 1980s, seeking to strengthen links between the ILO and the United States, in ways which did not involve ratifying Conventions but instead promoting the principles on which they were based.[42] Whatever its origins, the idea of a declaration was first raised in the ILO Governing Body by an Employers' delegate, Brian Noakes, in November 1996.[43] While there were certainly other factors

---

[40] Hansenne, op. cit., pp. 106–110.

[41] OECD: *Trade, employment and labour standards: A study of core workers' rights and international trade* (Paris, 1996).

[42] Abe Katz, Oral history interview.

[43] Hansenne, op. cit., p. 121.

involved, including the emphasis on core labour standards at the Social Summit, the idea also fitted well with the employer position that the ILO should shift towards statements of principles rather than multiplying the number of Conventions with specific obligations. The suggestion was originally opposed by the Workers' group, who were still aiming at a social clause, with "teeth", in the WTO. But when it became clear that there would be no social clause at the WTO at that time, workers rallied behind a new instrument within the ILO. The idea was elaborated further in the Director-General's Report to the 1997 International Labour Conference.[44] According to Jean-Jacques Oechslin, who led the Employers' group at the time and chaired the 1998 International Labour Conference, "this major text was mainly the outcome of a joint effort between the Employer and Worker members of the Governing Body".[45]

The Declaration was adopted in 1998, not without difficulty, since a number of major developing countries, including Egypt, Mexico and Pakistan, continued to argue, as they had in the WTO, that any initiative in this field carried with it risks of protectionism.[46] But, along with establishing the universal status of the fundamental rights at work, the Declaration also reiterated that labour standards should not be used for protectionist trade purposes. A year later, a Convention on the worst forms of child labour (No. 182), likewise seen as part of the social floor of the global economy, was unanimously adopted and rapidly achieved a large number of ratifications (169 out of 182 member States in October 2008). Opinion on the Declaration was not unanimous – some felt that it set a dangerous precedent by creating two classes of standards and reducing the priority of ratification.[47] However, in practice, the outcome has been an increase in the rate of ratification of the eight Conventions concerned, and all have now been ratified by more than 80 per cent of ILO member States.

During this period, the atmosphere in the ILO's governing organs was nevertheless strained. Other Office initiatives, such as proposals for further work on enterprise codes of conduct and social labels for internationally traded products,

---

[44] ILO: *The ILO, standard setting and globalization*, Report of the Director-General, International Labour Conference, 85th Session, Geneva, 1997.

[45] J.-J. Oechslin: *Tripartisme, dialogue social et démocracie: Perspectives du monde des employeurs*, paper prepared for the ILO Century Project, 2008, available at: http://www.ilocentury.org

[46] See the opening paragraphs of Chapter 2. Suspicion of the motives of industrialized countries persists among these countries, not without cause, because protectionist language persists in the domestic policy arena, especially in the United States. There is now a ritual incorporation of language of the type "labour standards should not be used for protectionist trade purposes" in all relevant ILO documents, including the most recent Declaration on Social Justice for a Fair Globalization.

[47] See, for instance, P. Alston: "'Core labour standards' and the transformation of the International Labour Rights Regime", in *European Journal of International Law* (2004), Vol. 15, No. 3, pp. 457–521. For a wider analysis, see C. La Hovary: *Les droits fondamentaux au travail: Origines, statut et impact en droit international du travail* (Paris, Presses universitaires de France, 2009).

which had also been considered in the Director-General's 1997 Report, met with considerable opposition in the Governing Body,[48] and there was no internal consensus on the priorities of the ILO's agenda – whether between workers and employers, or between North and South among government representatives. Behind the most politically visible issues the programme of the Office was diverse and lacked critical mass. And there had been little effective follow-up to many of the issues highlighted at the Social Summit.

## The Decent Work Agenda

The election of Juan Somavia as Director-General in 1998 was a logical consequence of his successful role as initiator and organizer of the Social Summit. Implicit in his election was the expectation that he would be well placed to take the Summit agenda forward, and to place the ILO strategically within it. Elected a year before he took up his post, he used that time to engage in a series of consultations with ILO constituents and others about their perceptions of the ILO's role and their demands on the Organization, and created a transition team – an innovation in the ILO – composed of people from within and outside the Office, to prepare the programme for the beginning of his term of office.

Recalling that period, Somavia has explained:

> I came out of the election campaign with the distinct feeling that ILO constituents were talking about very different ILOs. That somehow the combination of the end of the Cold War and a globalization model inimical to ILO's founding values was draining the energies of the institution. We needed to rekindle the spirit, reinvigorate tripartism and be perceived as relevant to the 21st century. That sentiment is the origin of the Decent Work Agenda.[49]

The strategy drew on the momentum created by the Social Summit. The political success of the Summit came from the adoption of a wide-ranging agenda which included the core concerns of the different actors involved, and the fact that these concerns were set within a common framework. The ILO's unbalanced initial

---

[48] See, inter alia, ILO: *Report of the Working Party on the Social Dimensions of the Liberalization of International Trade*, Oral report by the Chairperson of the Working Party, Governing Body, 273rd Session, Geneva, Nov. 1998.

[49] Juan Somavia, interview for this book.

follow-up to the Summit suggested that the Organization needed a more integrated programme. But the ILO constituency is – and always has been – diverse. The challenge was to find an overall frame of reference which could reflect the concerns of all of the ILO's constituents, spanning basic rights at work, employment and incomes, enterprise growth, security and protection, development and dialogue.

Decent work, summarized in box 5 (p. 224), was to provide that frame of reference, formulated in the following terms: "The primary purpose of the ILO today is to promote opportunities for women and men to obtain decent and productive work, in conditions of freedom, equity, security and human dignity."[50] This, of course, drew on the Declaration of Philadelphia, which refers to "conditions of freedom and dignity, of economic security and equal opportunity".

Decent work was a way of expressing the overall goal of the ILO, and a framework to bring its different programmes together. The ILO's work was grouped under four strategic objectives: rights at work, employment, social protection and social dialogue, which were to provide the substantive content of the Decent Work Agenda. Each of these objectives was valid in its own right, but each should also be considered as part of a common agenda. But decent work was also about understanding and reformulating economic and social goals in the changing global economy. As Amartya Sen, addressing the 1999 International Labour Conference, put it, "The economically globalizing world, with all its opportunities as well as its problems and difficulties, calls for a similarly globalized understanding of the priority of decent work and of its manifold demands on economic, political and social arrangements."[51]

Decent work was both a political and a substantive strategy. It was also a management strategy, providing a principle for internal organization that was intended to increase synergy between different parts of the Office. It reflected the concerns of workers with rights at work as well as those of employers around enterprise development, as a major determinant of employment creation. It responded to the needs of developing countries for better ways to embed labour and employment goals in development. At the same time, it offered a way to promote core labour standards in the global economy, which could satisfy industrialized countries without getting trapped in the contentious social clause issue. By making social dialogue a strategic objective, it underlined the particular contribution of the ILO's tripartite process to building consensus on these goals.

---

[50] ILO: *Decent work*, Report of the Director-General, International Labour Conference, 87th Session, Geneva, 1999.

[51] Address by Professor Amartya Sen to the International Labour Conference, 15 June 1999, available at: http://www.ilo.org/public/english/standards/relm/ilc/ilc87/a-sen.htm

## Box 5  The Decent Work Agenda

The concept of "decent work" was introduced in 1999 by the newly elected Director-General, Juan Somavia, in his first report to the International Labour Conference.
Decent work is seen as

*– a way of expressing the primary goal of the ILO in everyday language*

The word "work", wider than labour or employment, reflects the variety of ways in which people contribute to economy and society; the concept covers both formal and informal economies. The word "decent" reflects the idea of a realistic ambition which meets social norms of income, of conditions of work and security, of rights and dignity.

*– an overall goal which contains the priorities of all the ILO's constituents – employers, workers and governments – and so forms a basis for building consensus*

Decent work provides a focus for state regulation and public institutions, but can also be an attractive goal for employers, who can point to the need for productive work in viable enterprises if it is to be achieved, while encompassing the key demands of workers for rights and security.

*– an integrating concept with which to analyse and better understand the impact of more specific aspects of the ILO's work*

Decent work aims to bring together in a common framework both the quantity of work and its quality, legal and economic perspectives, security at work and a decent income. It directs attention to the positive and negative interactions between different aspects of work and social policy. It can be regarded as today's formulation of the permanent ILO concerns with peace, social justice, democracy and equality.

*– a means of organizing and managing the work of the Office*

In the ILO's programme, decent work is the sum of the Organization's work on four strategic objectives: rights at work, employment creation, social protection and social dialogue, and the Office is organized along these four axes, along with action for gender equality. The 2008 Declaration on Social Justice for a Fair Globalization confirms decent work as the organizing principle for the ILO's work, and recalls that the four objectives are inseparable and mutually supportive.

Decent work has been promoted by the Organization both as a way of building a social dimension into globalization, and as the framework for ILO action in support of national policy objectives. It is clearly an appealing point of reference in national politics, being quoted approvingly by the leaders of countries in all regions. It has now become an accepted global goal, having been endorsed at the international level at the United Nations and in many regional organizations.

Somavia started to implement this strategy immediately after taking office. His first Programme and Budget, which was adopted by the Governing Body in March 1999, was built around the four strategic objectives and incorporated strategic budgeting and results-based management.[52] The overall approach was presented in his report to the June 1999 International Labour Conference.[53] A strategic policy framework followed in November 2000, which called for simultaneous action at four levels: mapping out the concept of decent work; developing integration and coherence across the ILO within this framework; building decent work into policies for the global economy; and putting it into practice at the national level.[54] The strategic policy framework and the decent work goal received broad support from all tripartite constituents at the November 2000 Governing Body meeting.[55]

This all required a culture change in the ILO, both Organization and Office. Various forms of resistance could be observed, and practice did not always follow theory. New programmes tended to carve out their own space rather than build connections across the Office. The Sectors of the Office, which corresponded to the four strategic objectives, tended to become silos. Nevertheless, the common goal of decent work, even though sometimes paid lip service, required individual activities to be considered within a wider perspective and so promoted an increasingly integrated vision.

It was not enough to progressively embed decent work in the ILO's structures. The point was to convince a variety of policy actors, both within and outside the Organization, that an integrated approach built around decent work was needed; that it could provide a practical framework for connecting economic and social policy at both national and international levels; and that it was the way to take forward the aspirations of the Social Summit for poverty reduction, full employment and social integration.

The first step was to establish decent work on the international agenda. Somavia attended the ill-fated WTO Ministerial meeting in Seattle in November 1999, where, among other events, President Clinton – who had addressed the International Labour Conference the previous June and given substantial support

---

[52] ILO: *Programme and Budget Proposals for 2000–01*, Governing Body, 274th Session, Geneva, Mar. 1999, GB.274/PFA/9/1.

[53] ILO, *Decent work*, op. cit.

[54] ILO: *Strategic policy framework, 2002–05, and preview of the Programme and Budget proposals for 2002–03: Consolidating the decent work agenda*, Governing Body, 279th Session, Geneva, Nov. 2000, GB.279/PFA/6.

[55] The report on the discussion can be found at http://www.ilo.org/public/english/standards/relm/gb/docs/gb279/pdf/gb-10-3.pdf

to the ILO's work – signed the instrument of ratification for Convention No. 182 on the worst forms of child labour. Somavia's submission to the meeting spoke of the need for the benefits of globalization to reach more people, argued that there was a need for an integrated response built around decent work, and called for international collaboration. The failure of the meeting to launch a new round of trade negotiations, and the intense public protests and disruption around the meeting, reflected the widespread belief that the liberalization of the world trading system would not deliver on social and developmental goals. The Decent Work Agenda, it was argued, was a possible way out, because it offered a wider social development agenda to which all countries could subscribe whatever their level of development.

Somavia took this message to the UNCTAD X meeting in Bangkok in early 2000, which was much influenced by events in Seattle, where he spoke on decent work in the new global economy:

> Decent work ... is the most deeply felt aspiration of people in all societies, developed and developing. It's the way ordinary women and men express their needs. If you go out on the streets or in the fields and ask people what they want, in the midst of the new uncertainties that globalization has brought upon all of us, the answer is, work. Work on which to meet the needs of their families in safety and health, educate their children, and offer them income security after retirement, work in which they are treated decently and their basic rights are respected. That is what decent work is about.[56]

He subsequently promoted this idea both at the World Economic Forum in Davos, where international business leaders were increasingly receptive to ideas which would stabilize the global economy, and at the World Social Forum in Porto Alegre, where the protest movements gathered to promote "another globalization". As noted earlier in this book, in the ILO's world, employer representation of both the largest multinationals and of small enterprises is weak, while the international trade union movement, although a powerful force, is largely built on regular wage work in formal enterprises. The Social Summit had mobilized a much wider constituency, especially in the NGO world. Somavia argued that the promotion of decent work required the commitment and participation of economic and social actors beyond the ILO and that this would reinforce rather than weaken the existing tripartite governance structure. And he used these

---

[56] Juan Somavia, Presentation at UNCTAD X, Bangkok, 15 February 2000, http://www.ilo.org/public/english/bureau/dgo/speeches/somavia/2000/unctadx.htm

gatherings to promote the idea that, with the Decent Work Agenda, the ILO had a way to spread the benefits of globalization more fairly. There was coordination with the trade union movement, which also organized events and debates at the World Social Forum, but employers were sceptical about these gatherings to say the least, and both workers and employers were opposed to giving NGOs more space in the ILO.

Meanwhile, the follow-up to the World Summit for Social Development, the Social Summit +5, was held in Geneva in June 2000. It reaffirmed the 1995 commitments, while recognizing that globalization was rapidly changing the conditions for their achievement. The Summit endorsed the Decent Work Agenda, and in particular called on the ILO to develop a coherent and coordinated international strategy on employment.

It was natural for the ILO to focus its attention on the Social Summit +5, given the history of its involvement, and that of its Director-General, in the original Conference. However, it soon became apparent that this was not sufficient as a strategy. It was the Millennium Summit at the United Nations in September 2000 which set the priorities, and the Millennium Declaration focused, not on employment or decent work, but on ensuring that "globalization becomes a positive force for all the world's people", and on setting a number of specific targets for progress by 2015, the Millennium Development Goals (MDGs). The MDGs attracted the attention of the world community in a way that the follow-up to the Social Summit had failed to do. Yet the strategy was strangely different. Of the three goals identified by the Social Summit – poverty reduction, employment creation and social integration – only the first was an explicit target of the MDGs. Employment and social cohesion had disappeared. This appears to have been the result of a coordinated effort by the Bretton Woods institutions, along with the OECD and the UN, to redefine the international social agenda, and narrow its focus. A joint publication of these institutions at the time of the Social Summit +5 Conference, *A better world for all*, was widely criticized by NGOs and many governments as a step backward from the commitments of the Social Summit. Developing countries, in particular, insisted that the UN should promote all "agreed international development goals", which included full employment, and not only the MDGs.

The failure of the MDGs to recognize the central importance of employment for poverty reduction called for an ILO response. This took the shape of an effort to embed decent work better in both national and international policies. First, decent work had to be made into an operational instrument for policy at the national level. Successive reports of the Director-General to the International Labour Conference mapped out elements of this strategy. The 2001 report considered different types of action to reduce the decent work deficit, and the 2003 report examined how a decent work approach could contribute to national poverty reduction strategies.[57] A series of pilot country studies was launched to develop an integrated approach, based on the notion that there should be mutual reinforcement among progress on different dimensions of decent work. This work provided examples of the contribution of a decent work strategy at the country level to major national goals such as poverty reduction (Philippines and Ghana), facing up to global competition (Morocco and Bangladesh) and democratization (Bahrain).[58] In parallel with this work, ILO staff introduced decent work objectives into World Bank-led poverty reduction strategies in several countries.

The decent work goal was also widely adopted at the regional level, in statements and declarations from the European Union, the African Union, the Organization of American States, and the Asian Development Bank. For instance, the Declaration of the Fourth Summit of the Americas in November 2005 stated that "We are committed to building a more solid and inclusive institutional framework, based on the coordination of economic, labor, and social public policies to contribute to the generation of decent work ...".[59]

At the same time, it was obvious that social progress at the national level increasingly depended on the pace and pattern of globalization. The end of the twentieth century was a period of rapid expansion of cross-border flows of trade, foreign direct investment and financial capital, only briefly interrupted by the Asian Financial Crisis of 1997–99 (which gave some taste of things to come in 2008). In addition, the scope of globalization began to expand significantly, with a rapid spread of global production systems not only in agriculture and manufacturing but also in services. With the exponential growth in global connectivity, the offshoring of service sector jobs had begun to take off. Rapid growth in China and India, as well as steady economic performance in other emerging market economies, was beginning to have a widespread impact on the structure of the global economy. There were indications of a small decline in the numbers of people living in absolute poverty, but at the same time, it was a period of rising inequality both globally and nationally. Within many industrialized, transition and developing countries, wage and income inequalities were on the rise. Inequalities in wealth

---

[57] ILO: *Reducing the decent work deficit – A global challenge*, Report of the Director-General to the International Labour Conference, 89th Session, Geneva, 2001; ILO: *Working out of poverty*, Report of the Director-General to the International Labour Conference, 91st Session, Geneva, 2003.

[58] A. Berar Awad: *Decent work as a national goal: The experience of the Decent Work Pilot Programme and other related initiatives*, paper prepared for the 2nd South-East Asia and the Pacific Subregional Tripartite Forum on Decent Work, Melbourne, Apr. 2005.

[59] http://www.summit-americas.org/IV%20Summit/Eng/mainpage-eng.htm

increased even more, and the divergence in economic performance within the developing world increased substantially. In contrast to a minority of successful "globalizers", many developing countries – including most of the least developed countries – remained mired in economic stagnation, increasing poverty and a diminished capacity to benefit from globalization.

For these and other reasons globalization had become a highly contentious issue. Protest movements such as those at Seattle proliferated against the Bretton Woods institutions and the WTO, blamed for promoting a socially destructive process of globalization. Job losses in the face of rising imports from (and increased offshoring of jobs to) low-wage economies fuelled resentment and insecurity among workers in the rich countries. In developing countries, there was growing concern over issues such as the marginalization of many low-income countries from the global economy through rich country protectionism, agricultural subsidies and unfair global rules, the quality of employment in global production systems and the slow pace of job creation – even in situations of rapid GDP growth. The ILO was well placed to respond to these growing social ills and to strengthen the social pillar of the governance structure of an increasingly integrated and interdependent, yet unstable and underregulated global economy.

In November 2000, the Governing Body Working Party, renamed the Working Party on the Social Dimension of Globalization, discussed an Office paper on the development of an integrated approach to economic and social policy at the global level.[60] There was support for more work in this area, and in 2001 Somavia floated the idea of creating a world commission of independent personalities on the subject, which could help overcome the fractures in the globalization debate and develop viable consensual solutions. He developed this idea through several meetings of the Working Party in 2001,[61] and it was finally accepted at the November 2001 meeting.[62]

To overcome initial scepticism, it was necessary that employers, workers and governments all had a sense of ownership of and participation in the process. The Officers of the Governing Body (the Government Chairperson, Alain Ludovic Tou, the Employer Vice-Chair, Daniel Funes de Rioja, and the Worker Vice-Chair,

---

[60] ILO: *Framework for studies on integrated policies to achieve a wider sharing of the benefits of globalization*, Governing Body, 279th Session, Geneva, Nov. 2000, GB.279/WP/SDG/3; and *Report of the Working Party on the Social Dimension of Globalization*, Governing Body, 279th Session, Geneva, Nov. 2000, GB.279/16.

[61] ILO: *Report of the Working Party on the Social Dimension of Globalization*, Governing Body, 280th Session, Geneva, Mar. 2001, GB.280/17; and *Report of the Working Party on the Social Dimension of Globalization*, Governing Body, 281st Session, June 2001, GB.281/9.

[62] ILO: *Report of the Working Party on the Social Dimension of Globalization*, Governing Body, 282nd Session, Geneva, Nov. 2001, GB.282/12.

Bill Brett) were therefore made members of the Commission ex officio. There were also two additional members of the Commission from both trade unions and business. The Commission was chaired by two Presidents in Office, President Halonen of Finland and President Mkapa of the United Republic of Tanzania, and included a number of leading political and academic figures and representatives of civil society. Regular reports on progress were submitted to the Governing Body. The Commission's work was both substantively and politically complex, with intense negotiation in the final stages over the wording and balance of the final text, which was in the end unanimously adopted.

The report of the World Commission, *A fair globalization: Creating opportunities for all*, came out in February 2004. It presented a comprehensive review of the economic and social impact of globalization across the world, identified the major problems and their causes, and made a wide-ranging set of recommendations for bringing about a fairer and more inclusive pattern of globalization. The imbalances and disparities of globalization, stated the report, were "morally unacceptable and politically unsustainable".[63] The key messages included the importance of improved governance at both national and global levels, of more coherent international policies and, critically, of establishing decent work as a global goal – as the central means for strengthening the social dimension of globalization. It called for greater engagement by a range of actors, including the ILO's worker and employer constituents. Addressing the International Labour Conference in June 2004, President Halonen said:

> Our work was not always easy. Commissions are often composed of the people who are like-minded, but ours was largely one of "not like-minded" people: 26 people who came from different backgrounds, have different political views, are from different parts of the world and have their own strong opinions. The Commission was nevertheless able to publish a unanimous joint report. This is proof of the new attitude and desire to find common answers to common challenges. Our report is proof of the power of discussion and dialogue.[64]

This report has been widely cited, translated into some 18 languages, and a large number of global, regional and national policy statements, research studies, meetings and other activities have drawn on its findings and recommendations. There

---

[63] World Commission Report, op. cit., Synopsis, p. x.
[64] ILO: *Address to the Special Sitting of the International Labour Conference*, by Tarja Halonen, Record of Proceedings, Provisional Record No. 9, International Labour Conference, 92nd Session, Geneva, 2004.

were supportive statements and resolutions from the European Commission, the African Union and many other national and international bodies. At the United Nations, the work of the Commission was recognized and promoted by a Resolution of the General Assembly in December 2004,[65] which placed the report and its recommendations within the five-year review of the MDGs in 2005.

The report was received with varying degrees of enthusiasm in different parts of the ILO constituency. On the whole, there was strong support from workers, as well as from Africa, Latin America and continental Europe. Support was more selective in Anglo-Saxon countries, Asia and among employers. For instance, the United States supported the recommendations for improved national governance, but showed little interest in reforming international rules.[66] Employers were very reticent to accept any call for the extension of regulation, and pressed for a much narrower ILO follow-up agenda than the report proposed. It nevertheless became an important reference point for the development of the ILO's programme in the following years.

One conclusion of the report was the need for greater "policy coherence" among the organizations of the multilateral system. The background to this recommendation was the adverse social consequences of the policies advocated by the World Bank, IMF and WTO in the 1990s. The heads of all three of these bodies came to address the World Commission personally, with broadly conciliatory messages. The ILO then launched a "Policy Coherence Initiative" to try and build a common international policy framework for growth, investment and employment, involving the international financial institutions and the relevant agencies of the United Nations. But progress has been slow. The difficulty was exemplified at one of the meetings where the IMF representative asked whether coherence meant that "you are coherent with us, or we are coherent with you?" Policy approaches continue to diverge in significant respects among the international organizations concerned. A number of joint activities have nevertheless developed, notably a joint study undertaken by the ILO and WTO on trade

---

[65] United Nations, General Assembly: *A fair globalization: Creating opportunities for all* – report of the World Commission on the Social Dimension of Globalization, A/RES/59/57 (New York, 2004).

[66] Ms Chao, United States Secretary of Labor, speaking at the International Labour Conference in 2004, stated that: "The World Commission correctly concluded that efforts to achieve lasting benefits for the world's workers must begin at home, in each sovereign nation. Good national governance, democracy, respect for fundamental human rights and sound economic policies are the essential building blocks of sustainable development and brighter futures for workers and their families. ... But the creation of new international institutions, new international bureaucracies and new international instruments is not in itself a formula to achieve decent work and poverty reduction. Individual governments must and can step up to the responsibilities to address the root causes of these conditions in their own nations and within the framework of their own cultures."

and employment, in 2006–07. The study concluded that "trade policies and labour and social policies do interact and that greater policy coherence in the two domains can help to ensure that trade reforms have significantly positive effects on both growth and employment". [67]

A review of the impact of the World Commission Report three years after its publication concluded that "While the inadequate governance of globalization which so concerned the Commission persists, there is nevertheless progress to report in a number of specific areas – core labour standards, corporate social responsibility, global framework agreements, UN reform, a multilateral framework for labour migration …. there is no doubt greater acceptance today than in the past of the need for the rules [of the global trading system] both to be fair, and to be perceived as fair …. The call for decent work to become a global goal has received many echoes, and the challenge is now to translate this goal into country level action."[68]

At the 2005 UN World Summit, the follow-up meeting five years after the 2000 Millennium Summit, the importance of the Decent Work Agenda was recognized:

> We strongly support fair globalization and resolve to make the goals of full and productive employment and decent work for all … a central objective of our relevant national and international policies as well as our national development strategies, including poverty reduction strategies, as part of our efforts to achieve the Millennium Development Goals[69]

paving the way for the incorporation of decent work goals in the MDGs. A Ministerial Declaration of the Economic and Social Council in 2006 called on the multilateral system to mainstream employment and decent work, and the issue has been taken up in the Chief Executives Board, the top-level coordinating management group of the United Nations system. Agreement has been reached that all UN agencies will examine the implications of their actions for decent work. Of course, promises of coordination within the UN system are easier to make than to keep.

---

[67] M. Jensen and E. Lee: *Trade and employment – Challenges for policy research* (Geneva, WTO/ILO, International Institute for Labour Studies, 2007).

[68] H. Jenkins, E. Lee and G. Rodgers: *The quest for a fair globalization three years on: Assessing the impact of the World Commission on the Social Dimension of Globalization*, Discussion paper 175 (Geneva, ILO, International Institute for Labour Studies, 2007).

[69] United Nations, General Assembly: *2005 World Summit Outcome*, A/RES/60/1 (New York, 2005), para. 47.

The current strategy (2008) is to build the ILO's action at the national level around Decent Work Country Programmes (DWCPs), and to establish partnerships with other organizations of the multilateral system within coordinated country-level activities. DWCPs are designed as contributions to the national development strategy, and reflect both the demands and priorities of the ILO's constituents and the overall country assistance framework of the UN system. The number of such country programmes has expanded rapidly and regional ILO meetings in Asia, Africa and Latin America have all established "Decent work decades", to develop them more systematically over a ten-year time horizon.

A final element in this strategy is a new declaration, adopted by the International Labour Conference in 2008, the "ILO Declaration on Social Justice for a Fair Globalization".[70] This text is essentially concerned with underlining the importance of the Decent Work Agenda and its four components, which are "inseparable, interrelated and mutually supportive. The failure to promote any one of them would harm progress towards the others". Furthermore, efforts to promote them "should be part of an ILO global and integrated strategy" for decent work. Follow-up is proposed to include, inter alia, research into how the strategic objectives interact with each other, as well as regular reporting on progress towards decent work goals. This declaration is now being used to consolidate the Decent Work Agenda in the ILO's structures and programmes.

This is certainly the most intensive effort in the ILO's history to build and implement a coherent and integrated agenda at both national and international levels. The foregoing indicates that considerable progress has been made. But the complexity of the exercise can be seen in the fact that after almost ten years it is still not complete.

The notion of decent work as an expression of the ILO's purpose has not satisfied everyone. Some consider that the concept lacks analytical rigour and has not been given enough substantive and empirical content by the Office. The word decent is rather subjective and does not always translate easily into other languages than its original English. There is resistance among some of the ILO's employer constituents and certain governments also remain unenthusiastic.

There are also a number of empirical and conceptual difficulties. The notion of decent work includes many issues that are not usually covered in existing statistical systems, and some of them – for example freedom of association or economic security – are very hard to measure unambiguously. There is a much better information base on labour market variables than there is on respect for rights at

---

[70] http://www.ilo.org/public/libdoc/ilo/2008/108B09_147_engl_(4-14).pdf

work. Attempts to build overall measures of decent work using existing statistics therefore proved to be unsatisfactory, and there is a need for considerable investment in new statistical systems to measure progress on decent work adequately, especially in developing countries. This problem was for some time compounded by criticism from employers in particular (but also some developing countries) of the idea of developing indicators of decent work at all, since they feared that the Office would start to develop rankings of countries (or enterprises) of the type found in major international reports such as the *Human Development Report*. In 2008, efforts were under way to find solutions to these problems,[71] but the road is clearly long.

The Decent Work Agenda also raises research issues which need to be adequately addressed, in order to specify decent work goals unambiguously in any given setting. For instance, the extent to which there are trade-offs between different decent work goals needs to be better explored. To state, as the 2008 Declaration does, that the goals are mutually supportive is perfectly accurate as a political objective, because it is the fact that this is a package which makes it acceptable to all and therefore politically viable. But it is obviously not true of all relationships and in all situations; more social protection can be at the expense of employment, if it is not designed with the interrelationships in mind. More research is required to establish the conditions under which this mutual reinforcement can be realised. More generally, a stronger conceptual and empirical foundation for decent work is needed, and in 2008 there was a widespread sense in the ILO that the research capacity of the Office needed to be strengthened if this was to be possible. This will require reform in both internal incentives and recruitment criteria, which seriously undervalue substantive work and academic qualifications.

Despite these practical problems, the message of decent work has been highly successful in political terms. It has provided an important reference point for constructing a more coherent framework for the Organization's work and building a wider constituency around it. The notion of decent work is increasingly present in political discourse, and has modified policy agendas at the national level. It is regularly cited as a central goal of international action; it is specified as a goal in the Constitution of the International Trade Union Confederation, which has launched a World Day for Decent Work. It has raised the profile of the ILO as a global player. This has been achieved through a concentrated effort of high-level advocacy, built on a plausible argument about the connexions between different

---

[71] ILO: *Measurement of decent work*, Discussion paper for the Tripartite Meeting of Experts on the Measurement of Decent Work, Geneva, Sep. 2008.

social and economic goals. But it has also been achieved because decent work is a flexible concept which can be adapted to the aspirations of different actors. There is resistance to the agenda in some quarters, and the academic community has yet to pick up the concept – which is one reason why the research base is weak. In the history of the ILO and its ideas, however, the notion of decent work is clearly one which has had a substantial influence.

It can nevertheless be argued that some of the toughest issues still lie ahead. Decent work is today's formulation of the repeated calls throughout the ILO's history for an integration of economic and social perspectives and objectives. This has constantly been called into question. The shift in the international agenda, reported above, between the Social Summit +5 meeting and the Millennium Assembly, is a case in point. The struggle the ILO faced to retain its influence after the Second World War is another example. That is the nature of the political economy, with economic interests constantly putting social progress in question. How far can the ideas trump the political economy? Can we side with Keynes, who wrote that: "The ideas of economists and political philosophers, both when they are right and when they are wrong, are more powerful than is commonly understood. Indeed, the world is ruled by little else. ... soon or late, it is ideas, not vested interests, which are dangerous for good or evil ...."[72]

Whatever the power of ideas, and Keynes's ideas certainly had power, they clearly need to be constructed on a strong conceptual and empirical foundation if they are to resist political attack. The challenge is to build a rigorous unified framework which accommodates legal, social and economic concepts and approaches, all of them needed, to support the ILO's struggle to realize its overriding goals of social justice and decent work.

## Looking ahead

Anniversaries are a time for looking back, perhaps with satisfaction but also with a critical eye, and forward, hopefully with prescience. Looking back helps us appreciate the sources of success and failure, and identify the factors that made progress possible. And looking forward involves the anticipation of major changes in the global political and economic context in which the ILO operates and the identification of organizational responses that are required in the light

---

[72] J. M. Keynes: *The General Theory of Employment, Interest and Money* (London, Macmillan, 1936), last paragraph.

of this. These responses may involve, inter alia, reaffirmation of its core values and objectives in ways which are in step with the times, changes in the structure of the Organization and renewal of the content and method of its work. Such a process has in fact begun with the adoption of the Declaration on Social Justice for a Fair Globalization in June 2008, discussed above. The following remarks are thus merely an attempt to raise some supplementary points that are suggested by taking a longer time perspective than the reforms under way.

In drawing lessons from the past, we are of course creatures of the present. Interpretations depend on vantage points. But we can make a few general comments.

First, the core ILO philosophy and governance structure is surprisingly resilient. In a world which has changed radically, much of what was put in place in 1919, and firmly established in the period up to 1944, seems to be as valid today as it was then. Of course, the ILO is sometimes contested, its influence uneven, the legitimacy of its constituents questioned – yet it continues to be a vocal and visible player in global policy-making.

Second, that being said, the ILO's impact depends heavily on partnership and on economic and political context. It has neither the resources of the global and regional banks, nor the powerful economic instruments of the world bodies concerned with finance and trade. But the ILO often plays a strategic role for other global players, who need the integrated framework of social and economic progress that it can provide, the international legitimacy that comes from its universal membership and the social penetration that comes from the participation of workers' and employers' organizations. At key economic and political moments, its values and authority can give it a central role. Its periods of relative weakness came when political struggles were directed elsewhere, so that the ILO was on the sidelines, or when the Organization itself did not take advantage of the political space that was available.

Third, the ILO's instruments work – standards, policy research, technical cooperation – but they work best as part of a broader, coherent strategy, rather than on their own. That is the sense of the Decent Work Agenda; the same lesson can be seen in earlier times, when narrower approaches ultimately faced diminishing returns. Finding ways to strengthen the reinforcement between different domains and policy instruments is key. Not only does it make action in any one field more effective, but, perhaps even more important, it also widens the political coalition behind any particular action.

Fourth, the ILO's history shows that it is notably successful when it deploys knowledge-based strategies which connect the ILO and external networks of international expertise. Whether the topic was social insurance, employment or rights at work, it was when the Office invested in quality research and applied that research to major policy issues, in partnership with the Organization's own worker and employer constituents as well as with others, that it was at its most effective.

Fifth, achieving universality is the ILO's Achilles' heel. In every chapter of this book, ultimately we find that a limiting factor on the ILO's influence lies in the difficulty of reaching what we characterize as the informal economy or the informal sector. These terms are merely reminders of a distressing reality – that the world has yet to find the way to effectively include the population as a whole in social progress. The ILO is obviously not alone in failing to find the answers – but the fact is that we have yet to overcome the structural social and economic factors which perpetuate injustice and inequality in today's world.

Sixth, the ILO can play a particularly influential role when it aims to set the global policy agenda. Of course, there is an important agenda at the national and local levels too, where the ILO's ideas and assistance have made many important contributions, as this book shows. But the ILO's distinctive advantage comes when it acts as an advocate in global debates, and as a player in global action, in coordinating policy across countries and in constructing a universal vision that nevertheless accommodates the diversity of its membership.

There are many other lessons from the past, but the remaining paragraphs of this book look rather to the future – and not just tomorrow, but the coming decades, insofar as the crystal ball permits.

## An ethical framework for an interdependent world

Unless catastrophe intervenes, the steady increase in global interdependence among people, communities, firms and nations of the last few decades seems set to continue. It is this, in its many facets, which has rightly been defined as the major new challenge confronting the ILO. The shorthand term is globalization, but the word globalization evokes a vision of economic integration, whereas the forces that are emerging are wider, and raise fundamental questions about the key concepts and instruments that underlie the work of the Organization. In a far more interconnected world (and one that is likely to become even more so) conceptions of social justice and the instruments for attaining it, derived from an era where economies were largely national in scope, need to be reconsidered. Common principles for policies to be pursued in a coordinated way in individual nation states are still necessary but may no longer be sufficient. Action at the global level becomes increasingly important.

In this new global context, the view is rapidly gaining ground that the ethical foundation of today's world is seriously awry. The impact of the work of the

World Commission on the Social Dimension of Globalization, which called for a fair globalization, is but one sign of this. People are increasingly and acutely aware that the global economy does not deliver social justice. They observe the phenomenal rise in the wealth of a tiny minority, a widening gap between top and bottom, "golden parachutes" for failed business executives, billions to prop up disastrously managed financial institutions while resources to reduce global poverty stagnate or decline and speculative financial markets that have catastrophic effects on the lives and livelihoods of the world's poor.

Related issues have been raised in an emerging literature on cosmopolitan ethics within a globalized world. This is beginning to pose awkward problems of inconsistency in current conceptions of social justice that sanction large inequalities in remuneration for similar work across countries as well as the global labour market discrimination perpetrated through immigration controls. These seemingly utopian issues may well gain some resonance in a world where vast national differences in life-chances are plain for all to see. The ILO needs to be prepared to face the possibility that new conceptions of rights and associated claims to them may well continue to emerge. They have done so in the past with the broadening of the conception of rights to include social, cultural and economic rights that are taken for granted today.

If there is truly to be a reformulation of how social justice is conceived, the ILO must be at its heart. In its past, the ILO has played an important role at key times, promoting universality and human rights at one moment, embedding employment in development at another. Decent work is clearly a part of the way forward today. ILO notions of participatory democracy, and of mobilizing productive forces for both social and economic ends, and not just personal gain, are essential. So is a framework of academic freedom and open debate, as the basis for new thinking on routes to inclusion and universality, on how to put in place a universal minimum socio-economic floor, and on how to change the premises for global action. There are countries which have made great progress within their borders on these issues; the question is how to move up to a global scale.

## The global regulatory and policy instruments

A second domain that should engage the future ILO, and one which is central to its work, concerns the means of global regulation. This is a constant theme in the ILO's history. In Chapter 1 we wrote of the swings between state and market. The latest financial crisis has clearly swung us back towards a renewed belief in the need for regulation and so towards a more prominent role for the state. For it is now evident that the quest for social justice in the twenty-first century will require increasing efforts to tame global economic and financial forces that run rampant for want of an adequate regulatory framework at both the national and global levels. The financial crisis in the industrialized countries may well trigger off a political backlash that redresses the worst failings at the national level. But this will be far from enough unless there are similar efforts to regulate markets at the global level. Failing this the vast majority of the world's workers who live in developing countries will continue to be at the mercy of unaccountable and unregulated international actors operating in both the real and financial economy, and of states which pursue their narrow domestic interest in flagrant disregard for global principles of equity and shared interest.

The issues are wide and complex. A global labour market is rapidly emerging in which the welfare of workers is becoming more interrelated through the closer linkages that are being created by global production systems and increasing capital mobility. This has occurred even though the cross-border movement of workers still remains limited. In a world where politics is still national in scope this has resulted in the perception that there is intensifying competition for the jobs that are being created in the global economy. Fears over "offshoring" and declining wages are the latest manifestation of this in the industrialized world, while resentment over Northern protectionism is the counterpart sentiment in many developing countries. This groundswell of tension needs to be recognized and addressed by the ILO from a wider perspective than that of labour standards and a possible social clause. Issues such as the possibilities for coordinated international action to raise the rate of growth of decent jobs in the global economy and to accelerate the development of the least developed countries need to be confronted as ways of defusing this tension over jobs. New and complicated distributional issues raised by the emerging global labour market must also be addressed. These include the issue of what constitutes a fair distribution of the value-added generated within global production systems, especially between Northern capital and Southern labour. Subsumed within this is, of course, the issue of how to moderate the inequalities in market power between global economic and financial actors, on the one hand, and states and workers in the developing world, on the other.

It will be essential to deal with these conflicts of interest, otherwise they will undermine the potential for good of global interdependence. Yet it is apparent that the existing policy instruments are not enough. They must be complemented with new and imaginative means of intervention. Just as the 1998 Declaration on Fundamental Principles and Rights at Work opened the door to the universal recognition of those rights, so new means must be found to confront these new and complex issues of growth and distribution. There is a need for both better and more effective regulation to prevent abuse and injustice, not only in financial markets, but in all the domains of the global economy – trade, investment, environment and labour markets. And alongside regulation, global policy instruments are needed to pursue the common interest and ensure that all contribute according to their means. In today's world this may look implausible; political and economic power is too heavily concentrated. But the tensions are such that even implausible solutions may in the end appear inevitable, and the ILO will have to confront this issue. To do so the ILO will obviously require new competencies in a range of global economic and social policy issues.

## Representation, voice and governance

In order to equip itself to face this challenge the ILO will have to reach out beyond its traditional constituents and engage with a wider set of powerful new actors on the world stage. These actors include global enterprises, regional bodies, international groupings of parliamentarians and public authorities, and the increasingly global organization of specific interests beyond those already within its walls. It will also have to engage with economic and financial interests within countries which are inadequately represented. These actors will not engage with the ILO unless they have a stake in its work, which sets a challenge to the Organization as a whole to respond in ways that expand tripartite capabilities and partnerships. There is also a need to give voice to the interests of those who are presently excluded because they lack organization or their forms of organization fall outside the traditional tripartite model. Tripartism has stood the test of time; but it must be able to adapt to new realities.

This is not an issue for the ILO alone – it must be part of a broader rethinking of global governance. There is growing support for the view that the current system of international organizations that has evolved since 1945 needs to be reformed in order to respond adequately to current and emerging global challenges. A number of piecemeal and marginal reforms have been adopted but there is still a deep divide over how far and how fast governance structures of key international organizations should change to reflect shifts in political and economic power that have occurred since their establishment. Nevertheless, the issue is being widely discussed in official, non-governmental and academic circles. It is important for the ILO not to shy away from this process. Instead, it should be proactive and prepared to confront fundamental issues such as: what is the optimal structure of global governance for advancing global social justice? How should the ILO position itself within scenarios based on different extents of reform? And what do these analyses imply for the way the ILO should reform itself?

Institutional reform is, sadly, difficult except in times of crisis. This is borne out by the ILO's own history, where the key times of change, for better or worse, have followed war, economic turmoil or political crisis. We may be again entering such a period, and how the ILO responds, not only in its policies, but also in its structures and methods, will surely make a difference to whether the emerging global economy meets the goals of people around the world for rights, jobs and security. It has done it in the past. It can do it again.

# A chronology of the ILO

| | |
|---|---|
| 1900 | Creation of the International Association for Labour Legislation (IALL) |
| 1906 | First international labour Conventions adopted by the IALL (diplomatic) conference at Berne on the prohibition of the use of white phosphorus in match manufacturing and the prohibition of night work of women |
| 1913 | Two draft Conventions adopted by the IALL (technical experts) conference at Berne on the general prohibition of night work for young persons |
| 1916 | Inter-Allied Trade Union Conference, Leeds (with trade unionists from Great Britain, France, Belgium and Italy) |
| 1917 | International Trade Union Conference, Berne |
| 1919 | Paris Peace Conference<br><br>1 February–24 March 1919<br>Meetings of the Commission on International Labour Legislation (Labour Commission), Paris<br><br>11 and 28 April 1919<br>Adoption of the report of the Labour Commission by the Peace Conference<br><br>28 June 1919<br>Adoption of the Treaty of Versailles, of which Part XIII contains the Constitution of the ILO |

| | |
|---|---|
| 1919 | October–November |
| | First Session of the International Labour Conference, Washington, DC |
| | Admission of Germany and Austria to the ILO |
| | Election of Albert Thomas as the first Director of the ILO |
| | Adoption of the Hours of Work (Industry) Convention (No. 1), on the 8-hour working day and 48-hour working week, and five other Conventions |
| 1920 | The Office moves to Geneva (in the building currently occupied by the International Committee of the Red Cross) |
| 1920 –23 | *Enquiry into Production*, ILO international survey of trends in industrial production |
| 1926 | Opening of the new ILO building (currently occupied by the World Trade Organization) |
| 1926 | Creation of the Committee of Experts on the Application of Conventions and of the International Labour Conference Committee on the Application of Standards |
| 1928 | Adoption of the Minimum Wage-Fixing Machinery Convention (No. 26) |
| 1930 | Adoption of the Forced Labour Convention (No. 29) |
| 1930 | First edition of the ILO *Encyclopaedia on Occupational Health* |
| 1932 | Death of Albert Thomas (7 May) – Harold Butler becomes the second Director of the ILO |
| 1933 | Germany sends for the first time a Nazi trade union representative to the International Labour Conference; after contestation, the German delegation leaves the ILC |
| 1934 | Admission of the United States (20 August) and of the USSR (18 September) |
| 1935 | Withdrawal of Germany from the ILO |
| 1936 | First Regional Conference (of the American States), Santiago (Chile) |
| 1937 | Withdrawal of Italy from the ILO |
| 1939 | John G. Winant becomes the third Director of the ILO |

| | |
|---|---|
| 1940 | The USSR ceases in practice to be an ILO member as a consequence of its expulsion from the League of Nations in 1939<br><br>August–September<br>ILO moves operations to Montreal |
| 1941 | Edward Phelan becomes Acting Director of the ILO (appointed Director retrospectively in 1946)<br><br>27 October–6 November<br>Special Session of the International Labour Conference, New York (Columbia University)–Washington, DC (White House) |
| 1942 | First Inter-American Conference on Social Security, Santiago (Chile) |
| 1944 | 12 May<br>Adoption of the Declaration of Philadelphia during the 26th Session of the International Labour Conference |
| 1945 | January<br>Creation of the first Industrial Committees by the Governing Body: Inland Transport, Coal-Mines, Iron and Steel, Metal Trades, Textiles, Petroleum, Building Trades (including Public Works) |
| 1946 | ILO becomes the first specialized agency of the United Nations and incorporates the Declaration of Philadelphia in its amended Constitution |
| 1947 | First (Preparatory) Asian Regional Conference, New Delhi (India) |
| 1948 | David Morse becomes the fifth Director-General of the ILO<br><br>Adoption of the Freedom of Association and Protection of the Right to Organise Convention (No. 87)<br><br>Adoption of the Manpower Programme for Europe, Asia and Latin America |
| 1949 | Adoption of the Right to Organise and Collective Bargaining Convention (No. 98)<br><br>Start of the ILO Technical Assistance Programme |
| 1950 | Asian Regional Conference, Nuwara Eliya (Ceylon) |
| 1951 | Migration Conference, Naples<br>Adoption of the Equal Remuneration Convention (No. 100) |

| | |
|---|---|
| 1951 | Governing Body creates a committee to examine complaints of violations of freedom of association and a Fact-Finding and Conciliation Commission |
| 1952 | Launch of the Andean Indian Programme (AIP) |
| | Adoption of the Social Security (Minimum Standards) Convention (No. 102) |
| 1954 | Re-admission of the USSR |
| 1957 | Adoption of the Abolition of Forced Labour Convention (No. 105) |
| 1958 | Adoption of the Discrimination (Employment and Occupation) Convention (No. 111) |
| 1959 | Opening of the first field office in Africa, Lagos (Nigeria) |
| 1960 | Creation of the International Institute for Labour Studies |
| | The so-called "African Year": First African Regional Conference, Lagos (Nigeria); fifteen African countries were admitted simultaneously |
| 1963 | Creation of a committee on apartheid by the Governing Body |
| 1964 | Adoption of the Declaration on Apartheid, followed by the South African delegation leaving the International Labour Conference (official withdrawal of South Africa from the ILO in 1966) |
| | Adoption of the Employment Policy Convention (No. 122) |
| 1965 | Creation of the International Centre for Advanced Technical and Vocational Training (Turin) |
| 1969 | ILO is awarded the Nobel Peace Prize; celebration of 50 years of ILO |
| 1970 | C. Wilfred Jenks becomes the sixth Director-General of the ILO |
| | Launch of the World Employment Programme (WEP) |
| | Publication of Colombia mission report, *Towards full employment: A programme for Colombia* (WEP) |
| 1972 | Publication of Kenya mission report, *Employment, incomes and equality: A strategy for increasing productive employment in Kenya* (WEP) |
| 1973 | Francis Blanchard becomes the seventh Director-General of the ILO |
| | Adoption of the Minimum Age Convention (No. 138) |

| | |
|---|---|
| 1975 | Launch of the ILO International Programme for the Improvement of Working Conditions and Environment (PIACT) |
| | Opening of the new (current) ILO building (Geneva, route des Morillons) |
| | Adoption of the Declaration on Equality of Opportunity and Treatment for Women Workers |
| 1976 | World Employment Conference |
| 1977 | Adoption of the Tripartite Declaration of Principles concerning Multinational Enterprises and Social Policy (MNE Declaration) (revised in 2000 and 2006) |
| | Withdrawal of the United States from the ILO |
| 1980 | Re-entry of the United States |
| 1981 | 5 June |
| | Speech of Lech Wałęsa to the 67th Session of the International Labour Conference |
| 1983 | Creation of a Commission of Inquiry to investigate complaints against the Polish Government concerning freedom of association in Poland (and suppression of the Solidarność trade union movement) |
| 1984 | Publication of the first ILO *World Labour Report* |
| 1987 | High-Level Meeting on Structural Adjustment |
| 1989 | Michel Hansenne becomes the eighth Director-General of the ILO |
| 1990 | 8 June |
| | Nelson Mandela addresses the International Labour Conference shortly after his release from prison on 11 February 1990 |
| 1992 | Launch of the ILO International Programme on the Elimination of Child Labour (IPEC) |
| | The first Multidisciplinary Team is established in Budapest |
| 1994 | Re-admission of South Africa |
| | Creation of the Governing Body Working Party on the Social Dimension of the Liberalization of International Trade (renamed in 2000 as the Working Party on the Social Dimension of Globalization) |

| | |
|---|---|
| 1995 | Publication of the first ILO *World Employment Report* |
| | United Nations' World Summit for Social Development ("Social Summit") (Copenhagen) endorses goals of employment and core labour standards |
| 1996 | Creation of a Commission of Inquiry to investigate complaints against forced labour in Myanmar |
| 1998 | Adoption of the Declaration on Fundamental Principles and Rights at Work |
| 1999 | Juan Somavia becomes the ninth Director-General of the ILO |
| | Launch of the Decent Work Agenda |
| | The American President Bill Clinton addresses the International Labour Conference |
| | Adoption of the Worst Forms of Child Labour Convention (No. 182) |
| | Launch of eight InFocus Programmes (on socio-economic security, safe work, skills, crisis, follow up to the 1998 Declaration, child labour, social dialogue and small enterprises) |
| 2000 | Start of the ILO Programme on HIV/AIDS and the World of Work |
| 2001 | Launch of the Global Campaign on Social Security and Coverage for All |
| | World Employment Forum and launch of the Global Employment Agenda |
| 2002 | Convention No. 182 (Worst Forms of Child Labour) is ratified by over 100 member States (the fastest ratification in the history of the ILO) |
| 2002 –04 | World Commission on the Social Dimension of Globalization (presents its final report in 2004, *A fair globalization: Creating opportunities for all*) |
| 2005 | Decent Work Agenda is endorsed by the United Nations World Summit |
| 2007 | First joint ILO–WTO report *Trade and employment: Challenges for policy research* |
| 2008 | Adoption of the Declaration on Social Justice for a Fair Globalization |

## Appendix II
# Selected official documents

### Constitution of the International Labour Organization: Preamble, 1919

*The full text of the Constitution may be found at:*
*http://www.ilo.org/ilolex/english/constq.htm*

Whereas universal and lasting peace can be established only if it is based upon social justice;

And whereas conditions of labour exist involving such injustice, hardship and privation to large numbers of people as to produce unrest so great that the peace and harmony of the world are imperilled; and an improvement of those conditions is urgently required; as, for example, by the regulation of the hours of work, including the establishment of a maximum working day and week, the regulation of the labour supply, the prevention of unemployment, the provision of an adequate living wage, the protection of the worker against sickness, disease and injury arising out of his employment, the protection of children, young persons and women, provision for old age and injury, protection of the interests of workers when employed in countries other than their own, recognition of the principle of equal remuneration for work of equal value, recognition of the principle of freedom of association, the organization of vocational and technical education and other measures;

Whereas also the failure of any nation to adopt humane conditions of labour is an obstacle in the way of other nations which desire to improve the conditions in their own countries;

The High Contracting Parties, moved by sentiments of justice and humanity as well as by the desire to secure the permanent peace of the world, and with a view to attaining the objectives set forth in this Preamble, agree to the following Constitution of the International Labour Organization:

...

## General Principles from the Constitution, 1919

*The original ILO Constitution is Part XIII of the Treaty of Versailles. Article 427 of that Treaty laid out nine general principles for the work of the ILO, as follows:*

The High Contracting Parties, recognising that the well-being, physical, moral and intellectual, of industrial wage-earners is of supreme international importance, have framed, in order to further this great end, the permanent machinery provided for in Section 1 and associated with that of the League of Nations.

They recognise that differences of climate, habits, and customs, of economic opportunity and industrial tradition, make strict uniformity in the conditions of labour difficult of immediate attainment. But, holding as they do, that labour should not be regarded merely as an article of commerce, they think that there are methods and principles for regulating labour conditions which all industrial communities should endeavour to apply, so far as their special circumstances will permit.

Among these methods and principles, the following seem to the High Contracting Parties to be of special and urgent importance:

**First.** The guiding principle above enunciated that labour should not be regarded merely as a commodity or article of commerce.

**Second.** The right of association for all lawful purposes by the employed as well as by the employers.

**Third.** The payment to the employed of a wage adequate to maintain a reasonable standard of life as this is understood in their time and country.

**Fourth.** The adoption of an eight hours day or a forty-eight hours week as the standard to be aimed at where it has not already been attained.

**Fifth.** The adoption of a weekly rest of at least twenty-four hours, which should include Sunday wherever practicable.

**Sixth.** The abolition of child labour and the imposition of such limitations on the labour of young persons as shall permit the continuation of their education and assure their proper physical development.

**Seventh.** The principle that men and women should receive equal remuneration for work of equal value.

**Eighth.** The standard set by law in each country with respect to the conditions of labour should have due regard to the equitable economic treatment of all workers lawfully resident therein.

**Ninth.** Each State should make provision for a system of inspection in which women should take part, in order to ensure the enforcement of the laws and regulations for the protection of the employed.

Without claiming that these methods and principles are either complete or final, the High Contracting Parties are of opinion that they are well fitted to guide the policy of the League of Nations; and that, if adopted by the industrial communities who are members of the League, and safeguarded in practice by an adequate system of such inspection, they will confer lasting benefits upon the wage-earners of the world.

## Declaration concerning the aims and purposes of the International Labour Organization (Declaration of Philadelphia), 1944[1]

The General Conference of the International Labour Organization, meeting in its Twenty-sixth Session in Philadelphia, hereby adopts, this tenth day of May in the year nineteen hundred and forty-four, the present Declaration of the aims and purposes of the International Labour Organization and of the principles which should inspire the policy of its Members.

I. The Conference reaffirms the fundamental principles on which the Organization is based and, in particular, that:

(a)  labour is not a commodity;

(b)  freedom of expression and of association are essential to sustained progress;

(c)  poverty anywhere constitutes a danger to prosperity everywhere;

(d)  the war against want requires to be carried on with unrelenting vigour within each nation, and by continuous and concerted international effort in which the representatives of workers and employers, enjoying equal status with those of governments, join with them in free discussion and democratic decision with a view to the promotion of the common welfare.

---

[1] In 1946, the Declaration of Philadelphia was incorporated into the ILO Constitution, where it is reproduced as an annex.

II. Believing that experience has fully demonstrated the truth of the statement in the Constitution of the International Labour Organization that lasting peace can be established only if it is based on social justice, the Conference affirms that:

(a)   all human beings, irrespective of race, creed or sex, have the right to pursue both their material well-being and their spiritual development in conditions of freedom and dignity, of economic security and equal opportunity;

(b)   the attainment of the conditions in which this shall be possible must constitute the central aim of national and international policy;

(c)   all national and international policies and measures, in particular those of an economic and financial character, should be judged in this light and accepted only in so far as they may be held to promote and not to hinder the achievement of this fundamental objective;

(d)   it is a responsibility of the International Labour Organization to examine and consider all international economic and financial policies and measures in the light of this fundamental objective;

(e)   in discharging the tasks entrusted to it the International Labour Organization, having considered all relevant economic and financial factors, may include in its decisions and recommendations any provisions which it considers appropriate.

III. The Conference recognizes the solemn obligation of the International Labour Organization to further among the nations of the world programmes which will achieve:

(a)   full employment and the raising of standards of living;

(b)   the employment of workers in the occupations in which they can have the satisfaction of giving the fullest measure of their skill and attainments and make their greatest contribution to the common well-being;

(c)   the provision, as a means to the attainment of this end and under adequate guarantees for all concerned, of facilities for training and the transfer of labour, including migration for employment and settlement;

(d)   policies in regard to wages and earnings, hours and other conditions of work calculated to ensure a just share of the fruits of progress to all, and a minimum living wage to all employed and in need of such protection;

(e)   the effective recognition of the right of collective bargaining, the cooperation of management and labour in the continuous improvement of productive efficiency, and the collaboration of workers and employers in the preparation and application of social and economic measures;

(f)   the extension of social security measures to provide a basic income to all in need of such protection and comprehensive medical care;

(g)   adequate protection for the life and health of workers in all occupations;

(h)   provision for child welfare and maternity protection;

(i)   the provision of adequate nutrition, housing and facilities for recreation and culture;

(j)   the assurance of equality of educational and vocational opportunity.

IV. Confident that the fuller and broader utilization of the world's productive resources necessary for the achievement of the objectives set forth in this Declaration can be secured by effective international and national action, including measures to expand production and consumption, to avoid severe economic fluctuations to promote the economic and social advancement of the less developed regions of the world, to assure greater stability in world prices of primary products, and to promote a high and steady volume of international trade, the Conference pledges the full cooperation of the International Labour Organization with such international bodies as may be entrusted with a share of the responsibility for this great task and for the promotion of the health, education and well-being of all peoples.

V. The conference affirms that the principles set forth in this Declaration are fully applicable to all peoples everywhere and that, while the manner of their application must be determined with due regard to the stage of social and economic development reached by each people, their progressive application to peoples who are still dependent, as well as to those who have already achieved self-government, is a matter of concern to the whole civilized world.

## ILO Declarations

The Declaration of Philadelphia, 1944, is reproduced above.

The Apartheid Declaration, first adopted in 1964, can be found at: http://www.ilo.org/public/libdoc/ilo/P/09604/09604(1964-47)373-376.pdf
This Declaration is discussed in the paper by Neville Rubin, *From pressure principle to measured militancy: The ILO in the campaign against apartheid*, paper prepared for the ILO Century Project, 2008, available at: http://www.ilocentury.org

The Declaration on Equality of Opportunity and Treatment for Women Workers, 1975 can be found at: http://www.ilo.org/public/libdoc/ilo/P/09604/09604(1975-A-1)96-100.pdf

The Tripartite Declaration of Principles concerning Multinational Enterprises and Social Policy, adopted in 1977 and revised in 2000 and 2006, can be found at: http://www.ilo.org/public/libdoc/ilo/2006/106B09_303_engl.pdf
More information on this Declaration can be found at: http://www.ilo.org/public/english/employment/multi/tripartite/index.htm

The Declaration on Fundamental Principles and Rights at Work, adopted in 1998, can be found at: http://www.ilo.org/public/libdoc/ilo/1998/98B09_234_engl.pdf
More information can be found at: http://www.ilo.org/public/english/standards/relm/ilc/ilc86/com-dtxt.htm

The Declaration on Social Justice for a Fair Globalization, adopted in 2008, can be found at: http://www.ilo.org/public/libdoc/ilo/2008/108B09_147_engl_(4-14).pdf

## Appendix III

# Selected further reading

## ILO history

Alcock, A. 1971. *History of the International Labour Organisation* (London and Basingstoke, Macmillan).

Barnes, G. 1926. *History of the International Labour Office* (London, Williams and Norgate Ltd).

Béguin, B. 1959. *ILO and the tripartite system* (New York, Carnegie Endowment for International Peace).

Blanchard, F. 2004. *L'Organisation internationale du travail: De la guerre froide à un nouvel ordre mondial* (Paris, Seuil).

Bonvin, J.-M. 1998. *L'Organisation internationale du travail: Etude sur une agence productrice de normes* (Paris, Presses Universitaires de France).

Brett, B. 1994. *International labour in the 21st century: The International Labour Organisation, monument to the past or beacon for the future?* (London, European Policy Institute).

Carew, A. et al. (eds). 2000. *The International Confederation of Free Trade Unions* (Bern, Peter Lang).

Cox, R.W. 1977. "Labor and hegemony", in *International Organization*, Vol. 31, No. 3, pp. 385–424.

—. 1973. "ILO: Limited monarchy", in R.W. Cox; H. Jacobson; G. Curzon (eds). *The anatomy of influence: Decision making in international organization* (New Haven and London, Yale University Press), pp. 102–138.

Endres, A.; Fleming, G. 2002. *International organizations and the analysis of economic policy, 1919–1950* (Cambridge, Cambridge University Press).

Follows, J.W. 1951. *Antecedents of the International Labour Organisation* (Oxford, Oxford University Press).

Galenson, W. 1981. *The International Labor Organization: An American view* (Madison, University of Wisconsin Press).

Ghebali, V.-Y. 1988. *The International Labour Organisation: A case study on the evolution of UN specialised agencies* (Dordrecht, Nijhoff).

Guinand, C. 2003. *Die Internationale Arbeitsorganisation (ILO) und die soziale Sicherheit in Europa (1942–1969)* (Bern, Peter Lang).

Haas, E. 1964. *Beyond the nation-state: Functionalism and international organization* (Stanford, CA, Stanford University Press).

Hansenne, M. 1999. *Un garde-fou pour la mondialisation: Le BIT dans l'après-guerre froide* (Brussels and Geneva, Quorum and Zoë).

Harrod, J. 1987. *Power, production, and the unprotected worker* (New York, Columbia University Press).

Helfer, L.R. 2006. "Understanding change in international organizations: Globalization and innovation in the ILO", in *Vanderbilt Law Review*, Vol. 59, No. 3, pp. 649–726.

Hislop, R. 1961. *The United States and the Soviet Union in the ILO* (Ann Arbor, MI, University Microfilms).

International Labour Organization (ILO). 2009. *Edward Phelan and the ILO: The life and views of an international social actor* (Geneva, ILO Century Project).

—. 1996. "75 years of the *International Labour Review*: A retrospective", in *International Labour Review*, Vol. 135, Nos. 3–4 (special anniversary issue with selected articles from 1921 to 1975).

—. 1954. "The composition of the Governing Body of the International Labour Office", in *International Labour Review*, Vol. 70, No. 6, pp. 496–525.

—. 1947. "One hundred sessions of the Governing Body of the International Labour Office", in *International Labour Review*, Vol. 55, Nos. 3–4, pp. 201–226.

—. 1931. *The International Labour Organisation: The first decade* (London, George Allen and Unwin).

Jacobson, H. 1960. "The USSR and the ILO", in *International Organization*, Vol. 14, No. 3, pp. 402–428.

Jenks, C.W. 1976. *Social policy in a changing world: The ILO response* (Geneva, ILO).

—. 1970. *Social justice in the law of nations: The ILO impact after fifty years* (London, Oxford and New York, Oxford University Press).

—. 1969. *Universality and ideology in the ILO* (Geneva, ILO).

Johnston, G.A. 1970. *The International Labour Organisation: Its work for social and economic progress* (London, Europa Publications).

Kott, S. 2008. "Une 'communauté épistémique' du social? Experts de l'OIT et internationalisation des politiques sociales dans l'entre-deux-guerres", in *Génèses, Sciences sociales et histoire*, No. 71, pp. 26–46.

Lee, E. 1994. "The Declaration of Philadelphia: Retrospect and prospect", in *International Labour Review*, Vol. 133, No. 4, pp. 467–484.

Lorenz, E.C. 2001. *Defining global justice: The history of US international labor standards policy* (Notre Dame, IN, University of Notre Dame Press).

Maul, D. 2009. *Human rights, social policy and decolonization: The International Labour Organization (ILO) 1940–1970* (Geneva, ILO Century Project).

—. 2007. "The International Labour Organization and the struggle against forced labour from 1919 to the present", in *Labor History*, Vol. 48, No. 4, pp. 477–500.

Morse, D. 1969. *The origin and evolution of the ILO and its role in the world community* (Ithaca, NY, Cornell University Press).

Moynihan, D.P. 1960. *The United States and the International Labour Organization, 1889–1934* (Doctoral Dissertation, Fletcher School of Law and Diplomacy).

Oechslin, J.-J. 2001. *The International Organisation of Employers: Three-quarters of a century in the service of the enterprise (1920–1998)* (Geneva, International Organisation of Employers).

Phelan, E. 1949. "The contribution of the ILO to peace", in *International Labour Review*, Vol. 59, No. 6, pp. 607–632.

—. 1936. *Yes and Albert Thomas* (London, The Cresset Press).

Riegelman Lubin, C.; Winslow, A. 1990. *Social justice for women: The International Labor Organization and women* (Durham, NC, Duke University Press).

Rodríguez-Piñero, L. 2005. *Indigenous peoples, postcolonialism, and international law: The ILO regime (1919–1989)* (Oxford, Oxford University Press).

Ruotsila, M. 2002. "'The Great Charter for the Liberty of the Workingman': Labour, liberals and the creation of the ILO", in *Labour History Review*, Vol. 67, No. 1, pp. 29–47.

Scelle, G. 1930. *L'Organisation internationale du travail et le BIT* (Paris, Librairie des Sciences Politiques et Sociales).

Schaper, B.W. 1959. *Albert Thomas: Trente ans de réformisme social* (Paris and Assen, Presses Universitaires de France and Van Gorcum). Translated as: Schaper, B.W. Forthcoming. *Albert Thomas: Thirty years of social reform* (Geneva, ILO Century Project).

Sengenberger, W.; Campbell, D. (eds). 1994. *International labour standards and economic interdependence* (Geneva, ILO).

Shotwell, J.T. (ed.). 1934. *The origins of the International Labor Organisation* (New York, Columbia University Press), 2 vols.

Thomas, A. 1948. *International social policy* (Geneva, ILO).

Tortora, M. 1980. *Institution spécialisée et organisation mondiale: étude des relations de l'OIT avec la SDN et l'ONU* (Brussels, Bruylant).

Tosstorff, R. 2005. "The international trade-union movement and the founding of the International Labour Organization", in *International Review of Social History*, Vol. 50, No. 3, pp. 399–433.

Van Daele, J. 2008. "The International Labour Organization (ILO) in past and present research", in *International Review of Social History*, Vol. 53, No. 3, pp. 485–511.

—. 2005. "Engineering social peace: Networks, ideas, and the founding of the International Labour Organization", in *International Review of Social History*, Vol. 50, No. 3, pp. 435–466.

Waline, P. 1976. *Un patron au Bureau International du Travail, 1922–1974* (Paris, France-Empire).

## Papers prepared for the ILO Century Project (2008)

*All these papers are available on the ILO Century Project website: http://www.ilocentury.org*

Akpokavie, C. *Tripartism, social dialogue and democracy.*

Böhning, W.R. *A brief account of the ILO and policies on international migration.*

Cayet, T.; Rosental, P.-A.; Thébaud-Sorger, M. *Histoire du Service d'Hygiène Industrielle du BIT.*

Chigara, B. *The ILO's contribution to the development of international human rights law and human security in sub-Saharan Africa.*

Dahlén, M. *The ILO and child labour.*

Hughes, S.; Haworth, N. *The ILO involvement in economic and social policies in the 1930s.*

Kott, S. *De l'assurance à la sécurité sociale (1919–1949): L'OIT comme acteur international.*

Lapeyre, F. *The ILO contribution to the development of policies and strategies for growth, employment and poverty reduction.*

Lieten, K. *The ILO setting the terms of the child labour debate.*

Marinakis, A. *The role of the ILO in the development of minimum wages.*

Maul, D. *The ILO involvement in decolonization and development.*

McCann, D. *Contemporary working time law: Evolving objectives, subjects and regulatory modes.*

Murray, J. *ILO and working conditions: An historical analysis.*

Oechslin, J.-J. *Tripartisme, dialogue social et démocratie: Perspectives du monde des employeurs.*

Pimenta, C.; Tortell, L.; Wolfson, O. *Colonialism, forced labour and the International Labour Organization: Portugal and the first ILO Commission of Inquiry.*

Rubin, N. *From pressure principle to measured militancy: The ILO in the campaign against apartheid.*

Seekings, J. *The ILO and social protection in the Global South, 1919–2005.*

Trebilcock, A. *From social justice to decent work: An overview of the ILO's guiding ideals 1919–2008.*


## International labour standards

*There is an extensive bibliography of works detailing the functioning of the ILO's international labour standards. Here are a few representative examples.*

Bartolomei de la Cruz, H.; Von Potobsky, G.; Swepston, L. 1996. *The International Labor Organization: The international standards system and basic human rights* (Boulder, CO, Westview Press).

Basu, K. et al. (eds). 2003. *International labor standards: History, theory, and policy options* (Malden, Blackwell).

Boivin, I.; Odero, A. 2006. "The Committee of Experts on the Application of Conventions and Recommendations: Progress achieved in national labour legislation", in *International Labour Review*, Vol. 145, No. 3, pp. 207–220.

Dahl, K.N. 1968. "The role of ILO standards in the global integration process", in *Journal of Peace Research*, Vol. 5, No. 4, pp. 309–351.

ILO. 2006. *Handbook of procedures relating to international labour Conventions and Recommendations* (Geneva). Available on the ILO website.

—. 2005. *Rules of the game: A brief introduction to international labour standards* (Geneva). Available on the ILO website.

Landy, E.A. 1966. *The effectiveness of international supervision: Thirty years of ILO experience* (London, Stevens and Sons).

Valticos, N.; Von Potobsky, G. 1995. *International labour law* (Deventer, Kluwer).

Internal ILO reports include:

*Report of the Committee of Experts on the Application of Conventions and Recommendations*, which is published annually;

*Report III (1A)*, submitted to each Conference, which contains general and individual observations concerning particular countries;

*Report III (1B)*, incorporating the General Survey, which examines the application in law and practice of a particular set of Conventions and Recommendations in ILO member States;

*The Report of the Conference Committee on the Application of Standards*, which is published annually in the *Provisional Record* of the International Labour Conference.

These documents are available at the ILO website at http://www.ilo.org. The ILOLEX CD-ROM, which is published biannually, is a database of ILO standards including Conventions, Recommendations, reports of the Committee of Experts, reports of the Committee on Freedom of Association, General Surveys and numerous related documents.

# Index

Note: Page numbers in **bold** refer to boxes;
those in *italics* to figures.